The Spaces of Renaissance Anatomy Theater

Edited by
Leslie R. Malland
University of Texas Permian Basin

Series on the History of Science

www.vernonpress.com

In the Americas:	*In the rest of the world:*
Vernon Press	Vernon Press
1000 N West Street, Suite 1200	C/Sancti Espiritu 17,
Wilmington, Delaware, 19801	Malaga, 29006
United States	Spain

Series on the History of Science

Library of Congress Control Number: 2022931466

ISBN: 978-1-64889-141-0

Cover design by Vernon Press. Cover image by Francisca Esteve Barranca.

Table of contents

List of Figures and Tables

List of Figures

List of Tables

Acknowledgements

After the 2020 *Renaissance Society of America* conference was postponed due to COVID, William Whitehead reached out to me with an invitation to assemble an edited collection of essays themed around my planned conference panel, "Amputation, Queer Anatomy, and Winter Cadavers from Italy to England." This project came together through our common interest in anatomy: the spaces of intersections within the anatomy theater - such as botany and anatomy, - aspects of gender present in anatomical discourse and images, and our shared interest in the physical body and its parts. Thus, this project would not be possible without the support and encouragement of William Whitehead, Javier Rodriguez, Victoria Echegaray, and Argiris Legatos of Vernon Press. I am thankful for each scholar and all their hard work for this collection. I am also thankful for Emily DeHaven, Whitney Sperrazza, Emily Shortslef, Joyce G. MacDonald, and Lauren Cagle for their expertise and guidance.

Though the list is too long to include here, we would like to thank our friends and family for their support. In addition, we thank:

Molly Seremet

Rafael F. Narváez

Damara Carpenter

Francisca Esteve Barranca

Doug Raybuck

Athena and Elliot Malland

Danell Hetrick

Jenn Murray

Professor Evelyn Welch

Edinburgh University

Museums of the Royal College of Surgeons of England

Sheena Stief and *Stief Editing*

About the Authors

Giulia Mari, Independent Researcher, Aberdeen, Scotland, UK

Giulia holds a doctorate in English and History from King's College London for her thesis, *'Talking Legs in the English Renaissance': Shifting Concepts of Masculinity in Tudor and Stuart England, 1550-1700*, and has held teaching positions at King's and the University of Dundee. Her research focuses on early modern masculinities and the early modern body as a carrier of gender, and she explores this topic through a study of fashion history, history of medicine, literature, and drama.

David Soulier, PhD Student, History, Université Côte d'Azur

David Soulier got a PhD in Early Modern History and a teaching degree in Classical Humanities in France. He published papers and gave lectures on the history of anatomy. One of his forthcoming publications is a translation of Andreas Vesalius' *Examen of Gabriele Falloppio's Anatomical Observations* (1564). He'd like to thank all reviewers of his included chapter for their relevant suggestions!

Carlos Fernando Teixeira Alves, Researcher at the Centre for Religious History Studies at the Catholic University and at the Centre for History of Society and Culture at the University of Coimbra

Carlos Fernando Teixeira Alves has a Master's degree in History from the Faculty of Arts of the University of Coimbra (FLUC). In 2016, as a FCT PhD fellow, he started his PhD in the Interuniversity PhD Program in History: change and continuity in a global world (PIUDHist) at the Institute of Social Sciences of the University of Lisbon (ICS-UL), with a thesis entitled, *The Natural Order in the University Reforms of Salamanca and Coimbra (1769-1820)*. Finished in 2021. He was a visiting researcher at the Instituto Figuerola de Historia Y Ciencias Sociales of the Universidad Carlos III de Madrid (2019) and is currently a researcher in the Project Franciscan Landscapes: The Observance between Italy, Portugal and Spain (UCP-CEHR jPICH/0003/2019), of the Center for Studies in Religious History (UCP-CEHR). Simultaneously, he is also a researcher at the Center for the History of Society and Culture of the University of Coimbra (CHSC-UC). His most recent publications reflect on the History of Universities, History of Teaching, History of Science, and also Religious, Medieval and Modern History.

Jennifer Lodine-Chaffey, Assistant Professor of English, Southeastern Oklahoma State University

Lodine-Chaffey earned her PhD in Early Modern Literature at Washington State University in 2017. She has explored early modern literary engagements with death and violence in articles published in *Parergon, The Journal of Marlowe Studies, The Ben Jonson Journal,* and *Quidditas*. Her monograph, *A Weak Woman in a Strong Battle: Women and Public Execution in Early Modern England,* is forthcoming with the Strode Studies in Early Modern Literature and Culture at the University of Alabama Press.

Leslie R. Malland, Visiting Lecturer in English, University of Texas Permian Basin

Leslie received her PhD in early modern British Literature from the University of Kentucky in 2021. Her research interests include anatomical study, biopower and its politics, and early modern medicine. She has worked with various publications, including *The Arkansas Philological Review, The Journal of Literary Humanities,* and *Mortality*.

Gilad Gutman, PhD Student, English, Tel-Aviv University

Gilad Gutman is a member of the Department of English Literature and American Studies at Tel-Aviv University. His research focuses on early modern English theater and its relation to territoriality, games, economics, and ideology. Currently, he is writing his PhD, in which he employs methods from the Digital Humanities to analyze the figurative language of the early Jacobean theater and its ideological significance concerning the rise of capitalism.

Elizabeth Anne Kirby, Postdoctoral Fellow, French Literature, New York University

Elizabeth Kirby is a postdoctoral fellow in the Department of French Literature, Thought and Culture at New York University. Her doctoral project took Montaigne's note to his reader verbatim when he says he would like to depict himself wholly naked and examined how Montaigne's self-writing is a kind of undressing. Her new project examines Montaigne's account of both human and nonhuman perception as fundamentally phenomenological and investigates how in the *Essais,* human embodiment preferences a visual engagement with the world in which to perceive is to divest phenomena.

Kaleigh Hunter, PhD Candidate, History, Bergische Universität Wuppertal

Kaleigh Hunter is a doctoral candidate of history at the Bergische Universität Wuppertal, currently working on her dissertation regarding engraved title pages of printed, botanical treatises from 1530-1650. Her research focuses on the intersection of art and knowledge in early modern natural history with a special interest in the concept of gardens and the ways in which they were visually depicted.

Introduction: Defining the Spaces of Renaissance Anatomy Theater

This collection offers insight into the myriad of conversations taking place in and around Renaissance anatomy theaters. The *space* of Renaissance Anatomy is not solely in the physical theater. As this collection demonstrates, the *space* of the theater encompasses every aspect of Renaissance culture, from its education systems, art, and writing to its concepts of identity, citizenship, and the natural world. Renaissance anatomy theaters were spaces of intersection that influenced every aspect of their cultures, and scholars should broaden their concept of anatomy theaters to include more than the physical space of the theater. Instead, we should approach the anatomy theaters as spaces where cultural expression is influenced by the hands-on study of human cadavers.

The primary materials for this book present a telling indication of the increasing importance and pervasiveness of medicalized representations of the body in early modern culture at large. We examine not just the power that anatomy itself swayed over society, but the power of the anatomist to codify terminology and establish societal norms, thus, discipling spaces beyond the anatomy theater, beyond the public sphere, and into the bedrooms and private lives of citizens. Many of our scholars turn to Jonathan Sawday's influential work, *The Body Emblazoned*, as a building block for discussion. In *The Body Emblazoned*, Jonathan Sawday shows how anatomical study fashions a new image of the human interior in the Early Modern period and argues that this leads to a reconfiguration of self-hood. In addition, Sawday argues, "because of the old correspondence between the microcosm and the macrocosm...the anatomists, then, interprets not just the corpse on the dissection table, but through that corpse he begins to interpret the world itself."[1] He views anatomies with a Foucauldian lens when he asserts, "the anatomist is not simply a disinterested investigator of the natural world; he is fully implicated, as the extension of the law's revenge, in the re-assertion of

---

[1] Jonathan Sawday, "Bodies by Art Fashioned: Anatomy, Anatomists and English Poetry 1570-1680." (PhD Diss, University of London, 1988): 16.

the rights of sovereign power over the body of the condemned criminal."[2] Building from this approach, we continue to situate the theater as a space of discipline, knowledge acquisition, and empirical understanding where early moderns used anatomy as a lens for better understanding themselves and the world itself.

In addition to Sawday's work, we build upon critics such as Gail Kern Paster, Katharine Park, Michael Schoenfeldt, Andrea Carlino, and Nancy. G. Siraisi. Each chapter demonstrates a thorough review of relevant literature to present a new and unique approach to the anatomy theater's role in Renaissance society. Padua in Italy is often viewed as the central hub for anatomical study throughout much of the Renaissance. Even before commissioning the first permanent anatomy theater, the University of Padua had a very old and illustrious tradition of anatomical education: "Annual anatomies (that is, dissections) became part of the formal academic curriculum" in the fourteenth century, and "[s]tatutes of the arts and medicine branch of the University of Padua, dating 1465, refer to the annual anatomy as a well-established practice."[3] The earliest anatomies took place in the houses of professors or students, and even after the first anatomy theater was built, anatomical demonstrations would take place in a variety of locations, including churches, pharmaceutical venues, and temporary theaters. Padua received its study material from executions and hospitals. People were eager to study the human body and challenge long-held traditions of anatomical research, so the occasional grave robbery took place.

In England, the Barber-Surgeons were established as a guild in 1540 and began anatomies whereas the College of Physicians was established by a Charter of 1518, but it did not receive bodies for dissection until 1565 through an order by Queen Elizabeth.[4] Because of Thomas Vicary's service to Henry VIII's gangrenous wound, the Company of Barbers and Surgeons was granted four bodies a year from Tyburn for the purpose of dissection by Henry's 1540 Act of Parliament. This act was later extended by James I to six bodies per year.

---

[2] Jonathan Sawday, "The Fate of Marsyas: Dissecting the Renaissance Body," *Renaissance Bodies: The Human Figure in English Culture c. 1540-1660*. Edited by Lucy Gent and Nigel Llewellyn. (Reaktion Books, 1990), pp. 111-35: 116.

[3] Nancy G. Siraisi, *Medieval & Early Renaissance Medicine: An Introduction to Knowledge and Practice* (Chicago and London: The University of Chicago Press, 1990): 88; Klestinec, "A History of Anatomy Theaters in Sixteenth Century Padua," *Journal of the History of Medicine and Allied Sciences* 59, no. 4 (2004): 394.

[4] For more on the history of England's Company of Barbers and Surgeons, see their website at barberscompany.org.

As a result, Vicary became the first Master of the Company of Barbers and Surgeons. Dr. Caius was "the first man to lecture in public on the new anatomical methods of Vesalius...He began a series of lectures in the Barber-Surgeons' Hall in 1546 at the personal request of Henry VIII."[5] Thus, Henry VIII remained directly involved in the lectures of the Barber-Surgeons after granting the bodies for dissection.

Like the Barber-Surgeons, the College of Physicians was eventually granted bodies for dissection. As the translators of William Harvey's *Prelectiones Anatomiae Universalis* note, the lectures of the College of Physicians were a direct result of an endowment from Queen Elizabeth in 1581.[6] In fact, all power endowed upon anatomists stems from the sovereign.[7] By sponsoring anatomies, the sovereign vicariously establishes the "truth" about the human body that anatomists discover. Italy and Spain quickly developed anatomical programs in universities in stride with anatomy's growing popularity across Europe. While anatomists were acting as agents of the sovereign in a public and political deployment of punishment, they were actively researching the bodies granted to them in order to discover knowledge of the human body. *The Space of Renaissance Anatomy Theater* locates how the advancement of anatomical research influenced European culture within the space of the theater, spaces of justice, spaces of education, and more.

---

[5] Antonia McClean. *Humanism and the Rise of Science in Tudor England.* (New York: Neale Watson Academic Publications, Inc., 1972): 196.

[6] Gabriel Harvey took over these lectures in 1615 (3-6). The College required Harvey to "dissect and lecture on the trunk and all the organs contained therein at the end of his second year (1617), on the head only at the end of the third year (1618), and on the leg and arm, with special reference to the muscles, sinews, and ligaments, at the end of the fourth year (1619)" (Charles D. O'Malley, F.N.L Poynter, and K.F. Russell, "Introduction," *Lectures on the Whole of Anatomy.* Translated by Charles D. O'Malley, F.N.L. Poynter, and K.F. Russell, [Berkeley: University of California Press, 1961], pp. 1-19: 8-9).

[7] Florike Egmond's work finds that "neither [executions nor public dissections] could have taken place without the active involvement of the authorities - who, after all, not only arrested, sentenced and executed, but also provided the physicians with dead bodies, contributed in various ways to the construction of the anatomy theaters, and sanctioned the public dissections with their presence" ("Execution, Dissection, Pain and Infamy- A Morphological Investigation," in *Bodily Extremities: Preoccupations with the Human Body in Early Modern European Culture*, edited by Florike Egmond and Robert Zwijnenberg. [Ashgate, 2003], pp. 92-127), 123.

Chapter Summaries

This collection is organized in three sections, each divided by unique artwork that adds visually compelling evidence to our written words. The first section, "The Intersections of Anatomy Theaters and Universities," investigates the educational spaces of anatomy theater. Those three chapters discuss the circulation of anatomical material, the relationship between the supply and demand of university cadavers, and the development of anatomy on the Iberian Peninsula. Chapter One traces the story of the anatomical tables that John Evelyn bought during a study trip in Padua and details their popularity. In this chapter, Giulia Mari argues that the level of celebrity achieved by these unique anatomical curiosities in learned and, most importantly, in non-learned circles, reflects how "medical knowledge could be and indeed was organically integrated into the early modern world" (2). Her work offers a unique contribution to the study of medical artifacts and their influence in early modern society.

Chapter Two challenges Jonathan Sawday's assertion as the theater as a space of justice by investigating the supply in criminal bodies from the administrator of local justice in Italy. David Soulier studies a valuable question in the history of anatomical research: how many bodies could an anatomist procure for dissections and lectures? He notes, the "condition of supply turned out to be so problematic that the selection criteria of anatomical material were not aimed at local criminal bodies and the anatomists had to pass through literal underground means...the difficulties the anatomists encountered in obtaining cadavers to dissect reflects a difference in fascination with death between academic world and State power" (26). The answers to his questions beg us to rethink the relationship between science and justice within the space of the Renaissance anatomy theater and to "redefine the space of anatomy theater in Renaissance Italy as dedicated to science and/or justice by taking into account the availability of the anatomical material from acts of justice" (26). Soulier offers archival research that reflects the supply and demand trends in Italian anatomical studies.

Carlos Alves examines the educational spaces affiliated with anatomical study in Spain and Portugal in Chapter Three. He sheds new light on the economic and educational considerations universities undertook to develop the study of anatomy on the Iberian Peninsula. Alves conducted extensive archival research and elegant translations of primary texts to share the universities' history, including the importance of the proximity of the anatomy theater to the hospital and cemetery, transportation costs, and textbook selections. He finds "a significant development of anatomical studies in Coimbra and Salamanca from the fifteenth century until much of the next, although it was marked by some problems. Both Universities, during this period, managed to modernize their teaching, getting it closer to the main European centers" (66). This original work offers an important contribution to the study of Western anatomical research and education.

The second group of chapters makes up the section "Spaces for Female Bodies in Anatomy Theaters." Though living females were excluded from the anatomy theaters, their cadavers were readily welcomed. Chapter Four locates correlations between the blazon as a textual form and the eroticizing of female executions through anatomical descriptions. Jennifer Lodine-Chaffey rediscovers a classic poem by Edward May to argue that May effectually silences the woman burned at the stake by partitioning her body, interpreting her physical reactions, and employing her corpse as an emblem of martyrdom. Building upon Chapter Four, Chapter Five argues that anatomical research furthered the suppression and oppression of women and their bodies. Malland finds evidence in the anatomy manuals of Andreas Vesalius, Thomas Raynalde, and others, and she applies biopolitical theories from Michel Foucault to argue, "early modern England witnesses state-authorized agents collecting knowledge from female cadavers that they codify into medical terminology in a new regime of knowledge whose audience is educated, wealthy men. In turn, those men (many members of court) use this knowledge to uphold beliefs about women's inferiority" (105). These two chapters share a particular interest in the male-dominance of not only female bodies, but interpretations of female bodies.

Chapter Six introduces the final and longest section, "The Anatomy Theater as a Space for Understanding the World." Gilad Gutman helps us understand Shakespeare's *Coriolanus* and the Midland Revolts of 1607 through the lens of anatomy theater, tracing the steps from the outer layers of the city to the inner layers of Coriolanus' body, somographically replicating the steps of an anatomical demonstration. His chapter "considers the enclosures [of land and city spaces] as a long-standing phenomenon and their relation to the social space of the dissected body in the anatomical demonstrations, situating this relation within a network of spatial relations in early modern England, through which *Coriolanus* constructs the Roman body politic" (110). He expertly cites historical documents alongside Shakespeare to offer both a historical and literary perspective.

Chapters Seven and Eight offer not just a thorough reading of Montaigne, but also beautiful translations of evidence from the texts. Elizabeth Anne Kirby's translations and contextualization of Montaigne's words work to seamlessly reflect Montaigne's interests in skin, nakedness, and boundaries as Montaigne and readers alike try to make sense of the human body's relation to the world around it. Kirby reads Montaigne's *Essais* alongside artistic renditions of "The Flaying of Marsyas" to craft a discussion of artistic expression, written words, and the various spaces where skin is laid bare. The final offers exquisite insight into the emerging importance of botanical gardens alongside anatomy theaters: "The theater was open for anyone who wanted to learn about the human body, themselves, wonderous aspects of nature, or God through both observation and contemplation, with both dissections and the collection of curiosity" (176). Universities began using the anatomy theaters to better understand botany, their relationship to the natural world, and their relationship to God. Kaleigh Hunter reveals how studies of the natural world were approached in The Netherlands during the sixteenth century, especially the ones of the botanical garden and anatomy theater.

The Conclusion to this collection offers a look forward at where anatomical research can lead us as we consider various spaces of intersection. Thus, this collection situations itself within the space of the Renaissance anatomy theater and locates cultural intersections from within that space, looking outward to spaces beyond the theater to identify the cultural impacts of anatomical research in Europe throughout the sixteenth century.

Chapter 1

Let His Body be Unburi'd: The *Tabulae Evelinianae* and the Allegory of the Anatomized Body in Early Modern England

Giulia Mari

Independent Researcher

Abstract: Giovanni Leoni d'Este prepared the *Tabulae Evelinianae* during his time as a dissector for the Professor of Anatomy at the University of Padua. The tables are currently owned by the Royal College of Surgeons and are on display in Hunterian Museum in London. This chapter looks at the *Tabulae Evelinianae*, unique anatomical tables of veins, arteries, and nerves that John Evelyn brought back from a period of study in Italy in the 1640s, following the paper trail that they left in their journey from anatomical specimens to celebrated curiosities. This chapter discusses the tables alongside other cultural products that demonstrate the pervasiveness that medicalized representations of the body stemming from universities had in early modern culture at large.

Keywords: John Evelyn, Evelyn Tables, Medical Curiosities, Anatomical Specimens

***

Introduction

In the winter of 1645-46, twenty-five-year-old John Evelyn, at the time in the midst of his European Grand Tour, spent Shrovetide – the last cathartic celebration before the beginning of Lent – in Venice, a city famous for its extravagant Carnival celebrations. A week into Lent, Evelyn took his leave from Venice and returned to Padua – where he had enrolled in the university over the previous summer, receiving his *matricula* on 30th July 1645 – in order "to be present at the famous anatomy lecture, celebrated [there] with extraordinary apparatus, lasting almost a whole month."[1]

Using this crucial part of John Evelyn's Grand Tour as a starting point, this chapter closely follows the acquisition, return to England, and subsequent history of the rare tables of veins and nerves, unique and fascinating anatomical souvenirs that Evelyn purchased during his time in Padua. The story of the tables' enthusiastic reception in the upper echelons of the early modern London society is paired with a reading of excerpts from Phineas Fletcher's *The Purple Island*, Edmund Spenser's *The Faerie Queene*, and William Shakespeare's *Coriolanus* – extraordinary literary works that merge allegorical poetry with masterful anatomical knowledge and painstaking somatic descriptions. Positioning itself at the intersection of history of medicine, material culture, and literary studies, this chapter discusses the burgeoning relevance that anatomical investigations and discourses gathered in medical and, crucially, non-medical circles in England throughout the early modern period, proving that medical knowledge could be and indeed was organically integrated into the early modern vision of the world.

'At the foot of the gallows': A Brief History of Anatomical Investigations in Early Modern England

Anatomy was a topic of enormous fascination in the seventeenth century, and historians have extensively mapped the demand in bodies to be anatomized for educational purposes, starting in the sixteenth century, and exponentially increasing after 1600. One of the first institutions to be granted access to cadavers was the Edinburgh Guild of Surgeons and Barbers, which in 1505 started receiving one body per year. In London in 1540, Henry VIII enshrined the surgeons' right to

> have and take, without contradiction, four persons condemned adjudged and put to death for felony by the due order of the King's laws of [the] realm for anatomies [...] to make incision of the same dead bodies [...] for the further and better knowledge, instruction, insight, learning, and experience in the said science or faculty of surgery.[2]

Another four bodies among those of the criminals hanged at Tyburn were allocated to the capital's physicians for the same purpose. Andrew Cunningham

---

[1] Evelyn, *The Diary of John Evelyn*, 215.

[2] Cunningham, *The Anatomist Anatomis'd*, 224 (citing George Charles Peachey, *A Memoir of William and John Hunter* [Plymouth: William Brendon and Son, 1924]), 2: 4.

argues that the right to the eight bodies was exercised irregularly during the sixteenth century. By the seventeenth century, however, anatomies were much more regularly performed, and "other City guilds and companies, including the butchers, the tailors, and the wax chandlers, seem to have had a more than passing interest in obtaining bodies to develop the (lucrative) skills of embalming."[3] The fear of becoming the subject of a post-mortem dissection gradually became ingrained in society as punishment even worse than the hanging itself. Such fear was capitalized on for its potential to act as a deterrent against the most heinous crimes, and in 1751 the English Parliament passed the Murder Act, instituting the practice of "penal dissection" and stating that "in no case whatsoever shall the body of any [executed] murderer be suffered to be buried," destining such corpses for anatomies or to be hanged in chains for the crowds to behold, reintroducing "to the spectrum of punishment available to the authorities something of the spectacle of [Elizabethan and Jacobean] public dismemberment."[4] In the same year, William Hogarth concluded his series *The Four Stages of Cruelty* with an engraving entitled "The Reward of Cruelty" that shows Tom Nero, the protagonist of the series, being dissected in the Cutlerian theater near Newgate prison, his bowels carelessly shoved in a large bucket and his stomach bitten into by a dog, an ever-present animal in dissection engravings (Figure 1.1).

In much different fashion but similar spirit, in 1759, the Master of Anatomy at the Royal College of Surgeons discussed the "moral role of anatomy" in one of his lectures.[5] Not only was dissection now being used as an "added dimension to capital punishment," but through the enactment of the Murder Act, "[t]he criminal could, even after the point of death, be made to perform a public service" by contributing to the advancement of medical and anatomical knowledge.[6] Despite this widespread fear of being subjected to dissection, throughout the early modern period and into the eighteenth century "viewers [...] were absolutely fascinated by it," displaying on the one hand "loathing for those who came to the foot of the gallows in order to claim the dead for science," and on the other, "intense interest" for the object and methods of their investigation.[7] Anatomical lectures were open to the public and while title pages such as that of Vesalius's *Fabrica* or images such as

---

[3] Sawday, *The Body Emblazoned*, 57.

[4] Cunningham, *The Anatomist Anatomis'd*, 225.

[5] Ibid., 225.

[6] Sawday, *The Body Emblazoned*, 55.

[7] Cunningham, *The Anatomist Anatomis'd*, 226; Sawday, *The Body Emblazoned*, 59.

Hogarth's *Reward* were idealized, the lecture theaters were always crowded with onlookers tightly pressed together to take a good look.[8]

Figure 1.1: William Hogarth, *'The Reward of Cruelty', The Four Stages of Cruelty*, 1751. Wikimedia Commons.

---

[8] Cynthia Klestinec discusses the role of academic and non-academic audiences at dissections in Padua, which took place in the same theater visited by Evelyn in 1645, as mentioned above and discussed at length below. Klestinec quotes the University's statutes from 1595 stating that, as well as students, also "Jews, teachers, tailors, shoemakers, sandal-makers, butchers, salted fish dealers, and [...] porters [perhaps funereal] and basket-bearers" and members "of almost the 'whole citizenry'" crowded the anatomy theater to assist the dissections and anatomical lectures. The entertaining value of these events was clearly recognized, and in 1597 the lesson was accompanied by lute players, led into the theater by a procession of medical students, and paid for by the audience (Klestinec, "A History of Anatomy Theaters in Sixteenth Century Padua," 401; 407).

Anatomical Curiosities: John Evelyn's Rare Tables of Veins and Nerves

The increased availability of bodies throughout the seventeenth century made it possible for anatomists to move past the exclusive use of illustrated two-dimensional *ecorchés*, and to experiment with and devise solutions for the preservation and the display of the human body as learning tools for medical students, artists, and non-specialized learned audiences. One of the most unique and unusual of such aids to the study of anatomy made its way to England from the University of Padua in the mid-seventeenth century as part of the collection of curiosities that John Evelyn accumulated in the course of his travels. The University of Padua in the North East of Italy was an international center renowned for its anatomical lectures, where Andreas Vesalius, forefather of early modern anatomy, had held the chair of surgery and anatomy from 1537 to 1543, and where the world's first permanent anatomy theater had been built in 1584.[9] Anatomies were performed on executed criminals or on bodies procured from the nearby San Francesco hospital – whence most of the female and all the children's bodies came from, and where the medical students had the opportunity to practice their skill. With its prestigious university and anatomy theater, Padua was a common destination for young men's European education and grand tours. Jerome Bylebyl writes that this university was especially favored by non-Italian students for two main reasons: "first, it was generally regarded as the best medical school in Europe, and second, the religious divisions of Europe had not been allowed to prevent Protestant students from studying and taking degrees at this nominally Catholic university."[10] Despite its Catholic allegiance, therefore, English Protestants came to Padua to learn from its famed anatomists.[11]

---

[9] By the time John Evelyn visited Padua, the anatomical lectures were being held in Padua's second anatomy theater, built in 1595 in Palazzo del Bò, the same location as the first theater. Whereas the first theater was a simple wooden structure with stable scaffolding for seating, the new theater was more elegant and extravagant and much larger than the original structure, thus making room for larger audiences while also distancing medical students from the dissector and diminishing their ability to see the demonstrations. Klestinec argues that this contributed to shift in the relevance from the cadaver being examined to the philosophical discussions of the lecturer (Klestinec, "A History of Anatomy Theaters in Sixteenth Century Padua").

[10] Bylebyl, "The School of Padua," 335.

[11] Even before commissioning the first permanent anatomy theater, the University of Padua had a very old and illustrious tradition of anatomical education: "Annual anatomies (that is, dissections) became part of the formal academic curriculum" in the fourteenth century and "[s]tatutes of the arts and medicine branch of the University of Padua, dating 1465, refer to the annual anatomy as a well-established practice." The

Padua was not the first institution that John Evelyn visited in order to deepen his knowledge of anatomy: in 1641, in Leyden, he wrote that

> among all the rarities of this place, I was much pleased with a sight of their anatomy-school, theater, and repository adjoining, which is well furnished with natural curiosities; skeletons, from the whale and elephant to the fly and spider; which last is a very delicate piece of art, to see how the bones (if I may so call them of so tender an insect) could be separated from the mucilaginous parts of that minute animal. Among a great variety of other things, I was shown the knife newly taken out of a drunken Dutchman's guts, by an incision in his side, after it had slipped from his fingers into his stomach. The pictures of the chirurgeon and his patient, both living, were there.[12]

This was however a much briefer visit than the month Evelyn spent in Padua, during which he had the opportunity to see "a woman, a child, and a man dissected with all the manual operations of the chirurgeon on the human body."[13] The anatomies that Evelyn witnessed were performed by Johann Vesling (latinised to Veslingius), professor of anatomy, surgery, and botany at the university, assisted by Giovanni Leoni d'Este (latinised to Dr. Jo Athelsteninus Leonœnas in Evelyn's diary).[14] During the procedures, the latter would extract "the Veins, and other Vessels which contain the Blood, Spirits, &c. out of Humane Bodies" and "apply and distend them on Tables, according to their natural proportion and position, as an Improvement which might be of use in Anatomy."[15]

There are only ten extant examples of such tables, divided into two sets, and there is no record of any other ever being created. The first set, pictured below

---

earliest anatomies took place in the houses of professors or students, and even after the first anatomy theater was built (especially in the period between its destruction and the construction of the new one), anatomical demonstrations took place in a variety of locations, such as churches (namely, the Church of St Catherine) or pharmaceutical venues, as well as temporary theaters built *ad hoc* at the students' expense (Siraisi, *Medieval & Early Renaissance Medicine*, 88; Klestinec, "A History of Anatomy Theaters in Sixteenth Century Padua," 394).

[12] Evelyn, *The Diary of John Evelyn*, entry for 28th August 1641, 26.

[13] Ibid., entry for 1645-46, 215.

[14] Anatomies would only be carried out in winter when the low temperatures would delay decomposition, whereas, during the summer, the abundance of plants and flowers would make it possible to lecture on medical botany.

[15] Evelyn and Cowper, "An Account of Divers Schemes of Arteries and Veins," 1178.

(Figures 1.2 to 1.5), was purchased by John Evelyn during his period as a student at the University of Padua. Of the four tables, for which he paid 150 scudi, three – displaying the nervous system, arteries, and lungs and liver of an adult human – were in possession of Leoni in 1645, whereas the fourth – the venous system – was commissioned by Evelyn especially in order to complete the collection. In a letter to the esteemed surgeon and anatomist William Cowper penned by the diarist in 1701 on occasion of Cowper's lecture on the tables at the Royal Society, Evelyn relates the circumstances surrounding his trip to Padua and the purchase of the tables in more detail than he does in his diary. After describing the lectures, during which Leoni "begun to apply and distend" the vessels extracted from the cadavers' bodies on tables, he adds,

> [s]ome of these Tables, being finish'd, with the Direction and Public Approbation of [Veslingius] and several other Learn'd Physicians and Anatomists, present at those Lectures and Operations; and understanding that Leoncenae was going shortly (I think) into Poland, and willing to dispose of his Tables, before he took his Journey; I desir'd the Late Dr Geo. Rogers, (Consul then at Padoa for the Students of our Nation in that University) to purchase and procure them for me; which he did, for, as I remember, 150 Scudi; with Condition, that he should add a Table more, namely, that of the Liver, Gastrick Nerves and other Vessels, to compleat the Fourth.[16]

The anatomical curiosities, which Evelyn always calls "the [or my] Tables of Veins and Arteries," figure several times in his journal. They are first mentioned in the 1645-46 log quoted above, where Evelyn describes attending the lectures at Padua and purchasing the tables. In the letter to Cowper, after repeating the circumstances in which he purchased the tables, Evelyn recounts their belated arrival in England. After Leoni completed the fourth table, Evelyn

> immediately sent them to Venice, from whence they were shipp'd for England: But, upon what Accident or Occasion I know not, the Vessel was carried into Holland, and lay there a year or two, (without any tydings about what was become of my Concerns being then my self at Paris) till coming at last to be unladen, Sir Richard Ford [...] finding by some Papers and Letters, with Directions on the Cases, and several Bales of Books, and other things (which I had been collecting in Italy,

---

[16] Ibid., 1178.

that they belonged to me) took care to have them all safely convey'd to me at London, to my no small charges.[17]

Evelyn proudly writes of having presented the tables, the first of their kind to ever have been produced, let alone brought to England, to the Royal Society. He describes subsequently lending them to the Royal College of Physicians as an aid for their anatomical lectures in 1652, as well as listing the various personalities who visited him to see such wonders. Most renowned in 1667, "after the happy Restauration, [...] his Majesty Charles the II. hearing of them, was pleas'd to come and see them himself to his great satisfaction."[18] Following such visit, as a celebration for his own fifty-seventh birthday, Evelyn donated the tables to the Royal Society, whence – via the stores of the British Museum – they made their way to the Royal College of Surgeon's Hunterian Museum in Lincoln's Inn Fields, London, where they are still preserved today.[19]

The second set is composed of six anatomical tables: a table of the nervous system, one of the veins, two arterial systems, one representing either the placenta or the portal venous system in an adult, and finally, the venous system of a quadruped animal. These tables were prepared just a few years after Evelyn's in the 1650s and belonged to the Earls of Winchelsea and Nottingham from the late seventeenth century until March 24th, 1823, when they were gifted to the Royal College of Physicians by George Finch, the then-current earl, with the following accompanying letter:

> Sir, I have in my possession some anatomical preparations which belonged to the late Dr. Harvey, which I have great pleasure in offering to the College of Physicians... these specimens of his scientific researches can be nowhere so well placed as in the hands of that learned body.[20]

Even if the claims that the tables were owned by William Harvey – discoverer of the circulatory system and University of Padua graduate – were questioned and disputed at the beginning of the twentieth century, these tables remain objects of extraordinary cultural value. They are still in possession of the Royal

---

[17] Ibid., 1178.

[18] Ibid., 1179.

[19] Special thanks to Hayley Kruger and Jo Clarke of the Royal College of Surgeons of England for securing images of the tables for this collection.

[20] The Royal College of Physicians website, "The Anatomical Tables."

College of Physicians and were the main objects on show in the award-winning 2012 exhibition "Curious Anatomys."

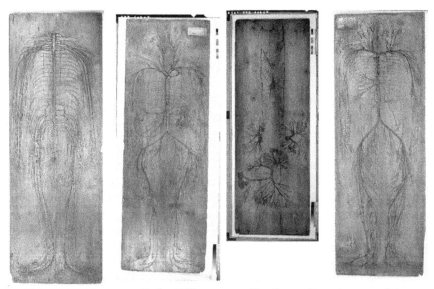

Figures 1.2, 1.3, 1.4, 1.5: Evelyn Tables, prepared by Giovanni Leoni, mounted dry tissue. From left to right: nervous system, arteries, nerves and veins of lungs and liver, and venous system. Hunterian Museum, Royal College of Surgeons, London.

Giovanni Leoni 's tables are exceptional. They are minutely detailed two-dimensional representations of a three-dimensional structure, demonstrating "an extraordinary high level of dissection technique, and also preservation techniques."[21] An analysis of the tables has revealed that the wooden surface has been both varnished and waxed. Traces of animal and fish glue, which may have been used as adhesive during the preparation of the tables, have been found, although experts suggest that if the tables were prepared with bodies dissected in the fresh state, as Evelyn's diary appears to suggest, the fluids from the bodies themselves would have been enough to glue the tissues to the panels.[22] These unique objects demonstrate great surgical skill, a fascination with the human body, and a strong commitment to the teaching of human anatomy and its advancement. However, the history and legacy of the tables, treated as they are as objects, albeit extraordinary, to be purchased,

---

[21] Royal College of Physicians, "The Story Behind 'Curious Anatomys," 4:00-4:04.
[22] Ibid., 10:38-11:34.

temporarily lost at sea, lent, borrowed, kept in storage, showcased, and gifted, rather than with the reverence that one would expect for human remains, may provide a clue to the reason why anatomy and the necessary objectification that came as a consequence of being the subject of a post-mortem investigation were regarded with terror in the early modern period.[23]

The tables were part of a collection of objects that Evelyn brought home from his travels; by comparison, he also wrote in his diary of having visited Murano: "famous for the best glasses in the world, where having viewed their furnaces, and seen their work, I made a collection of divers curiosities and glasses, which I sent for England by long sea."[24] Whereas while they were in possession of John Evelyn the tables were mainly treated as curiosities (not unlike the extraordinary glass artefacts from Murano) and they figure in their owner's diary together with the names of the important people who visited him to admire them, they finally achieved their original aim to be used "for the further and better knowledge, instruction, insight, learning, and experience in the [...] science or faculty of surgery" after Evelyn donated them to the Royal Society.[25] Discussing the tables during his 1701 Royal Society lecture, Cowper declared:

> [i]t is some satisfaction that I find the Arteries here so agreeable to a Figure which I Drew and Published not long since, from the Arteries of a Foetus Injected with Wax. But this Figure of the Veins differs so much

---

[23] Discussing anatomical examinations and the denial of burial as an "added dimension to capital punishment," Sawday writes that the "lack of a proper burial was not merely a disgrace to offenders and their families, but involved the posthumous punishment of the criminal's soul which would not rest whilst the remains lay ingathered within sanctified ground" (Sawday, *The Body Emblazoned*, 55). An example of the extreme lengths to which people may be willing to go in order to escape the blade of an anatomist's knife is that of Charles Byrne (1761-1783), the "Irish Giant." At a height of between 2.30 and 2.5o metres (depending on different accounts; his skeleton is 2.31 metres tall), Byrne was treated as a wonder for all his life, with a newspaper referring to him as a "modern living Colossus" in 1782. Afraid of being dissected by anatomists after his death, Byrne requested to be buried at sea. Unfortunately, the Bristol fishermen that he had entrusted with carrying out the procedure were bribed by John Hunter, who purchased the body for £130 (equivalent to £8,170.50 in 2005 currency). Over 200 years later, Byrne's skeleton is still part of the permanent exhibition in the Royal College of Surgeon's Hunterian Museum.

[24] Evelyn, *The Diary of John Evelyn*, entry for Venice, 210.

[25] Cunningham, *The Anatomist Anatomis'd*, 224 citing George Charles Peachey, *A Memoir of William and John Hunter*, 2; 4.

from any extant, as would incline one to suspect all of the subject hitherto published are Fictitious, not excepting even those of Vesalius.[26]

Richard Aspin calls this statement 'the high-point of the Evelyn tables' career,' but he adds that soon after this lecture, "the increasing use of the technique of injection in the preparation of anatomical specimens, particularly of the arteries and veins of the viscera, rendered the tables obsolete for scientific purposes, leaving them as objects of merely antiquarian interest."[27]

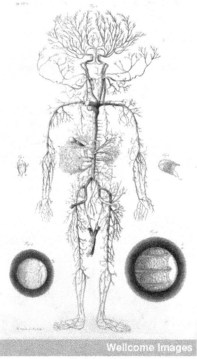

Figure 1.6: Arteries of the Human Foetus, from William Cowper, The Anatomy of Humane Bodies.

---

[26] Evelyn and Cowper, "An Account of Divers Schemes of Arteries and Veins," 1179. The "Figure" referenced in the passage quoted above was published in Cowper's *The Anatomy of Humane Bodies* in 1698 and represents Cowper's innovative look at the arterial system of an unborn foetus, compared and contrasted with a similar illustration by Govard Bidloo – the source of most of the plates printed in Cowper's book, provided in the *Anatomy* as figure 15) Cowper, *The Anatomy of Humane Bodies*, appendix, fig. 3).
[27] Aspin, "John Evelyn's Tables of Veins and Arteries," 494.

Whether renowned for their extravagance, usefulness as an aid to the teaching of anatomy, or as objects of antiquarian interest, John Evelyn's tables represent the multiplicity of varied and unconventional ways in which it was possible to engage with the study of human anatomy in the early modern world. The relevance they are granted within Evelyn's journal and the amount of interest they sparked amongst the diarist's acquaintances provide a clue to the fascination with which the mysteries of the human body and anatomy, the discipline most likely to uncover these secrets, were regarded in the seventeenth century. Additionally, the widespread enthusiasm with which the "tables of veins and arteries" were met in seventeenth-century London is a telling indication of the increasing importance and pervasiveness of medicalized representations of the body in early modern culture at large.

Somatic Epics and Anatomical Allegory in Early Modern English Literature and Culture

Interesting and compelling evidence of the appeal that new anatomical knowledge had in non-medical learned contexts is provided by Phineas Fletcher's 1633 masterpiece *The Purple Island*. Like the House of Alma in the second book of Edmund Spenser's *The Faerie Queene*, Fletcher's poem reveals itself to be a complex work of "somatic epic," painstakingly constructing a world that reveals itself to be an allegory of the human body.[28] *The Purple Island* is a long poem in 12 cantos, the first six of which are dedicated to a minute description of the island by the part of the poet and shepherd Thirsil. Like the early modern body, known and obvious to all but hiding under its surface secrets that only few can uncover, the island is

> A place too seldome view'd, yet still in view;
> Neare as our selves, yet farthest from our care;
> Which we by leaving find, by seeking lost;
> A forrain home, a strange, though native coast;
> Most obvious to all, yet most unknown to most.[29]

The first canto of *The Purple Island* narrates the creation of the island and parallels the biblical story of the fall of man,[30] establishing the theme of the

---

[28] Sawday, *The Body Emblazoned*, 170-82.

[29] Fletcher, *The Purple Island*, 1.34.3-7.

[30] Ibid., 1.49-54. In the third canto, Thirsil describes the island as not one but two islands, stressing the influence of the Book of Genesis on the description of how they were formed: "These two fair Isles distinct in their creation, / Yet one extracted from the

first half of the poem as a description of the anatomy of a Christianized, fallen yet redeemed, human body. It reveals a complex allegorical structure that sees the island working both as a metaphor for the human body and a dynastic realm/emerging nation (England).[31] In the second canto, Fletcher and Thirsil begin a systematic and coherent description of the geopolitical characteristics of the island that is distinctly influenced by the scientific and descriptive eye of anatomical treatises, but also by the "language of discovery and strangeness" that characterizes the early modern colonizing discourse: *The Purple Island* takes its reader on a journey into the human body, a land of strange, unknown geography. This creation of the body as the "uncanny familiar" may be understood as the direct creation of the anatomical gaze into the interior world of the body that objects such as Evelyn's tables permitted.[32]

The direct influence that non-narrative genres have on Fletcher is evident in the layout of his poem, which comes complete with long and detailed footnotes that carefully unpick the somatic metaphor for the reader and provides additional medical information regarding the function and appearance of the various bodily parts described. Fletcher's anatomical knowledge is clearly influenced by Galen's humoral theory, describing the bones as the "cold and drie" foundation upon which the island is built and focusing for several stanzas on bodily fluids and the same vessels that

---

others side." The difference between Arren, the masculine island, and Thelu, the feminine, is said to be evident only in the "sixt and last town" of the lowest region of the island, the seat of the genitalia, the islands being

Alike in all the rest, here disagreeing,

Where *Venus* and her wonton have their being:

For nothing is produc't of two in all agreeing.

(3.24-26).

[31] Mitchell, *The Purple Island and Anatomy in Early Seventeenth-Century Literature, Philosophy, and Theology*, 18.

[32] Sawday, *The Body Emblazoned*, 180. Peter Mitchell opens his extensive monograph on Fletcher's poem with an anecdote that substantiates Sawday's interpretation of *The Purple Island* as a piece of travel literature of sorts. In August 1645, historian and political writer James Howell, who was at the time detained in Fleet Prison due to his insolvency, wrote to Edward Benlowes thanking him for his visit and for the gift (or loan) of a copy of Fletcher's poem. In his letter Howell goes on to say, "you have enlarg'd my quarters 'mong these melancholy walls by sending me a whole Isle to walk in, I mean that delicate *purple Island* I received from you [...]; I stumble also ther often upon my self, and grow better acquainted with what I have within me and without me" (Mitchell, *The Purple Island and Anatomy*, 17).

Giovanni Leoni would extract and paste on wooden tables just over a decade
after the publication of *The Purple Island*.[33]

9
Nor is there any part in all this land,
But is a little Isle: for thousand brooks
In azure chanels glide on silfer sand;
Their serpent windings, and deceiving crooks
Circling about, and wat'ring all the plain,
Emptie themselves into th' all-drinking main;
And creeping forward slide, but never turn again.

> The whole body is as it were
> watered with great plenty of
> rivers, veins, arteries, and nerves.

10
Three diff'ring streams from fountains different,
Neither in nature nor in shape agreeing,
(Yet each with other friendly ever went)
Give to this Isle his fruitfulnesse and being:
The first in single chanels skie-like blue,
With luke-warm waters di'd in porphyr hue,
Sprinkle this crimson Isle with purple-colour'd dew.

> A vein is a vessel long, round, hollow,
> rising from the liver, appointed to
> contein, concoct, and distribute the
> bloud. It hath but one tunicle, and that
> thinne; the colour of this blood is purple.

11
The next, though from the same springs first it rise,
Yet passing through another greater fountain,
Doth lose his former name and qualities:
Through many a dale it flows, and many a mountain;
More firie light, and needful more then all;
And therefore fenced with a double wall,
All froths his yellow streams with many a sudding fall.

---

[33] Among the fluids described by Fletcher, venous blood, "purple-colour'd" and spreading
its "porphyr hue" to the island, is considered of greatest importance for the body and the
very title of the poem comes from it.

An arterie is a vessel long, round, hollow,
formed for conveyance of that more
spritely bloud, which is elaborate in the
heart. This bloud is frothy, yellowish, full
of spirits, therefore compast with a
double tunicle, that it might not exhale or
sweat out by reason of the thinnesse.

12

The last, in all things diff'ring from the other,
Fall from an hill, and close together go,
Embracing as they runne, each with his brother;
Guarded with double trenches sure they flow:
The coldest spring, yet nature best they have;
And like the lacteall stones which heaven pave,
Slide down to every part with their thick milky wave.

A nerve is a spermaticall part rising from
the brain and the pith of the backbone, the
outside skinne, the inside full of pith,
carrying the animall spirits for sense and
motion and therefore doubly skinned as the
brain: none of them single, but runne
in couples.

13

These with a thousand streams through th' Island roving,
Bring tribute in; the first gives nourishment,
Next life, last sense and arbitrarie moving:
For when the Prince hath now his mandate sent,
The nimble poasts quick down the river runne,
And end their journey, though but now begunne;
But now the mandate came, & now the mandate's done.[34]

The veins convey nourishment from the
liver, the arteries life and heat from the
heart, the nerves sense and motion from
the brain. The will commands, the nerve
brings, and the part executes the
mandate; all almost in an instant.

[34] Fletcher, *Purple Island*, 2.9-13 with Fletcher's original footnotes.

As evidenced from the excerpt above, "[t]he rhetoric of anatomical observations sometimes creates the effect of an imaginary presence of the anatomised body, as though the poetic description itself were methodically consistent with or even performing an anatomical dissection."[35] The thirteenth stanza (above) and relative commentary are particularly revealing of the rigorousness and accuracy of Phineas Fletcher's medical knowledge: in 1636, three years after the publication of *The Purple Island*, Alexander Read published his *A Treatise of all the Muscules of the Whole Bodie*, which, in its description of veins, arteries, and nerves, repeats Fletcher's words almost *verbatim*: Fletcher's poem reads "the first [veins] give nourishment, / Next [arteries] life, last [nerves] sense and arbitrarie moving,"[36] whereas Reid wrote "[t]he veines affoord nourishment, the arteries life, and the nerves motion."[37] After bones, veins, nerves, and arteries, the organs that spread to the whole of the body, Fletcher's narrator describes the island as divided into three main parts:

14
The whole Isle, parted in three regiments,
By three Metropolies is jointly sway'd;
Ord'ring in peace and warre their governments
With loving concord, and with mutuall aid:
The lowest hath the worst, but largest See;
The middle lesse, of greater dignitie:
The highest least, but holds the greatest soveraigntie.[38]

As explained in the related footnote, the three cities are identified, from the bottom up, as the belly, the breast, and the head: "In the lowest, the liver is sovereigne, whose regiment is the widest, but meanest. In the middle the heart reigns, most necessarie. The brain obtains the highest place, and is the least in compasse, so the greatest in dignitie."[39]

Edmund Spenser wrote *The Faerie Queene* at the end of the sixteenth century and imbued it with a similar interest in anatomy, which makes it possible to postulate that an anatomized view of society is not exclusive to the seventeenth century, but indeed endemic to the early modern construct of the world and its spaces. Spenser structures the ninth canto of the second book of

---

[35] Mitchell, *The Purple Island and Anatomy*, 17.
[36] Fletcher, *Purple Island*, 2.13.1-2.
[37] Read, *A Treatise of All the Muscules of the Whole Bodie*, 1-5.
[38] Fletcher, *Purple Island*, 2.14.
[39] Ibid., footnote to 2.14.

his epic poem as an extensive and detailed allegory in which the human body is transformed and described as a castle, the House of Alma (a witty pun, as the word *alma*, which means *nourishing* in Latin, is the root for the word *soul* in several Romantic languages – hence "House of Alma" would translate into "House of the Soul": the body). Spenser represents the body as similarly divided into three sections ordered in crescent degree of perfection, each section associated with a geometrical shape. The House of Alma is described as a castle "so high, as foe might not it clime":[40]

[t]he frame thereof seemd partly circulare,
And part triangulare, O worke diuine;
Those two the first and last proportions are,
The one imperfect, mortall, foeminine;
Th'other immortall, perfect, masculine,
And twixt them both a quadrate was the base.[41]

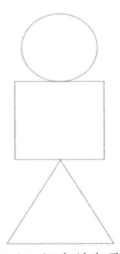

Figure 1.7: Geometric Shapes Associated with the Three Sections of the Body.

The shape described recreates the silhouette of a standing person, with head, trunk, and legs astride (Figure 1.7): "As a primary figure (Proportioned) without beginning or end, the circle is perfect, and immortall as it refers to God and eternity. Being less simple and stable, the triangle is imperfect, and,

---

[40] Spenser, *The Faerie Queene*, II.ix.21.2.
[41] Ibid., II.ix.22.1-6.

by contrast, mortall."[42] The union of the feminine and masculine by a quadrate indicates the androgynous state of the castle. Additionally,

> [t]hese three figures refer to the three human souls: the circle to the rational soul, the quadrate to the sensible, and the triangle to the vegetable. Further, the quadrate is associated with the four elements and the four humours that connect the body to the soul, indicating that the frame refers also to the body's temperament.[43]

Despite including the legs in the outline of the castle, Spenser's description of the House of Alma focuses on the same body parts that constitute the three cities of the Purple Island. Spenser carefully details the various steps in the process of digestion, framed by the mouth and the anus, lists the various organs involved, and sketches characters such as Diet, Appetite, and Concoction, respectively representing "the temperate course of life," hunger, and the first stage of digestion where the ingested foods are boiled or cooked together (from Latin *con+coquere*) in the stomach.[44] The heart is Alma's "goodly Parlour," or bedchamber, where nine fair ladies, representing the nine affections or moods dwell, and where Guyon and Arthur rest for a while, each courting a different lady.[45] Finally, Alma and the knights reach the brain, a

> chamber filled […] with flies,
> Which buzzed all about, and made such sound,
> That the encombred all mens eares and eyes,
> Like many swarmes of Bees assembled round,
> After their hiues with honny abound:
> All those were idle thoughtes and fantasies,
> Deuices, dreames, opinions vnsound,
> Shewes, visions, sooth-sayes, and prophesies;
> And all that fained is, as leasings, tales, and lies.[46]

The brain is contained in a 'stately Turret' (the head), that receives light from the eyes, "Two goodly Beacons, set in watches stead, / Therein gaue light, and

---

[42] Ibid., footnote to II.ix.22, 238-9.
[43] ibid.
[44] Ibid., footnote to II.ix.31, 240-1.
[45] Ibid., II.ix.33-43.
[46] Ibid., II.ix.51.

flamed continually," and is reached climbing ten alabaster steps (the ten vertebrae that separate the heart from the base of the skull).[47]

Spenser's and Fletcher's exclusive focus on the trunk and the head appears at first to be an odd choice, considering the painstaking attention to details that they display in their anatomical descriptions and, in Fletcher's case, footnotes. It is however a testament to the fact that both the poets subscribed to a typically early modern attitude that considered the limbs to be of a considerable lesser status and importance when compared to the body's internal organs and head, mirroring representations of the English society as a body politic. This social construct, which has its most striking visual representation on the cover of Thomas Hobbes' 1651 politico-philosophical masterpiece *Leviathan*, was based on the theory of the King's two bodies:

> the one whereof is a Body natural, consisting of natural Members as every other Man has [...]; the other is a Body politic, and the Members thereof are of his Subjects, and he and his Subjects together compose the Corporation [...], and he is the Head, and they are the Members, and he has the sole Government of them; and this Body is not subject to Passions [...] nor to Death.[48] (Figure 1.8)

Figure 1.8: Thomas Hobbes, *Leviathan*, 1651.

---

[47] Ibid., II. ix.44-46.
[48] Kantorowicz, *The King's Two Bodies*, 13.

In the context of the body politic, and most aptly considered in the passages from Fletcher and Spenser addressed above, the King was seen alternatively as the head (as in the head of state whose decisions govern the rest of society), the heart (without which the body would instantly die), or the stomach (an interpretation derived from Aesop's fable of the belly and revisited by Shakespeare in the first act of *Coriolanus*), and his subjects as the limbs, increasingly farther away from the kingly center of power ("What do you think? / You, the great toe of this assembly?" asks Menenius Agrippa to one of the citizens in *Coriolanus*).[49]

Menenius narrates a "pretty tale" of the time...

> when all the body's members
> Rebell'd against the belly, thus accused it:
> That only like a guld it did remain
> I' the midst o' the body, idle and unactive,
> Still cupboarding the viand, never bearing
> Like labour with the rest, where the other instruments
> Did see and hear, devise, instruct, walk, feel,
> And, mutually participate, did minister
> Unto the appetite and affection common
> Of the whole body.[50]

He clarifies the metaphor by identifying the Roman aristocracy with the belly, which has the right to access the most and the best food produced by the labor of the limbs:

> The senators of Rome are this good belly,
> And you the mutinous members; for examine
> Their counsels and their cares, digest things rightly
> Touching the weal o' the common, you shall find
> No public benefit which you receive
> But it proceeds or comes from them to you
> And no way from yourselves.[51]

As well as a clear literary declination of the theory of the King's two bodies – the senators have their own, individual bodies, but together they constitute

---

[49] Shakespeare, *Coriolanus*, 1.1.149-50.
[50] Ibid., 1.1.72-81.
[51] Ibid., 1.1.129-35.

the stomach of the Roman society – this passage, with its somatic details, extended corporeal metaphor, and careful bestowal of different degrees of importance to various individual body parts, represents another example of medicalized discourse making its way into the spaces of literature and drama.

Final Remarks

This chapter has examined and argued for the relevance of anatomical investigations and the knowledge they produced in early modern understandings of the world and society. By pairing considerations about the history of the "rare tables of veins and arteries" with an analysis of excerpts from texts such as *The Purple Island* and *The Faerie Queene*, this chapter demonstrates that the peering eye of the anatomist and his curiosity in revealing, layer after layer, the secrets concealed by the skin contributed not only to the circulation of anatomical curiosities such as – among countless examples of human and non-human preserved specimens – the Evelyn tables, but also to the creation of new literary styles heavily influenced by the language and practice of academic dissection.

The creation and circulation of anatomical knowledge depended on international academic networks that spanned the whole of Europe. Not unlike today, students would flock to universities renowned for their illustrious medical programs and celebrated lecturers, bringing home new knowledge, innovative methods and, in some cases, rare curiosities. The relevance acquired by the Evelyn tables in seventeenth-century London, as argued above, is evidence that the fascination with the knowledge created and spread through academic dissections wasn't confined to the spaces of academic circles, but on the other hand was common to all learned society. This fascination expressed itself throughout the early modern period in a variety of media and formats, such as *ecorchés* and paintings, but also literary works such as the somatic epics and corporeal allegories examined within this chapter.

No record of the identity of the people who were anatomized in Padua in the 1640s and 50s, and whose veins, arteries, and nerves are still on display today at the Royal Colleges of Physicians and of Surgeons in London survives today. We cannot know if they were outlaws whose crimes were so heinous, they were deemed unworthy of a proper burial and of the promise of resurrection, or if they were poor patients at San Francesco Hospital whose bodies nobody claimed. We cannot know if they approached death with terror and dread at the idea of becoming objectified under the dissector's knife, but we can presume that they would never have imagined that almost 400 years later and so far away from their home, we would still be looking at the remains of their bodies in wonder and amazement. Likewise, very little information about Giovanni Leoni survives beyond the few references made about him in John

Evelyn's diary and his letter to William Cowper. However, the works by Spenser and Fletcher analyzed in this chapter, with their rich and detailed somatic descriptions, demonstrate that the "rare tables of veins and nerves" that he created, and that Evelyn brought home from Italy, are both a perfect expression of the culture in which they were created, commissioned, and purchased, and unique artefacts that pushed the boundaries of early modern culture further.

Chapter 2

The Anatomy Theater in Renaissance Italy: A Space of Justice?

David Soulier

Université Côte d'Azur

Abstract: The supply of dissection material remained the main concern of anatomy professors in early modern times. In letters and publications, anatomists complained they had to be content with animal corpses because of the lack of human cadavers provided by the university. However, they were aware that the Renaissance anatomy theater was not only a space of science, but rather a space of intersection and even conflict between science and justice. The fascination with death was for some an opportunity to acquire knowledge through dissections, for others a deterrent through executions decreed as examples. But despite the large number of capital sentences, the bodies condemned to death were not always provided for anatomy lectures. The paradoxical difficulty for the *riformatori* to obtain anatomical material from the *podestà* challenges us to question the will of justice to supply corpses for dissection. Contrary to what one may believe, academic anatomical material was scarce, and some anatomists decided to secretly stock up from gallows or to pressure judges, as they admitted in their treatises. This chapter illustrates the attempt to reconcile science and justice within the Renaissance anatomy theater in northern Italy in the 1540s-1550s, namely those in Padua, Pisa, Ferrara, which attracted the most famous anatomists of the era, such as Andreas Vesalius, Gabriele Falloppio, Giovanni Battista Canani. Ultimately, this chapter challenges the notion that dissections were primarily seen as extensions of juridical punishment.

Keywords: Anatomy, Dissection, Corpse, Justice, Padua, Pisa, Ferrara

***

Introduction

Nowadays, any anatomical faculty may be obviously seen as a space of science only, inside which teaching anatomists produce knowledge by dissecting an anatomical material constituted by deceased persons who gave their own body to science itself. However, the anatomy theater in Renaissance Italy, where first flourished what is called the "anatomical Renaissance," has been once considered by the historiographic tendency as much a space of science as a space of justice, since the only legal prime source of material used for public anatomies was the corpses of executed people (besides frequent secret sources like unclaimed deceased in hospitals, victims of murder, suicides, postmortems, or especially grave robbing): in order to share science with his students, the dissector had to inflict several damages to the exposed criminal body that are likely to be perceived as a continuation or culmination of the capital punishment outraging the body as well as the soul.

In fact, according to Katharine Park, the Italian medical universities in the early sixteenth century saw a renewed interest in human anatomy resulting in an unprecedented hunger for cadavers, so that many asked for a legalization of dissection from judicial power.[1] This legalized source of anatomical material in public dissections suggests that complicity links between anatomists and the officials of criminal justice have been somewhat inflated.[2] So, despite its academic status, the Renaissance Italian anatomy theater might appear as a space inside which the anatomist would act not only as a teacher devoted to science, but also as an executive agent of the judicial power by applying, with his scalpel and before his students, an ultimate punishment to the criminal body drawn from the gallows, which receives from dissection a new mark of infamy making it unfit even for a decent funeral.[3]

This long-persistent discourse was first stated in the account of Jonathan Sawday, influenced by Michel Foucault's theories on state biopower controlling the life of the citizens as well as their bodies.[4] In *The Body Emblazoned*, Jonathan Sawday combines the teaching anatomist's traditional scientific function with a certain judicial duty in any Renaissance European anatomy theater (such as the English case with the 1752 Murder Act), by asserting that "the anatomist, in his scientific jurisdiction over and above the

---

[1] Park, "The Criminal and the Saintly Body," 14-5.

[2] Ibid., 20-1.

[3] For a brief historical review about the use of the bodies of the executed in anatomy teaching, see Sabine Hildebrandt's "Capital Punishment and Anatomy: History and Ethics of an Ongoing Association." *Clinical Anatomy* 21, no. 1 (2008): 5-14.

[4] Foucault, *Discipline and Punish*, 48.

criminal body, expressed the symbolic power of knowledge over the individual, a continuation of the process by which the individual was forced, on the gallows, to acknowledge the legitimacy of the sovereign power over his or her body."[5] Also, he connects public anatomies to public executions "as two acts in a single drama" whose mutual relationship was evident during the "ritual of investigation" taking place inside the theater, a ritual that "can only be understood when we recall that the corpse which was carried into the theater had been retrieved from a chaotic, violent, and hostile spectacle of judicial power."[6]

Thus, this interpretation puts together both scientific and judicial purposes inside the Renaissance anatomy theater so that the dissected criminal body allegedly served to extend juridical power from disordered tribunals and gallows to the ordered academic world. Such a conception reduces the pedagogical role of any anatomist to the role of a mere civil servant imbricated in a hierarchy of power between the medico-judicial authority and the dissected body. From this point of view, any anatomy theater may be regarded as a space of expression for secular punishment within which public anatomies would only serve to reflect the State power over the criminal body with the same deterrent effect as public executions. Thus, the idea of a politico-academic link tends to bring to the forefront an intimate association between anatomist and executioner in the frame of the expansion of absolutist governments in Early Modern era.[7]

However, this Foucauldian conception of the anatomy theater as a judicialized academic space and of the anatomy professor as an agent of power has already been partly questioned in the case of Renaissance Italy. Though supposing the new enthusiasm for anatomy there brought anatomist and executioner into closer association, Katharine Park pointed out, "there is no evidence here that dissection itself, at least in this period, was considered part of the criminal's penalty,... nor does it seem to have been seen by either judges or criminals as specifically punitive in intent."[8] More recently, Cynthia Klestinec argued that to regard public anatomies as expressions of secular punishment on criminal bodies is "to overlook the theological significance of execution and the role of public anatomies within the extended social ritual of punishment," a ritual to which contributed brotherhoods of comforters

---

[5] Sawday, *The Body Emblazoned*, 64.

[6] Ibid, 62-3.

[7] For more about the vision of the criminal body in English literature and Renaissance anatomical iconography, see Powell.

[8] Park, "The Criminal and the Saintly Body," 20.

consoling the condemned, so that "the connection between executioner and anatomist appears so fleetingly."[9]

Actually, the question whether or not this Foucauldian concept is valid should depend instead on a key point that seems to have received little emphasis so far: the supply in criminal bodies from the administrator of local justice or *podestà* in Italy. Indeed, a supposed collaboration between the anatomy professor and the judicial authority normally implies a regular supply in anatomical material to dissect – admitting that the provided material was exclusively composed of hanged or decapitated bodies and that the judicial officer participated directly in public anatomy as well as in public execution.

Nevertheless, in Renaissance Italy, this condition of supply turned out to be so problematic that the selection criteria of anatomical material were not aimed at local criminal bodies and the anatomists had to pass through literal underground means. As a rule, the difficulties the anatomists encountered in obtaining cadavers to dissect reflects a difference in fascination with death between academic world and State power. So, this underrated problem, which is likely to compromise the idea of a judicialized anatomy theater, leads us to redefine the space of anatomy theater in Renaissance Italy as dedicated to science and/or justice by taking into account the availability of the anatomical material from acts of justice.

So, this chapter reconsiders, through the problem of supply in anatomical material from justice, the Foucauldian concept of the Renaissance Italian anatomy theater as a space of intersection between science and justice on the base of various and mostly unpublished mid-sixteenth century documents concerning especially the illustrious anatomy university in Padua and the renowned anatomists Andreas Vesalius (1514-1564), Realdo Colombo (1515-1559), and Gabriele Falloppio (1523-1562). I shall try to answer a couple of still-unanswered questions regarding the eventual interactions between science and justice inside the Renaissance anatomy theater: Were public anatomies of criminal bodies really used as a crime deterrent (as that will occur in England two centuries later)? Did the actors and participants of these public anatomies consciously grant more importance to science or to justice? I shall first analyze a famous engraved depiction of the Renaissance Italian anatomy theater hiding a space that may be dedicated to justice, then examine the regulations established by the university statutes regarding the preparation and holding of anatomy lectures, and finally note their results on the courses given by the aforesaid anatomists through a selection of letters.

---

[9] Klestinec, *Theaters of Anatomy*, 130-1.

The Renaissance Italian Anatomy Theater in Picture: What Place for Justice?

The well-known and largely discussed frontispiece of Andreas Vesalius' 1543 *De humani corporis fabrica* (Figure A) offers a spectacular (in the etymological sense), though hardly faithful, representation of a temporary anatomy theater built at the Studium in Padua towards 1540, in whose center the author himself is shown performing a public dissection before a large and varied audience.[10] Different spaces within this depicted anatomy theater can be localized through the places given to the spectators according to their different social conditions (students, laymen, clerics). Among them, a symbolic space of justice may be defined with the character standing in the place of honor on the right in the foreground. Judging by his honorary dress, one might identify an eminent figure of the local criminal justice at that time: Marcantonio Contarini,[11] podestà of Padua and member of the Venetian Senate.

Vesalius respectfully mentioned Contarini in his treatise when talking about the heads of decapitated men provided after their execution: he expresses his gratitude for receiving a "rich abundance of bodies for the practice of anatomy" from this podestà, who was a "very studious and assiduous spectator of the human fabric."[12] Thus, Contarini is said to have supplied the Flemish anatomist, whose classes this judge assiduously attended with criminal bodies. This supply may be implied in the *Fabrica*'s frontispiece: Contarini is pointing directly at the body dissected by Vesalius and lying on the table in the very center of the theater, the body of a woman who undoubtedly had been condemned to death. This woman, according to the author, had tried in vain to avoid hanging by falsely declaring herself pregnant before being examined by midwives on orders of Contarini, who then handed her body over to Vesalius after the execution.[13] More generally in this judicial sphere, as well as through torture, the judge extracted from a body the truth regarding some human fault; similarly through dissection, the anatomist extracts from this same body the truth regarding the creative Nature, so that

---

[10] For a description of the *Fabrica* frontispiece, see Cunningham, *The Anatomical Renaissance*, 124-30; Carlino, *Books of the Body*, 39-53; Mandressi, *Le regard de l'anatomiste*, 107-8; Klestinec, *Theaters of Anatomy*, 32-5.

[11] Fontana, 231-2. On Contarini, see O'Malley, *Andreas Vesalius of Brussels*, 113.

[12] Vesalius, *De humani corporis fabrica*, 650-1: "qui nunc Patavinae urbis Praetor vigilantissimus, uberem profecto nobis ad Anatomes administrandas copiam suppeditat, ipse humanae corporis fabricae studiosissimus indefessusque spectator" (personal translation). Reference to Contarini omitted in the 1555 edition because of his death nine years prior.

[13] Vesalius, *Fabrica*, 539.

justice and science both somehow help the corrupted soul rehabilitate itself
on its way to redemption according to theological view.[14]

As his gesture suggests, the podestà appears here as the one who provided this
criminal body, presumably so it could receive an ultimate punishment from the
Flemish anatomist. Thus, this depicted anatomy theater might be viewed as a
space of intersection between dissection and execution, justice being a source
of supply in anatomical material. This source of supply may be also pictorially
implied in some of the initial letters scattered throughout Vesalius' treatise: the
letter L (Figure 2.1), for example, shows a hanged man lowered from the scaffold
before the eyes of the crowd and a priest carrying a cross.[15]

Figure 2.1: The Letter L from Vesalius' Andreae Vesalii Bruxellensis.

---

[14] See Silverman, 9. For more about the links between torture and surgery, see 133-52.
[15] Vesalius *Fabrica*, 55, 153. On this letter, see Carlino, *Books of the Body*, 218.

Likewise, the assumption of a complicity between judges and anatomists in Renaissance Italy has often been induced by a long-quoted personal anecdote Vesalius recalled in his 1546 *China Root Epistle*, alluding probably to Contarini himself: "I will no longer bother judges to have people killed by this or that execution, or to reserve them for this or that time suited to our dissections."[16] Therefore, this apparent confession of connivance of Vesalius with the Padua podestà might lead us to visualize the Renaissance Italian anatomy theater not only as a space of science, but also as a space of justice: the same deterrent intention as in public executions would be expressed in these public dissections before the eyes of students somehow warned by the teaching anatomist, who would act as a Foucauldian agent of power.

However, this presumed collaboration between both judiciary and academic worlds requests at least three conditions: a direct participation of the judicial officer in the public dissection as in the public execution; anatomical material exclusively composed of criminal bodies used as a crime deterrent; and especially a regular and constant supply of corpses of the executed. But this last key condition faces the main problem encountered by more than one anatomist: the supply in anatomical material, about which many dissectors were particularly concerned.

In fact, if Vesalius claimed to have insistently solicited Contarini to obtain some criminal body and even suggested the method and moment of execution, that should reveal instead less a zeal in completing the podestà's role than an unceasing concern, namely a scarcity in anatomical material. Conversely, if Contarini, according to his afore-cited mention in the *Fabrica*, provided Vesalius with dissection material, the reason is less about some care in applying his deterrent power even before the eyes of anatomy students than (as said above) his exceptional interest in anatomical science.

Likewise, to interpret Contarini's gesture as dissuasive in the *Fabrica*'s title page is to ignore his gaze oddly turned away from the dissection scene. Actually, the podestà's attention is attracted by a dog, doubtless female, brought inside the theater in case it may serve as some substitute anatomical material, same as for the little rhesus monkey on the left (or to compare with Galen anatomy based on animals). The judge, contemptuously looking at the dog shown by a participant, seems to respond with a refusal by pointing at the

---

[16] Vesalius, *Fabrica*, 194: "Non modo iudicibus molestus ero, ut hoc aut illo supplicio homines necari curent, sive in hoc aut illud tempus nostris sectionibus opportunum conservent" (personal translation). Mentioned in Martinotti, 44; Park, "The Criminal and the Saintly Body," 20.

dissected female cadaver as to enhance the value of this rare human material for scientific knowledge.

So, this famous picture of the Renaissance Italian anatomy theater hides without doubt a double message the author wanted to convey: the frequent lack of human material to dissect from justice, and, as a result, the recurrent need to fall back upon animal corpses. Indeed, contrary to what this title page might suggest, the human corpses available to Vesalius for his anatomy lectures were in extremely limited number, especially the female ones (less numerous among the criminal bodies), and not always appropriated.[17]

Vesalius remained concerned by this problem of unavailability and unsuitability of the anatomical material until the very last public dissection he performed at the Paduan Studium. In a letter to Benedetto Varchi, secretary to the Duke of Florence, written on December 11th, 1543 in Padua, Vesalius appears anxious to give his anatomical lecture on some corpse he luckily acquired from another source than executions that provides less healthy subjects: "Since I think this will be the last of all dissections I will have ever performed, I will have to fulfill it with the greatest diligence and correctness and therefore to devote more time than usual, besides the fact we have to conceal here the suitability of cadavers."[18]

Vesalius expressed similar complaints regarding the unavailability in corpses of pregnant women, so he very often had to be content with canine or caprine uteruses and fetuses as makeshift material. In his *China Root Epistle*, he admits he had only once or twice the occasion to observe a human fetus in utero before his *Fabrica* was printed, but never for his last course given in winter 1543.[19] Similarly, in his 1564 *Examination of the Anatomical Observations of Gabriele Falloppio*, the Flemish anatomist regrets not to have had the opportunity of dissecting a pregnant woman when his *Fabrica* was being republished in 1555.[20]

Because of the frequent lack in criminal bodies, it is no surprise Vesalius felt obliged to search for human material by risky underground means at night, such as going on peregrinations in cemeteries or near gibbets to carry

---

[17] See for example Vesalius, *Fabrica*, 538-9.
[18] Biblioteca Nazionale Centrale di Firenze (BNCF), Fondo Palatino, Autografi, II 118, f. 139r: "Quandoquidem hanc omnium, quas forte unquam obiturus sum, postremam fore coniicio, mearum erit partium pro mea virili illam sedulo & diligenter aggredi, ac proinde solito plus temporis impendere, praeterquam quod cadaverum opportunitas nobis hic sit operienda" (personal translation).
[19] Vesalius, *Examination of the Anatomical Observations*, 143.
[20] Ibid., 154.

subjects he then kept at home.[21] Among findings by grave robbing, Vesalius mentioned in his *Fabrica* the body of the mistress of a monk that had been removed from its grave by Paduan students and then entirely flayed so that it could not be recognized.[22]

Thus, since Contarini was a judge acting more for science than for justice, and Vesalius an anatomist concerned with the lack of anatomical material, the Foucauldian concept granting a place of justice in any Renaissance anatomy theater already needs at this point some reassessment. However, the cause of this problem of scarcity in anatomical material lay nowhere else than in the university statutes regarding the preparation and holding of anatomy courses.

University Selection Criteria for the Anatomical Material: The Foreign Criminal Body

The supervision of anatomy teaching as well as the supply of anatomical material in the Renaissance Italian anatomy theaters were ordered by formal codes instituted by university statutes which were similar from one Studium to another. In the case of the Padouan Studium, whose statutes may have served as a model for other Italian gymnasiums, the preparation of public anatomies was organized by a rector (elected student representative), two *consiliarii* (presidents of the student Nazioni), and two *massarii* (graduate student assistants and elected through their affiliation to the Nazioni) responsible for setting up the event that was then held in a temporary theater built of wood (before the erection of a permanent one at Fabrizi d'Acquapendente's initiative in 1594). While the consiliarii were at the head of a general assembly that directed the entire institution, the massarii, also called *anathomistae* or *anatomistini*, were in charge of providing dissection material to professors as well as collecting instruments, regulating the entrance to the session and collecting a fee covering the preparation costs, and lastly, filtering and monitoring the audience — composed of students, academics, and magistrates, among whom was at least one of the Venetian *riformatori* or administrators of the Studium.[23]

Regarding the period of anatomy courses, the Paduan university statutes stipulated the holding of one dissection per year, which normally took place during the winter, namely from January to February, and could last up to six

---

[21] Ibid., 194.

[22] Ibid., 538.

[23] Archivio Antico dell'Università di Padova (AAUP), filza 665, Raccolta Minato, seria 20, Teatro anatomico, De Anatomia singulis annis facienda XXVIII (Status 28 regulating the annual holding of Anatomy), f. 263v.

weeks. The choice of this season took into account both a practical concern (better conservation of cadavers) and a certain liberty of morals (Christmas vacations and Carnival festivities) that favored tolerance for an act some might find scandalous, and therefore left little room for the deterrence spirit the judiciary would maintain in people's minds.

Yet the supply in anatomical material depended on strict university regulations imposing rigorously restrictive selection criteria. The number of provided bodies was limited to two: depending on availability, two corpses of a man or woman, or only one of either sex. The corpse had to be that of a criminal (*delinquens*) sentenced to death (*supplicium capitis*) by the podestà or officers of justice (*praetores*). But to this criterion was added another that could prove particularly frustrating: in order to divert any dishonor from the town, the supplied criminal body had to be that of a foreigner, namely neither a native of Padua nor a Venetian citizen (Padua being then under the Serenissima's dependence); there was a penalty of a very high fine (1,000 lire) for failure to meet this criterion.[24]

The university administrators remained uncompromising about the origin of the provided material, even if, when local justice had no criminal executed during the preparation and holding of anatomy courses (i.e., from the beginning of the academic year to the end of February), they could authorize, exceptionally and without any hindering decree, the dissection of an executed person coming from the citadel of Padua or from any other place in its territory. In short, the body of a foreign criminal perfectly fit the selection criteria, which thus drastically reduced the field of search for dissection material.

Because of this regulation aiming exclusively at foreign bodies, it is hardly conceivable to see the Renaissance Italian anatomy theater as a space for the extension of capital punishment inflicted by the local justice system whose deterrent power is supposed to be efficiently applied when executing local criminals. By the way, the university statutes did not imply any direct participation of the podestà in public dissection as in public execution. Indeed, the rules stipulated that the praetores intervened only at the request of the rector, a consiliarius, and the students to provide them with criminal bodies: the officer of justice thus played a part only outside the theater, being less a direct actor than a source occasionally solicited by the university administration and not solely by the anatomy professor.

Likewise, the university statutes imply a pedagogical rather than dissuasive scope of anatomical teaching: the Studium intends to authorize public

---

[24] Ibid., f. 263r. See Annex 1. Transcribed in *Statuta*, f. XXVIIr. See Klestinec, 132.

dissections "not only for the interest of [its] students, but also for the health of the whole human race" (*non modo ad nostrorum scholarium utilitatem, sed etiam totius humani generis salutem*), thus acting for science and medicine only. From this angle, the anatomy theater easily appears more as a space of science than as a space of justice.

The conditions and challenges for the organization of anatomy courses were practically the same in some other Italian universities. The Nuovo Studio Pisano, whose statutes were established by the Duke of Florence, Cosimo de' Medici, stipulated, also for the good of medicine and the human race's health, that every winter the university administrator (rector) procure for public anatomy two cadavers of criminals (delinquentes) condemned to death, one male, the other female, or at least one of either sex, by submitting a request to the justice officer (*commissarius*) in Pisa. Similarly, in the Pisan case, the provided body had to be that of a foreigner, namely neither a Florentine or Pisan citizen, nor a master or student – no doubt in response to desperate attempts at supplying that could be prejudicial to the university staff itself!

Likewise, in the absence of any criminal body in Pisa during the period of the anatomy, the administrator had to write to the jails' directors in Florence to obtain the required material.[25]

At the Ferrara Gymnasium, the statutes also provided, for the good of students, that the rector would request a single criminal body from the town's podesta each year, specifying that in order to put an end to the usual brawls and rumors during the search for material, no master, student or any other person would attempt to procure any dead body for the anatomy without first obtaining the rector's permission.[26] At the Alma Studiorum in Bologna, the rector and the consiliarii had to request two cadavers for anatomy, one male, the other female, or two men if there was no female body from the podestà or conservator *iustitiae* of the town each year on the sole condition that the executed were born at least 30 miles away from Bologna.[27] At the Studium Urbis in Rome, the Vicar Cardinal, the Senator, or the Governor of the City in

---

[25] Fabroni, 73-4, n. 1. See Annex 2. See also Zampieri, 201-4.

[26] Biblioteca Classense di Ravenna, ms. 426, De Anathomia quolibet anno fienda, f. 35v. See annex 3. Transcribed in Borsetti, 436. See also Muratori, 98-100.

[27] Riforme degli Statuti dell'Università di Medicina e d'Arti promulgate nel 1452, rubr. XIX, p. 318 (De subjectis per Potestatem singulo anno dandis pro Anothomia). See Martinotti, 50; Ferrari, 54. Baldasar Heseler relates that Vesalius, passing by the Bologna faculty in January 1540, gave an anatomy lecture in collaboration with Matteo Corti on six living dogs and three criminals hanged on the occasion and carried from the gallows to the Ospedale della Morte (see Eriksson).

connection with the courts had to provide the material for the gymnasium, the only selection criterion being that the supplied body had to be of a person condemned to death.[28]

In most of these Italian university statutes, we easily observe that public dissection did not have the same purpose as public execution: instead of extending the deterrent power of justice under the students' eyes, anatomy courses only aimed at students' interest (*utilitas*) in the sense of both scientific and medical profit. Moreover, these statutes relegated the officer of justice, whether podestà, praetor, or commisarius from one town to another, to the role of a mere external supplier of dissection material, expressly stipulating he was bound to assign some criminal body to every request issued at least by the university's rector. Above all, it was clearly ordered that the procured criminal body should preferably be that of a stranger or unknown person (*ignotus* or *ignobilis*) with no ties to the town and distant enough from it. These strict regulations and selection criteria, which diminished the range of availability in criminal bodies and the chances of dissecting one in the theater, could only cause significant difficulties in the supply of anatomical material, especially since this material did not necessarily come from the gallows.

Condemned Bodies and Dissected Bodies: A Divergence of Fascination with Death

According to the remaining registers kept in Padua archives, it seems impossible to report any systematic transfer of selected bodies of the executed to the Studium theater, at least towards the mid-sixteenth century.[29] The health registers, not starting until the century's end, do not specifically indicate whether some corpses of condemned criminals were destined for university dissection, especially since it is uncertain whether the executed bodies were all recorded there.[30] On the other hand, the documents left by the

---

[28] This was according to the remaining statutes of the Roman College of Physicians (Carlino, *Books of the Body*, 79-93).

[29] The search for documents regarding university dissections in the bb.183-4 of Studio Patavino at the Archivio di Stato di Padova (ASP) turned out to be unfruitful (except, in b.184, a letter by the *Riformatori* allowing the holding of a dissection at the *Studium* in 1584). I wish to thank its curator, Dott.ssa Cristina Roberta Tommasi, for her kind assistance in consulting its archivistic registers.

[30] In Ufficio di Sanità (ASP), the bb. 464-513 (1598-1806) give a list of persons condemned to death with a more or less synthetic description of the kind of execution. The n.2bis presents references to autopsies performed in 17th and 18th centuries. The Libri dei morti register all deceased before funerals with indication of some capital punishments.

Confraternity of San Giovanni della Morte, in charge of the spiritual comfort of the condemned and of their burials in Padua, do not disclose the destination of their bodies.[31] In short, the absence of any systematic list of death sentences and capital executions (except a few incidental references), or even of transferred criminal bodies for anatomical use, should prove the absence of any constant cooperation between justice and academy in Padua, especially considering the low frequency of public executions at that time.

Indeed, though the perception of the Renaissance anatomy theater as a space of science and justice remains persistent, it has already been pointed out that, as far as Renaissance Italy is concerned, death sentences, as for dissection material, turned out to be as a rule much rarer than one might imagine.[32] In the case of Padua, then part of the Venetian territory, the podestà's authority as well as his ability to satisfy the demand of anatomy professors depended on the judicial authority of the Serenissima. However, although one might think death sentences were frequent because of a supposedly high risk of criminality at that time, the number of public executions then ordered by the Council of Ten appears less frequent than expected according to the extant judicial registers.

The executions that took place in the Venetian Republic were recorded in a manuscript currently kept at the Biblioteca Marciana and entitled *Registro dei giustiziati in Venezia* (Class VII, cod. DII); its content has later been identically copied in a publication without date or editor's name. The year and sometimes the month of execution, the name of the executed person, the reason for the conviction, and the type of imposed sentence are there summarily indicated, though this register, which lists cases of sure memory, does not specify whether it presents all the carried-out executions or only the most significant ones. For the mid-sixteenth century, it records just about fifteen executions in the public square, a relatively little number for a rather long period of time, and which narrowed the margin of maneuver in getting anatomical material.

In his confession stated in the *China Root Epistle*, Vesalius actually implies that he urged the podestà to postpone the execution of sentenced criminals at another time of the year for his winter classes and to provide him preferably (for obvious reasons) with bodies that had undergone execution by hanging or beheading rather than being burned at the stake. However, according to the Registro, not only the limited number of executions in random months, but

---

[31] ASP, I/73B, bb.53 (1361-1806). On the Confraternity of San Giovanni Decollato in Rome, which sometimes indicated the sending of criminal bodies to the Sapienza, see Carlino, *Books of the Body*, 98-108.

[32] Park, "The Criminal and the Saintly Body," 13-4, 20-1; Carlino, *Books of the Body*, 94.

also the types of execution and the identities of the executed made it difficult to permit a regular and acceptable supply in anatomical material.

For the 1540s-1560s, this codex reports the following executions: three spies in the pay of the French court were hanged (1540); two murderers of a patrician father-in-law were beheaded, one being from Bologna (1546); a Venetian priest was beheaded and then burned for incest with his daughter (February 1557); a foreigner who had outraged a public image of the Virgin after losing at gambling was condemned to be pulled by a horse, to have his tongue and one ear cut off, and then to be beheaded and quartered (1557); a thief from Locato who stole from the Camerlenghi's money box was condemned to have one hand cut off and be hanged in Rialto square (May 1560); two criminals beheaded in public, one being from Treviso (August or November 1564); a Venetian confessor beheaded and then burned for "scoundrels" committed in his monastery (November 1565); and a patrician beheaded between the columns of St. Mark Square for falsely fomenting a rebellion (January 1566).[33]

The printed version of this document adds a few executions from other codices: a Venetian priest beheaded and then burned for sodomy (May 1545); a patrician hanged for shooting his associate with a harquebus (1562); and a foreigner hanged without trial for killing a Neapolitan nobleman during a council of the Collegio e magistrati inside the ducal palace (1565).[34] Giuseppe Tassini, who took up especially the Marciana codex's content by correcting some dates, adds two cases (not without stressing on the lacunar state of the remaining registers kept in Venice archives): the execution of a band of murderers, one a nobleman from Padua, another from Bologna (August 1541),[35] and a citizen of Brescia beheaded for murdering his associate, then divided into quarters and dragged on horseback between St. Mark columns (May 1544).[36]

In total, there were at least 18 criminal bodies for 14 known public execution events in Venice during more than 25 years between 1540 and 1566. Thus, the chances of obtaining anatomical material are reduced not only by this low number, but also by the non-winter months in which many of these executions took place, by certain common kinds of execution that damaged the criminal body's integrity, and by the gravity of the crimes committed by some executed who tried to challenge the security of the republic. The Serenissima therefore wanted to make an example of these condemned as a crime deterrent in the eyes of its citizens in the public square, even if the

---

[33] Raccolta, 12-3.
[34] Ibid., 75.
[35] Tassini, 174.
[36] Ibid., 182.

delinquents were foreigners. Once again, one might regret the absence of any mention of some transfer of executed bodies to the Paduan faculty.

Because of the low number of executions, male and female criminal bodies, or even one of either sex, could not always be provided for the anatomy courses given each winter. In fact, the difficulty for the rectors to obtain dissection material from the podestà can be explained by the willingness of justice to be feared by deterring crime in the eyes of the entire crowd rather than only of the students. In the academic world, the fascination with death was an opportunity to acquire knowledge of the secrets of human fabric through dissection; in justice, however, this fascination was an effective deterrent expressed through executions decreed as examples on the gallows.

Consequently, the difficulty of the constraints linked to the low availability in criminal bodies was then felt within the anatomical theater itself, with the rise of secret search practices to make up for the lack of anatomical material. As a result, the university administration had to make some changes reflecting the problem of supply in anatomical material to its statutes, a material whose availability became more crucial than ever. The Paduan Studium was the first Italian anatomy university in the middle of the century to update its statutes, which informed that anatomy courses had for several years rarely been held with a shortage of cadavers (*cadaverum defectu*).

While reaffirming that the executed criminal body, provided this time by the governor of Padua and the praetores of all districts, should not be that of a Paduan or Venetian citizen, the statutes added a much more restrictive selection criterion: the social affiliation of the supplied body. Henceforth, it was stipulated that the criminal body, neither Paduan nor Venetian, should not be that of a member or even a close relative of a noble or distinguished family in the territory, under penalty of a fine; all matriculated students had to be informed in order to avoid eventual protests from the victim's relatives (which must have often been the case).[37] As a result, the availability in anatomical material from justice was compromised not only by traditional religious concerns regarding the soul of the dissected person, but also by common social shame felt by esteemed families because of some criminal family member somehow punished by the anatomist's scalpel. Such obstacles may explain the disturbing number of desperate attempts in searching for anatomical material at all costs and by secret means (maybe at the instigation

---

[37] AAUP, filza 665, Raccolta Minato, seria 20, Teatro anatomico, Cap. 17 super 28 de Anatomia facienda singulis annis, f. 264r. See Annex 4.

or imitation of Vesalius), so that the town itself was forced to take action against this near threat.

Indeed, on February 8th, 1549, the General Council of Padua passed a decree prohibiting the theft of corpses from cemeteries for private dissection and the sale of bones. Violators of burials, whether they were townsmen or countrymen of any rank or condition and acted by any imaginable means, were exposed to very heavy fines newly instituted by the Senate as well as prosecutions applied by the podestà. These exceptional regulations attribute the reason for these reckless acts to the increasing infatuation commonly manifested by young students who did not even spare graves in case of a lack of university material, which could push them to act in the shadows by moving from the public to the private sphere.[38]

This growing problem of lack in anatomical material was also felt in other Italian universities so that they had to adapt to the rising need of anatomists. At the Alma Studiorum in Bologna, which was more flexible than its Paduan rival, a reform of the statutes in 1561 abolished the previous selection criteria to authorize public dissection on the cadavers of persons born in the suburbs of the town and therefore within Bologna's territory so long as they were not honored citizens and the university had the consent of their relatives.[39] At the Studium Urbis in Rome, following a decree issued by the Congregation of Roman Deputies in 1569, the administrators broadened the range of selection for material by including the bodies of marginalized non-Christians or those judged to be infidel.[40]

Thus, the difficulty in obtaining anatomical material due to the rarity of public executions in addition to strict and restrictive university regulations gave rise to various statutory changes intended to curb the actions of those who sought to circumvent the criteria. So, this permanent problem of unavailability in anatomical material is very likely to invalidate the alleged implicit relationship that has been forged between dissections and executions as well as between science and justice within the anatomy theater. The situation may appear more clear if observed from the point of view of the anatomists themselves facing the constraining effects of these university regulations.

---

[38] Ibid., f. 271 (see Annex 5). Facciolati, 208-9 (see Annex 6). See also Klestinec, *Theaters of Anatomy*, 134.

[39] Riforme degli Statuti dell'Università di Medicina dell'anno MDLXI. See Ferrari, 66.

[40] Carlino, *Books of the Body*, 95.

The Anatomy Course and the Lacking Subject: An Unsatisfied Hunger for Bodies

The enduring conception of the Renaissance Italian anatomy theater as a space both of science and justice can be further questioned by considering the preparations for an anatomy course by professors or university administrators. In this allegedly judicialized academic place, the supply in anatomical material could be so problematic because of the statutory criterion that the officer of justice was often unable to provide the university with a lawful foreign criminal body.

In case the podestà could not immediately satisfy a request for material issued by the university, an eminent princely authority had to intervene. For example, Cosimo de' Medici, a patron keen on anatomy, invited Vesalius to give a dissection course at his academy in January-February 1544. Once the Flemish anatomist arrived in Pisa, the Duke, no doubt because of the lack of bodies of executed criminals foreign to the town and Florence, was in a hurry to call upon another source of supply.

In a letter to the ducal secretary in Pisa, Pier Francesco Riccio, dated January 22nd, 1544,[41] Marzio de Marzii, bishop of Marsico and intendant of the Nuovo Studio Pisano, tells of the Duke's order to get from the Ospedale di Santa Maria Nuova in Florence two bodies of dead men, if possible young, or one of a woman, and then transport them in two crates on a boat across the Arno to the Convent of San Francesco in Pisa in the deepest secrecy and (for obvious reasons) as quickly as possible. Shortly afterwards, the secretary learns from a new letter, written on January 30th by the supervisor Vincenzo Riccobaldi,[42] that Florence sent only one corpse (of a nun, according to Vesalius[43]), which moreover had broken ribs, so the Flemish professor who started with osteology was unable to reconstruct her entire skeleton. This peculiar episode shows not only that the provided anatomical material was not exclusively criminal, but also that the difficulty of its supply could lead to attempts of obtaining it discreetly from institutional sources where the identity of the bodies was not always certain, such as hospitals, though this method did not guarantee the sending of sufficient or intact material.

---

[41] ASF, Archivio Mediceo del Principato, filza 1171, fasc. VI, c. 286. See Annex 7. Quoted in Corsini, 5. The letter is dated 1543 following the Florentine calendar.

[42] Ibid., c. 283. Quoted in Corsini, 6.

[43] Vesalius, *Epistola*, 140. The author shortly mentions this episode and that of the corpse of a hunchback young girl taken from a cemetery in Pisa.

Thus, like the Paduan gymnasium, the Nuovo Studio Pisano also respected the selection criterion for an executed foreign criminal body to avoid any infamy. Cosimo de' Medici must have taken into account this criterion when he had the occasion to procure for Realdo Colombo, Vesalius' successor at the Pisan academy from 1546, the corpse of a woman named Santa di Mariotto Tarchi, a native of Mugello in Tuscany whom the Duke had sentenced to death by suffocation for having strangulated her two illegitimate twin sons, as later reported in Colombo's treatise.[44] The scarcity of foreign criminal bodies in Pisa undoubtedly prompted Colombo to leave for another position at the Roman Studium Urbis two years later, where he thought he would find an abundance of anatomical material, as he claims in a letter to the Duke dated April 17th, 1548 from Rome.[45]

Gabriele Falloppio, Colombo's successor at the Pisan university from September 1548, sustained this frustrating scarcity with more difficulty. For his first anatomy course at the ducal academy, it seems the anatomical material was long in being provided, and it is uncertain whether Falloppio, like his predecessor, had the opportunity to dissect a foreign female criminal body. In a letter to Cosimo de' Medici dated January 14th, 1549, the Rector of the Pisan Academy, Antonino Frosino, requests the Duke's intervention to obtain from the commissarius in Campiglia, another Tuscan town, the bodies of two women condemned to death, an unexpected opportunity for the utilità of the students of Falloppio, though the latter made no mention of it afterwards.[46] Until the end of his stay in Pisa, Falloppio was concerned mainly with the supply of dissection material in the following winters, so he complained to the academy administrators about missing, insufficient, or unsatisfactory human material and he felt obliged to make do with animal material, undoubtedly because of lacking foreign criminal bodies.

In a letter to Francesco Torelli, advisor (*auditore*) to the Duke in Florence, dated January 5th, 1550 in Pisa, Falloppio tells that, for his anatomy course this

---

[44] Colombo, 60, 173-4. The author adds the body of this woman offered one more rib that surprised his theologian auditors and menstrual veins of an odd shape.

[45] ASF, Archivio Mediceo del Principato, filza 386, f. 267r: "Onde considerando io questo, me ricorsi da V[ostra] E[ccellentia] a pregarla se degnasse concedermi licentia che io me ne venisse a stantiare a Roma; si perché la fortuna mi apresentava il primo pittor del mondo [Michelangelo] a servirmi in questo, si per la gran copia de' corpi nelli quali bisogno quasi decontinuo haver li la mano, per considerare bene le cose."

[46] Ibid., filza 391, f. 490r-v: "Habbiamo inteso qui in Pisa che il comessario di campiglia ha condennate dua donne amorte et per essere aproposito alla anatomia io in nome di tutti scolari supplico V. Ecc^a se degni commettere che havendo a morire dette donne si habbino da mandare a pisa perch' sara cosa utile et desiderata ascolari."

winter, he has at his disposal only one human subject that he considers insufficient (one, he says, does not last very long), and therefore asks Torelli to commission another cadaver, if possible female, or at least a pair of monkeys and a goat in kid.[47] However, in a later letter written on November 27th of the same year to Giacopo Guidi, ducal secretary in Livorno, the Italian anatomist tells this single human subject was an old man who had long been ill with fever quarte and whose body was quickly corrupted – no doubt a patient from a local hospital or a tramp with unknown identity – and he received for galenic anatomy one monkey he was unable to dissect in time. In this letter, Falloppio remains unaware of the availability or not in subjects and wishes to know if it would be possible to obtain at least one healthy body among the criminals recently executed in Florence.[48]

These unfavorable teaching conditions caused by the statutory criterion may have prompted Falloppio to leave Pisa in his turn the next year and permanently hold an appointment at the Studium in Padua. There, however, his compliance with this criterion again compromised his teaching on many occasions. After successful courses, the risk of unavailability in anatomical material in the following winters led the section of students in medicine (*università artista*) to approach the university administrators more than once. For two consecutive academic years, the vice-rector and the consiliarii asked the riformatori dello Studio in Venice by letters written on January 21[st][49] and December 2nd 1555,[50] to commission a body of some (implicitly foreign)

---

[47] ASF, Archivio Guidi, 571, n. c.: "incominciaro l'Anatomia, et di gia è qua un soggietto, il quale stimandomi che non sia sofficiente, perchè uno non dura tanto, prego sua signoria, voglia dar' commissione d'un'altro, et che sia femina. o ver non si potendo questo, commetta al proveditor' di dogana che ci compri un paio di simie, et una capra pregna a quei di ricercato che sara se pero la dimanda mia è giusta."

[48] Ibid., Annex 8.

[49] AAUP, Atti dell'Università Artista, filza 675, busta 12, f. 171v: "Si che per le cause predette, e perchè anchora il tempo il permette, et oltre il clarissimo Podestà ha un corpo da giusticiare quale ci ha promesso de novo supplichiamo Vostre magnificentie clarissime, che in questo voglino sodisfare al comune desiderio et utile di questo Studio" (Quoted in Favaro, 225).

[50] Ibid., f. 199v: "et acciochè tal bono intento per commune utilità sia esequito, le pregamo vogliano favorir li massari del'anatomia per noi electi facendoli havere provisione de corpi o in venetia o in altro luoco scrivendo una lettera over commissione generale per li luochi subditi al dominio accio dove si trovassero suggecti atti se potessero togliere e commectendo che durante dicta anatomia publica non se ne faccia altra privata in padoa per disturbo e di questo ultra gli altri infiniti oblighi ne li restaremo obligatissimi" (Quoted in Favaro, 225).

executed criminal at the podestà in Venice or in another place of the territory for the benefit of the students' utilità.

Nevertheless, as a result, the anatomy teaching was cancelled twice on end, according to Falloppio, who, more frustrated than ever, decided the following winter to write a letter directly to the riformatori on December 12nd, 1556, to warn them of the effects of this double cancellation and the constant lack of dissection material at the Studium.[51] The Italian anatomist informs them that many German and Polish students, seeing no preparation and doubting the course would take place without a human subject, began to organize their departure for universities in Bologna or Ferrara. Tired of making promises, Falloppio asks his recipients to solicit the podestà for a subject as soon as possible, even suggesting the massarii may secretly procure the body of some unknown (*ignobile et non conosciuta*) person for public dissection.

Three days later, the riformatori in Venice relayed Falloppio's urgent request to the podestà in Padua with a letter in which they give him the commission of a body of a person condemned to death (implicitly a foreign one) to be handed over to the professor for the dissection expected of his students unless the massarii may search for some body of an unknown person.[52] Probably after the failure of their approach or for greater efficiency, the university administrators stated the same request the following winter, this time to the Padua rettori with a letter sent on December 7th, 1557,[53] in which they ask once again for the sending of some subject for the good of the students' utilità. Having quickly obtained one, the riformatori repeated their action eight days later with another letter informing the governors that the provided subject was judged unfit for dissection by Falloppio, who received the

---

[51] Archivio di Stato di Venezia (ASV), Lettere dei Riformatori dello Studio, 1555-1559, filza 63, n. c. Annex 9. (Quoted in Favaro, 226-7).

[52] Ibid., n. c.: "Essendo l'anatomia utilissima a quelli studiosi la medicina, et essendo al presente li tempi opportunissimi, pregamo la Magnificenza Vostra che havendo alcun suggieto condennato alla morte vogli accomodarlo all'eccellente Faloppio che con grande aspettation et satisfattion di quei scolari farà essa anatomia, et non havendo suggieto da far morire vogli permetter che li massari possino covratamente procaciarsi di qualche corpo quando li venga occasione di persona ignobile et non cognosciuta, per che questo sarà di gran giovamento a tutto questo studio" (Quoted in Favaro, 227).

[53] Ibid., n. c.: "Essendo questa stagion di tempo opportunissima di far l'anatomia che si vuol fare ogni anno per utilità di quei scolari, pregamo le magnificenze vostre che per beneficio del studio voglino far accomodare gli scolari anatomisti che venirano a ricercarle di qualche soggietto acciochè si possi far una cosi buona, et utile opera" (Quoted in Favaro, 228).

corrupted cadaver probably of an aged unknown patient or vagabond instead of some healthy criminal body.[54]

Conclusion

The persistent Foucauldian concept of the Renaissance anatomy theater as a space for symbolic interaction between science and justice seems to me difficult to apply to the Italian case. The three aforesaid conditions of the idea of a judicialized academic space turned out to be seriously compromised by various factors in the problem of supply of anatomical material from justice. Indeed, the frequent difficulty of this supply caused by university selection criteria for exclusively foreign criminal bodies had multiple consequences: the body supplied to the theater could be that of an executed criminal as well as that of a sick person obtained from a hospital or a dead one stolen from a cemetery; the podestà was much less a direct actor of the dissection than an external supplier occasionally solicited by the university administration, and his intervention could be insignificant or even nil because of the rarity of public executions; and the dissection material could not be procured regularly every winter because of this criterion, which considerably limits the chances of obtaining the physical material for the anatomy course.

The closer view of the Renaissance Italian anatomy theater I have given here reassesses the alleged complicity between anatomist and executioner and hardly allows for attributing any deterrent function to a presumably judicial academic space. Instead, it turned out that the prevalent interest at issue inside this theater, that should easily be regarded as a purely academic space, was science rather than justice: the teaching anatomist played the part less of an agent of power extending public execution into public dissection than of a pedagogue acting for the intellectual profit of students (despite the specter of the phantom body).

---

[54] Ibid., n. c.: "Essendo l'Anatomia di gran beneficio a quel studio et specialmente a quelli che studiano in medicina pregamo le Magnificenze Vostre che voglino dar favor et suffragio alli scolari anatomisti accomodandoli di alcun sugietto che si trovassi de l'aver scrivendo per le Castelle quando che quello che hanno havuto de qui non fusse a proposito si come le potrano certificarsi dall'eccelente Faloppio che deve legger et tagliar l'anatomia" (Quoted in Favaro, 228).

Chapter 3

The Teaching of Anatomy at the University in the South of Europe: The Case Study of the Universities of Coimbra and Salamanca (XIV-XVI)

Carlos Fernando Teixeira Alves

University of Lisbon

Abstract: This work aims to understand the anatomical theaters, anatomy, and the teaching of anatomy in a very specific space, the University, more precisely, in the classrooms of the medical faculty. These medical faculties were guided by their ability to modernize themselves. In this sense, we have witnessed slow introductions from the fourteenth century that eventually last until the eighteenth century. In Europe, the University of Montpellier was the first to perform dissections and Paris followed shortly afterwards. The issue of dissections, limited by Roman law, delayed the systematic introduction of the anatomy in the European universities. However, in the sixteenth century we already see anatomy chairs in many universities. Later, the anatomical theaters appear and soon multiply. Therefore, this period witnesses the appearance of recognized anatomists as the University of Padua becomes the central place for medical studies in Europe. Thus, this work analyzes the introduction of the chair of anatomy in European universities from the fourteenth to sixteenth centuries. It offers case studies of the Universities of Coimbra and Salamanca. Furthermore, this chapter identifies the anatomical publications adopted by these universities, how anatomy was complemented by other disciplines such as botany and surgery, the origin of the bodies and body parts, and, finally, resistance to the evolution of the anatomy discipline.

Keywords: Anatomy, Medical Studies, Coimbra, Salamanca, Iberian Peninsula

***

Introduction

In the scholar year of 1574-1575, the Doctor of Medicine Rodrigo Soria declared that "in the house of the anatomy were made anatomies in two bodies of men, and a universal anatomy in veins and arteries in a dog. And another universal in bones, reading through the skeleton. And they have particulars of the heads of men ... And they have in the school two eyes, two hearts, two kidneys."[1] The previous passage shows us that the anatomies were a common practice at the University of Salamanca, and what the historiography call the 'revival' in the fifteenth century.[2] The reference to human cadavers and the anatomical theater were an important indication that the students could learn directly from the dissections conducted by a professor.

Three decades later, the same professor shows us that the practice of anatomy in Salamanca in the seventeenth century was already in decline.[3] These complaints increased and the professor of anatomy, Domingo Vázquez, delivered a complaint where he indicated that he had more and more difficulties in finding instruments for his dissections.[4] Based on the actual historiography, the main conclusion is that until c.1620 the teaching of anatomy grew at the University, and then went into decline.[5]

These few decades represent a rapid and accelerated decline, even more so after accepting the conclusions of Carreras Panchón that indicated that until the end of the sixteenth century, the University of Salamanca was one of the most advanced European Universities in anatomy teaching.[6] So, what changed in a few decades at the University of Salamanca? And did the University of Coimbra go through the same process of decline?

In the Reformation of 1612 (in Coimbra), the number of anatomical demonstrations on human corpses was reduced to only one per year.[7] Previously, the number of obligated universal anatomies (meaning the anatomies practiced in all the body and not only in parts) were three per year.

---

[1] Archivo Historico de la Universidad de Salamanca, AUSA, Libros de Visitas de Cátedras, Años 1560-1838, 947, fl. 77v., 123.

[2] García Ballester, "Medical Science and Medical Teaching at the University of Salamanca in the 15th Century," 37–64.

[3] Rodriguez-San-Pedro Bezares 1986, 2:134.

[4] Carreras Panchón, 332.

[5] Prieto Carrasco, "La enseñanza de la Anatomía en la Universidad de Salamanca," 188.

[6] Carreras Panchón, 303.

[7] Lemos, *História da Medicina em Portugal. Doutrinas e Instituições*, vol. I, 153.

Without the stimulus or even the obligation, and the fact that the Universities should finance all the costs involving a dissection, the lack of pressure works as a discouragement to this practice.

Seven years later, an inquiry was made in the University of Coimbra and the criticism was severe:[8] the students attacked the negligence of the anatomy professor (Martim Gonçalves) and the lack of dissections in cadavers; they were also very unhappy that the only dissection they had seen was performed on a sheep and that the dissections took place in the professor's house. The relaxation of the professors was another reason for this decline. The criticisms directed to Martim Gonçalves are very similar to others directed to his predecessor, João Bravo Chimaço.[9]

Manuel Alves Carrilho, professor of anatomy at the University of Coimbra in the school year of 1623-24 needed to demand a new authorization to make dissections in cadavers and animals. The fact that the professor needed to ask for a new authorization (beyond the statutes or the existing legislation) shows that in the recent years the practice of the dissection was insignificant or even inexistent and, at best, performed mainly on sheep or pigs. An internal document from the University of Coimbra, dated 1746, confirms this idea and the students' indignation with this situation.[10] As in the case of Salamanca, this image does not say it all. Before the end of the sixteenth century, the University of Coimbra made a serious investment to bring its anatomical teaching closer to other European centers.[11]

These few examples are at the core of what historiography calls the 'period of decline' of the anatomic studies at these Universities. This decline took place at the end of the sixteenth century and continued until the reforms of the eighteenth century. Through this long period, the decline of these studies was significant, although with punctual exceptions. In the 1770's decade, the anatomy in both Universities had a revival with a new study plan, new books, and, even more important, with new anatomical theaters.[12]

---

[8] Lemos, *História*, I:157.

[9] Correia, "Esboço da História da Anatomia em Coimbra," 11–12.

[10] A. da Rocha Brito, "As primeiras dissecações humanas na Universidade de Coimbra. O primeiro Teatro Anatomico," 15.

[11] Teixeira Rodrigues and Fiolhais, "O ensino da medicina na Universidade de Coimbra no século XVI," 441.

[12] Rui Pita, "Medicina, Cirurgia e Arte Farmacêutica na Reforma Pombalina da Universidade De Coimbra," 141–78; Demerson, "La chaire et le Théâtre d'Anatomie de L'Université de Salamanque (1771-1792)."

However, even after the decline of the end of the sixteenth century and the revival of the eighteenth century, it is impossible to forget the important efforts that allowed the vital developments of the fifteenth and part of sixteenth century. This chapter demonstrates that since the middle of the fifteenth century until the late sixteenth century, both Universities made serious efforts to incorporate new ideas, books, and even the construction of anatomical theaters similar to the main European models. The fifteenth and sixteenth centuries were important milestones in the study of anatomy in these Universities where there had been an important effort to follow the main centers of the time, like Padova or Bologna. However, the lack of resources, the absence of pressure by the authorities, and the negligence of some professors were decisive factors for the delay of progress for centuries to follow.

Two main questions guided this research and, simultaneously, indicate the originality of this work. The first is trying to understand how the studies of anatomy appeared and evolved in two of the most important Universities of the Iberian Peninsula. For this purpose, it will be necessary to focus this analysis on the late fourteenth, fifteenth, and sixteenth centuries and on the first steps in the reform of medical studies in Portugal and Spain. At the same time, it is possible to answer another, no less important question: how advanced was the study of anatomy in Coimbra and Salamanca in relation to the main Europeans centers? The following text seeks to answer these questions.

Anatomy in the Universities of Salamanca and Coimbra: The Beginning of a Long Project

The first direct observation on a cadaver for anatomical purposes is usually attributed to Mondino de Liuzzi (1270-1326) in Bologna (1315).[13] Although, a few years later, Gentile da Foglino in 1341 and Leonardo da Bertipaglia in 1429-30 also conducted dissections' (in Padua).[14] However, since the end of the thirteenth century, a few professors from Universities like Bologna, Paris, or Montpellier had already shown some familiarity with the dissections even before the legalization of this practice.[15] The resort to private dissections at the houses of students and mainly professors but also in convents or hospitals was the norm.[16]

---

[13] Carlino, *Books of the Body*, 151.

[14] Ongaro, "La medicina nello Studio di Padova e nel Veneto," 95–96; Carlino, *Books of the Body*, 85.

[15] Diana, "Anatomy between Public and Private in 14th-16th Century Europe," 337.

[16] Martinotti, "L'insegnamento dell'anatomia in Bologna: prima del secolo XIX," 3–146; Zaccagnini, *La vita dei maestri e degli scolari nello Studio di Bologna nei secoli XIII e XIV* (Genève: L.S. Olschki, 1926).

The transition from the thirteenth to fourteenth century was a very important stage in the development of the study of anatomy. The circulation of the translations of the Greek and Arabic texts, the development of forensic medicine, and the development of the European Universities had a great impact in this process.[17] The Medical School of Salernitana was the first institution to officialize the unification between surgical studies and anatomical practice. In 1241, Federico II determined that the study of anatomy and the practice of dissections on animals were compelling to all the students of surgery.[18]

Later, the brief of Pope Sixto IV in 1482 addressed to the University of Tübingen provided the 'methodological rules' that had a significant impact on European Universities and established that: the dissections could only be practiced in the corpses of executed criminals, they had to be strangers to the social ambient of the city in which they were executed, and they were mainly from the lower classes.[19] These rules regulated the anatomical practice through the fourteenth century until the fifteenth century. Coimbra and Salamanca were no exceptions, and many of these rules remain after the sixteenth century.

The first authorization for human dissections (1546) addressed to professor Rodrigo de Reinoso of the University of Coimbra demanded the practice of dissections in corpses of criminals and in deceased patients from the Hospital.[20] This authorization shows not only that Coimbra followed the same pattern in the selection of corpses for the dissections at European Universities, but it also displays a prudent approach from the Monarch in this sensible matter.

---

[17] Diana, "Anatomy between Public and Private in 14th-16th Century Europe," 329. For a more detailed analysis of the contribution of Universities to the development of various disciplines, including medicine, see Olaf Pedersen, "Tradition and Innovation," in *A History of the University in Europe: Universities in Early Modern Europe (1500-1800)*, vol. 2 (Cambridge: Cambridge University Press, 2003), 452–88; Lewis Spitz, "The Importance of the Reformation for the Universities: Culture and Confessions in the Critical Years," in *Rebirth, Reform and Resilience, Universities in Transition 1300-1700* (Columbus: The Ohio State University Press, 1984), 42–67; Laurence Brockliss, "Curricula," in *A History of the University in Europe: Universities in Early Modern Europe (1500-1800)*, vol. 2 (Cambridge: Cambridge University Press, 2003), 565–620.

[18] Carlino, *Books of the Body*, 178.

[19] Diana, "Anatomy between Public and Private in 14th-16th Century Europe," 334.

[20] Rodrigues, *Memoria Professorum Universitatis Conimbrigensis, vol. 1: 1290-1772*, 42; Brito, "As Primeiras Dissecações Humanas na Universidade de Coimbra," 3. Note that in Coimbra the authorization for dissections is prior to the creation of the discipline of anatomy. The professor Rodrigo de Reinoso was the professor of prima, and for some authors this is the proof that the anatomies were a practice even before the creation of the discipline of anatomy in 1556. So, in this ten-year gap, it is possible that some anatomies were done.

In the year 1552, a letter from the University of Salamanca asking for a permission to obtain corpses of the executed criminals and the deceased in the city Hospital arrived at the Council of Castile.[21] The city Hospital (of Salamanca) limited the access to cadavers, only provide cadavers of executed criminals (demanded by law) and corpses of people who had committed suicide.[22]

It is not difficult to conclude that public health has a main impact in the mind of the public entities and the University authorities. Both agreed that this special event that is anatomies can be applicated as a supplementary punishment to someone who was punished for criminal behavior, reflecting a reality also present in other countries.[23]

Coimbra and Salamanca followed the same path related to the regulation of this activity in the fourteenth and fifteenth centuries as some of the European Universities. The majority of the Italian Universities like Bologna,[24] Padua, Venice,[25] Florence,[26] Genoa,[27] or Rome[28] in the statutes from the fifteenth through the sixteenth century only accepted cadavers from foreigners. The same happened in Montpellier,[29] Barcelona,[30] Vienna,[31] Prague,[32] and Paris.[33] Siena was probably an exception, not mentioning the origin of the cadavers in the General Reform of 1589.[34] The main point shared among almost all these institutions seems to be the fact that anatomies could only be made in cadavers of executed people.

---

[21] Carrasco, "La Enseñanza de la Anatomía en la Universidad de Salamanca," 188.

[22] Carreras Panchón, 332.

[23] Diana, "Anatomy between Public and Private in 14th-16th Century Europe," 334.

[24] Ferrari, "Public Anatomy Lessons and the Carnival," 52. Florence goes further in the Major Decree Council of 1368, stipulating that it should be provided two cadavers (one from a woman and another from a man) but only of the executed that were hanged.

[25] Ongaro, "La Medicina Nello Studio di Padova e nel Veneto," 94-96.

[26] Nardi, "Statuti e Documenti Riflettenti la Dissezione Anatomica Umana e la Nomina di Alcuni Lettori di Medicina Nell'antico Studium Generale Giorentino," 242.

[27] Isnardi and Celesia, *Storia della Università di Genova* (Genova: Coi tipi del R.I. de'sordo-muti, 1867).

[28] Carlino, *Books of the Body*, 77.

[29] Dulieu, *La médecine à Montpellier*, vol. I, 134.

[30] López Piñero, "The Vesalian Movement in Sixteenth Century Spain," 47.

[31] Corradi, *Dello Studio e Dell'insegnamento Dell'anatomia in Italia nel Medioevo e in Parte del Cinquecento* (Milano: [s.n.], 1873).

[32] Edmondo Solmi, "Per gli Studi Anatomici di Leonardo da Vinci," 347.

[33] Carlino, *Books of the Body*, 211.

[34] Piccinni, "Tra Scienza ed Arte: lo Studio di Siena e L'insegnamento della Medicina (sec. XIII-XVI)," 149.

The steps followed in Portugal and Spain were similar. The authorities benefited from the fact that in both cities existed a local Hospital. In 1546 Coimbra received the first authorization and the city Hospital was obligated to provide corpses. And in 1552, the University of Salamanca appealed to the King to obligate the Hospital to deliver the cadavers of the deceased. But, despite that, the Hospitals were dissatisfied and did not always comply. One of the earliest problems in Salamanca was the opposition of the city Hospital who wanted the University to perform anatomies only on executed cadavers and not on deceased patients.[35] The sources tell us that this problem persists until very late in both Universities. In the case of Salamanca, the statutes foresaw this situation and in 1594 established that with the impossibility of obtaining cadavers, the prints and figures of the work of Andreas Vesalius would be used as an alternative.[36]

In relation to the cadavers, it is certain that the anatomies in human bodies were made in Salamanca, but in Portugal, the doubts led to a debate. Some authors argued that dissections were not performed on human cadaver and some sources of the seventeenth and eighteenth centuries were very critical of the teaching of anatomy.[37] However, to better answer this question, it would be better to look at other sources, particularly in the sixteenth century.

After the Royal authorization in 1546, it seems that the dissections didn't start right away. The first discipline of anatomy created in Coimbra was created almost a decade later and the first professor was the Spanish Alfonso Rodriguez de Guevara.[38] Some authors defend that this professor indeed did his dissections (including in human cadavers, although fewer in number) in the short time that he was in Coimbra.[39] And even after this professor left, dissections could have been continued by other professors.[40] Further, we see the expenses of anatomies in the books of income and expense of the University (1633-1634).[41]

---

[35] Carreras Panchón, 332.

[36] Rodríguez-San Pedro Bezares, *La Universdiad Salamantina del Barroco*, 2:364.

[37] Taveira da Fonseca, "A Medicina," 871.

[38] Teixeira de Carvalho and Costa, *A Universidade de Coimbra no séc. XVI: Guevara: Notas e Documentos* (Coimbra: Imprensa da Universidade de Coimbra, 1922).

[39] Alfonso Rodriguez de Guevara, according to some authors, left the University shortly after because he was not allowed to dissect a human corpse.

[40] Correia, "Esboço da História da Anatomia em Coimbra," 7–8.

[41] Brito, «As primeiras dissecações humanas na Universidade de Coimbra. O primeiro Teatro Anatomico», 1–16.

In the scholar year of 1626-1627, the University paid 12,000 *réis* (Portuguese currency) for the professor's expenses related to the anatomies. Even more elucidative was the register for the year 1632-1633. The University paid 12,000 *réis* to Professor António Pacheco de Fabião and a bonus of 1,200 for the expenses with cadavers.[42] It is possible to conclude that human dissections were performed at the University of Coimbra, although it is also possible to recognize that the number of these dissections was not high.

The Content of the Discipline of Anatomy in Salamanca and Coimbra

Through the thirteenth to the fifteenth century, the work in the academy allowed the development of medicine and one of the main aspects was the creation of an environment that would end up legitimizing this practice.[43] And in the fifteenth century, the Universities had a main role in establishing the rules and norms for the consistent practice of dissection as an important part of the activity of the professor.[44] Later, in the sixteenth century, medical humanism flourished in the academy,[45] and the medical curricula of a wide-ranging number of Universities indicates a significative effort from these institutions and some individuals to recover and critically evaluate the ancient texts from Hippocrates, Aristoteles, and Galen.[46]

Anatomy won space in the courses of medicine and was intrinsically linked to other matters, mainly surgery. In our cases of study, this tendency is evident. Coimbra creates the Chair of Surgery in 1558 (only two years after anatomy began in the University) and Salamanca in 1566 (fourteen years after anatomy began in the University). Thus, neither Coimbra nor Salamanca chose to unite anatomy and surgery as it happened in Roma or Padua, for instance.[47] Although, both share human and material resources. The first

---

[42] In the statutes of 1559 of the University of Coimbra, we see that if the professors did not perform anatomies, they could be fined by the University. For each universal anatomy they could be fined 20 cruzados (Portuguese currency) and partial anatomies could go up to six cruzados. The same happened if they didn't respect the stipulated duration for each anatomy (Leite, *Estatutos da Universidade de Coimbra [1559]*, 302).

[43] Siraisi, *Medieval and Early Renaissance Medicine*, 190.

[44] Romero et al., "La cátedra 154.

[45] Bylebyl, "Medicine, Philosophy, and Humanism in Renaissance Italy," 27–49; Bylebyl, "The School of Padua: Humanistic Medicine de Cirugía y Anatomía en el Renacimiento," in the Sixteenth Century," 335–70; Schmitt, "The Problem of Continuity," 104–23; Schmitt, "Science in the Sixteenth and Early Seventeenth Centuries," 35–56.

[46] Klestinec, "A History of Anatomy Theaters in Sixteenth-Century Padua," 377.

[47] Siraisi, *The Clock and the Mirror,* 96; Romero et al., 156.

professor of anatomy in Coimbra, Alfonso Rodríguez de Guevara, was simultaneously the first professor of surgery in the same University.

The link with other subjects with a major practical approach explains the importance of observation, recollection, and description for the discipline of anatomy. In the sixteenth century, anatomy was distinguished by a greater frequency in performing dissections, improved techniques, importance of observation, and a greater importance of illustrations.[48] This also represents an important aspect of medical studies: the union between practice and theory. Tomás Rodrigues da Veiga, in a book published posthumously in 1586 (*Opera Omnia*), defends this same idea.[49] Unfortunately, this 'harmonic concept' doesn't survive the exit of this professor.[50]

The growing importance of the discipline of anatomy in the curricula of medicine in the sixteenth century was clear but also variable from university to university.[51] In the University of Coimbra, since 1556 to 1615, the Chair of Anatomy had four substitutes and six professors.[52] As some of these professors taught for a short period of time (one to four years on average), it is possible to conclude that there was some degree of instability.[53] More than that, the Salamanca case shows the trend to select professors in the early stages of their career to the Chair of Anatomy.[54] It is not hard to explain this situation: the Chair of Anatomy struggled to have the same status and neither did it provide the same financial returns as other Chair positions. The professors looked at the Chair of Anatomy as a way to reach the main and better paid Chairs in the course of medicine, like prima or vespera.[55]

Nonetheless, all the advances and retreats in the sixteenth century demonstrate not only a very complex reality in these Universities but also a closer relationship between the national and University authorities. The content of the discipline of anatomy is nothing more than the result of this relationship.

Despite the first authorization for anatomies dating from 1546, the course of medicine of the University of Coimbra only had two disciplines, prima and

---

[48] Siraisi, *The Clock and the Mirror,* 95.
[49] The original text was transcribed by Fonseca, "A Medicina," 873.
[50] Fonseca, "A Medicina," 871.
[51] Siraisi, *The Clock and the Mirror,* 95.
[52] Rodrigues, *Memoria Professorum Universitatis Conimbrigensis,* 1: 1290-1772:47.
[53] In the case of the substitutes the average is even shorter, just one year.
[54] Martínez-Vidal and Pardo-Tomás, "Anatomical Theaters in Early Modern Spain," 258.
[55] Carreras Panchón, 332.

vespera.[56] This number increased with the statutes of 1559 and was maintained with the statutes of 1597.[57] This increase represents the effort and the pressure felt by the authorities to improve the formation of physicians and surgeons.

Salamanca, for instance, is a good example of this tendency. In the second half of the sixteenth century, new and more practical disciplines were created, and anatomy represented the incorporation of the ideas of Vesalius based in direct dissection and empirical observation influenced by the University of Valencia.[58]

On the 6th of September (1550), the University Claustrum reunited and discussed a royal order.[59] The School Master was invited to gather the professors of medicine and arts to provide the creation of the Chair of Anatomy in the same year. This discussion continued through the next month until finally both parts agreed that the anatomy discipline should be created.[60] The Spanish crown had a main role in motivating and pressuring the University.[61]

In March of 1552, two years later after the first notice, the first professor for anatomy, Cosme de Medina, was appointed and performed his first dissection.[62] He had considerable freedom, mainly because of the novelty of anatomy in the University of Salamanca.[63] Because anatomy was a new addition, the public and university authorities needed to rely on the skills and capacity of qualified people that were trained in other Universities (and

---

[56] "Statutos d'el Rei Dom Manoel para a Universidade de Lisboa," in *Noticias Chronologicas da Universidade de Coimbra*, 2ª, vol. 1 (Coimbra, 1937); Rodrigues, *Os primeiros Estatutos da Universidade de Coimbra* (Coimbra: Arquivo da Universidade de Coimbra, 1991).

[57] Leite, *Estatutos da Universidade de Coimbra (1559); Estatutos da Universidade de Coimbra. Confirmados por ElRey Dom Philipe Primeiro deste nome nosso senhor em o ano de MDXCVII 1597.*

[58] For the importance of the University of Valencia, see López Piñero, "The Faculty of Medicine of Valencia: Its Position in Renaissance Europe," 65–82; O'Malley, "Pedro Jimeno: Valencian Anatomist of the Mid-sixteenth Century," 69–72.

[59] Archivo 54istórico de la Universidad de Salamanca, AUSA, Libros de Claustros, 19. F.128v.

[60] Ibid., f.120v. Archivo 54istórico de la Universidad de Salamanca, AUSA, Libros de Claustros, 20, fl.6 and 7.

[61] Santander, 256–57; Martínez-Vidal and Pardo-Tomás, "Anatomical Theaters in Early Modern Spain," 256.

[62] Archivo Historico de la Universidad de Salamanca, AUSA, Libros de Claustros, 21. F.78r; Santander, 257.

[63] After Cosme de Medina, the list of professors until the end of the sixteenth century was: Cosme de Medina, 1551-61; no professor from 1561-62; Agustín Vázquez, 1562-67; Rodrigo de Soria, 1567-75; Agustín Vázquez, 1575-96; Diego Ruiz de Ochoa, 1597-1607; Domingo Vázquez Mexía, 1607-11.

sometimes outside the country). Medina, for instance, knew well the ideas of Vesalius and had worked closely with Luis Collado in Valencia.[64] In Salamanca, he introduced a more practical teaching method and provided a solid training in anatomy.[65] One of his disciples, Francisco Micó, is a good example of the excellence of the teaching of Professor Cosme de Medina.[66]

The same happened in Coimbra. The monarch João III needed to create new disciplines in medicine at the pace that it was possible to find qualified people.[67] In 1555, anatomy was created and the Spanish professor Alfonso Rodríguez de Guevara, who did his training in Spain and in Italy, was appointed. He started teaching anatomy at the University of Valladolid and came to Coimbra afterward. Although Guevara remained in Coimbra for a short time, he had considerable freedom in the exercise of his function.

Another aspect related to the content of the Anatomy Chair was the number of anatomies. In 1559, the statutes of Coimbra demanded the realization of two universal anatomies and six partials.[68] A few decades later in 1591, the number of universal anatomies increased to three.[69] This demand persists until late 1653 when the professor needed to execute three universal anatomies.[70]

For the Portuguese University, the number of anatomies is not particularly high, especially compared with Salamanca. A resolution from March 1552 mentions a high number of anatomies (thirty).[71] However, the number of corpses delivered (from the city Hospital) was never that high, and the number of anatomies conducted by Medina was lower. In a more realistic approach, in 1561, it was specified that six general anatomies and twelve partials should be done. In 1591 this number was reduced, and the professor needed to conduct six universal and six partial anatomies per year.[72] Three years later, the mandatory anatomies changed again: 12 partial and six general.

---

[64] Santamaría Hernández, "Collado, Luis," in *Diccionario Biográfico y Bibliográfico del Humanismo Español (Siglos XV-XVII)* (Madrid: Ediciones Clásicas, 2012).

[65] Martínez-Vidal and Pardo-Tomás, "Anatomical Theaters in Early Modern Spain," 256.

[66] Fernández Luzón, *La Universidad de Barcelona en el siglo XVI*.

[67] Rodrigues and Fiolhais, "O Ensino da Medicina na Universidade de Coimbra No Século XVI," 439.

[68] Leite, *Estatutos da Universidade de Coimbra (1559)*, 300–301.

[69] *Estatutos da Vniuersidade de Coimbra confirmados por el rey Dom Phelippe primeiro deste nome, nosso Senhor em o anno de 1591* 1593, 74.

[70] *Estatutos da Universidade de Coimbra (1653)*, 143-144.

[71] Santander, 257.

[72] *Estatutos Hechos por la Muy Insigne Universidad de Salamanca, año MDLXI* 1591.

The numbers presented in the statutes of both Universities is high. However, it is not wrong to say that the real number of anatomies is lower than stipulated. The lack of human cadavers made it impossible to reach the demanded anatomies. In 1634, the professor Sebastián Ruiz indicated that the number of anatomies performed in a year was no more than three.[73] Only Coimbra seems near the required number in other Universities between one and two.[74] For instance, the statutes of Bologna of 1442 demanded two per year.[75] Cambridge, in 1570, indicated only one a year.[76] Salamanca was indeed different due to the high number of mandatory anatomies imposed by national authorities.

The procedure for dissections appears in the statutes several times. In the statutes (1550) of Salamanca, the general anatomies had to follow the following form: one demonstration only of the muscles, another of the bones, and another of the nerves and only then it passed to the complete dissection of the body.[77] For the anatomies of body parts, the teacher should perform two of the head, two of the eyes, two of the kidneys, two of the heart, two of the muscles and two of the veins of the arm and leg.[78]

Another interesting feature is the timeframe allowed for the performance of anatomies, and neither Coimbra nor Salamanca were different from their counterparts. The reason is simple: due to the impossibility of preserving the cadavers, the anatomies could only be performed during the winter months. In 1559, Portuguese authorities demanded that an anatomy should be done in four days (even if it is a holiday) due to the speed of decomposition of the corpses.[79] During these days, the professor should give four lessons a day, two hours in the morning and two in the afternoon. After 1562, the morning anatomies held in winter should begin at 6:30 am.[80] Salamanca performed dissections during the period between October 18th and March 8th. In the case of Coimbra, we know from a 1562 letter that dissections began on October 1st.[81]

---

[73] Carreras Panchón, 332.

[74] Diana, "Anatomy between Public and Private in 14th – 16th Century Europe," 354-5.

[75] Ferrari, "Public Anatomy Lessons and the Carnival," 52.

[76] Spicci, *Corpo e Ibridazioni Discorsive nell'Inghilterra Elisabettiana*, 25; Macalister, "An Address on the History of Anatomy in Cambridge,"449.

[77] *Estatutos Hechos por la Muy Insigne Universidad de Salamanca, Año MDLXI* 1591.

[78] *Estatutos Hechos por la Muy Insigne Universidad de Salamanca*, 1595. The professor was obliged to perform vivisections on animals to show the movements of the heart and nerves (see French 1999).

[79] Leite, *Estatutos da Universidade de Coimbra (1559)*, 300.

[80] In this letter, it seems that it was also possible to perform anatomies in the summer, but they should start earlier at 5:30 am. However, it is possible to conclude that it is very improbable that any anatomy happened in the summer due to the high temperatures.

[81] Brito, "As Primeiras Dissecações Humanas na Universidade de Coimbra," 10.

Salamanca and Coimbra evolved positively and shared characteristics of anatomy teaching in other Universities, although this reality begins to change towards the end of the sixteenth century. The development of anatomy was marked by the degree of interest not only of individual anatomists but also of local authorities.[82] The lack of attention of some professors was decisive and the Portuguese and Spanish authorities also abandoned a more involved attitude in the promotion of the study of anatomy. Besides the lack of resources, it seems that this lack of commitment is the main reason for the long decline of anatomical studies in the Universities in this study.

The Anatomical Theaters in Salamanca and Coimbra

As a rule, the first anatomies took place in private houses of teachers. This situation changed in the fourteenth century with the transfer to a (temporary) installation at the University.[83] Anatomical practice could follow two lines of conduct: 1) the official, public, and educational dissection where this practice was approved and regulated; 2) the private (illegal) dissection which represented an excellent opportunity to train with few restrictions.[84]

Anatomical theaters played an essential role in the development of medical education and in the dissemination of anatomy as performance.[85] Salamanca and Coimbra had many similarities and some differences with the anatomy theater trends across Europe.[86]

Little is known about the structure of the theater in Coimbra. Although, nothing indicates that it was very different from the elliptical form. Coimbra had a distinctive characteristic: there were two spaces for anatomies. Regarding the date of construction of these anatomical theaters, Salamanca stands out for having built its theater relatively early in relation to other European Universities.

With the creation of the anatomy discipline in Salamanca, the first dissections were performed in a provisional structure in the building of the *Escolas Maiores*.[87] This first dissection, realized by Cosme de Medina, used a dog, a pig,

---

[82] Siraisi, *The Clock and the Mirror,* 95.

[83] Brockbank, "Old Anatomical Theaters and what Took Place Therein," 371.

[84] Diana, "Anatomy between Public and Private in 14th-16th Century Europe," 334.

[85] Brockbank, "Old Anatomical Theaters," 371.

[86] Underwood, "The Early Teaching of Anatomy at Padua,"1–26; Gamba, "Il Primo Teatro Anatomico Stabile di Padova non fu Quello di Fabrici d'Acquapendente," 157–61; Semenzato, Piaz, and Rippa Bonati, *Il Teatro Anatomico. Storia e Restauri* (Padua: Università degli Studi di Padova, 1994); Stolberg, "Learning Anatomy in Late Sixteenth-century Padua," 381–402.

[87] Santander, 257. AUSA, Libros de Claustros, 20, 71v-73v.

and body parts of a sheep.[88] It was Medina who had a determinant role on the construction of a permanent and specialized space at the University of Salamanca.[89] Probably the first permanent theater for dissections for educational purposes in Spain (built between 1552 and 1554).[90]

In March 1552, the Vice-Chancellor received a royal order to begin searching for the theater's construction site. The construction of this theater sought to respond to two motivations: the reform movement of Vesalius in Spain[91] and a cultural policy related to the teaching and practice of medicine initiated in the reign of Carlos V and continued by Philip II.[92] On June 23rd, the new site was found, and a commission (which included Cosme de Medina) was appointed to handle the necessary preparations.[93] The new theater cost around 50,000 Maravedis (Spanish currency), which was equivalent to the annual salary of a professor. It was located between the Church of San Nicolás and the cemetery; its walls were stone, it had a slate roof, and the floor, benches, and panels were made of wood.[94] Near the Tormes River and far from the city, its stone structure gave it greater resistance compared to other anatomical theaters built with wood.[95]

The University faced some difficulties in the maintenance of the building: maintenance expenses, problems with the chaplaincy of the church of San Nicolás,[96] floods, damage caused by nearby residents, humidity, and an inefficient infrastructure that allowed animals to enter, especially at the time of dissections.[97]

In the case of the anatomical theater of Coimbra, information is scarce. At a meeting of the University Council in June 1560, rector Jorge de Almeida and his advisors decided to go ahead with the construction of the building requested in

[88] Carreras Panchón, 332.

[89] Martínez-Vidal and Pardo-Tomás, 257; Pardo Tomás, *Un lLugar para la Ciencia. Escenarios de Práctica Científica en la Sociedad Hispana del Siglo XVI* (Tenerife: Fundación Canaria Orotava de Historia de la Ciencia, 2006).

[90] Santander, 257–59.

[91] López Piñero, "The Vesalian Movement in Sixteenth-century Spain."

[92] Martínez-Vidal and Pardo-Tomás, 256.

[93] Santander, 258.

[94] Martínez-Vidal and Pardo-Tomás, 258. The rector and professor of medicine, Lorenzo Alderete, was responsible for directing the construction of the theater (Carreras Panchón, 332).

[95] Carreras Panchón, 332.

[96] Martínez-Vidal and Pardo-Tomás, 258–59.

[97] Carreras Panchón, 332.

the 1559 statutes.[98] The new building should be installed in the *Paço das Escolas* in the bell house due to the good state of the building and the clarity.[99] Curiously, this building should not be used for dissections of human cadavers.

A letter from the monarch in 1562 indicated that the University should finance the acquisition of houses close to the Hospital for anatomy. The reason: the authorities preferred that dissections on human cadavers took place as close as possible to the hospital where they came from. This process was long because the costs were all to be borne by the University. By the end of 1562, no houses had yet been purchased. The process of selection and acquisition of the houses for the theater was only resolved on July 13th, 1566, when a new royal order demanded this matter to be finalized.[100] It is possible to assume that the few dissections performed in this period had occurred in the first building, the school hall, probably with animals.[101]

Both universities experienced financial burdens from performing dissections. From the moment a corpse was handed over to the University until it was buried, all the expenses were paid by the institution. Besides the anatomy professor who almost always had a demonstrator for assistance and a substitute, when necessary, there was also a person responsible for cleaning the theater and the table, providing water and towels for the teacher after dissection, and cleaning the instruments. Another expense was the purchase of animals for dissections. But the main expense, besides the construction of the anatomical theaters, was human cadavers. The statutes (of Coimbra) well demonstrate the complex and expensive process involved in obtaining the cadavers assigned to the University by the city Hospital.[102]

The Hospital physician was obliged to notify the rector of the deaths at the hospital, then the rector would send the conservator of the University and the anatomy professor to choose the bodies for the anatomy. Soon after, the conservator would send the corpse to the anatomical theater (from 1566, next to the hospital); when the corpse was in place it would be the responsibility of

---

[98] The whole process of creating this theater and the main sources, were presented in Brito, "As Primeiras Dissecações Humanas na Universidade de Coimbra," 9–13.

[99] The rector was commissioned to make the central table and the benches (Brito, 8; Mário Brandão, *Actas dos Conselhos da Universidade de 1537 a 1557*, vol. II, 3.ª parte (Coimbra: A. U. C., 1969).

[100] The regent D. Henrique donated the houses near the Hospital to the University, so that finally the dissections could be performed (Nuno Grande, 484).

[101] João Bravo Chamisso, professor of anatomy, mentioned this theater in one of his books (Rodrigues and Fiolhais, 443).

[102] Leite, 300–302.

the anatomy teacher to start the dissection. If during the four days of the demonstration the corpse showed a high degree of decomposition, the teacher would have to warn the rector who in turn would ask two medical professors to decide what to do; the rector would decide what to do according to the advice of the two professors and could order the anatomy to continue or conclude.

When the anatomy was finished, the teacher had to ask the *Santa Casa da Misericórdia* of Coimbra to arrange the burial of the cadaver. The University would then have to pay for the transportation of the corpse, the burial, the holding of masses and still had a stipulated amount (600 *réis*, Portuguese currency) for the wax of the candles used in the ceremony. The proximity of the anatomy theater to the hospital and cemetery made transportation costs lower and prevented cadavers from decomposing before the anatomy.

Books and Authors

An important feature of Renaissance anatomy was the institutional and personal effort, visible in the medical curricula of many European universities, to recover and evaluate ancient texts.[103] The translation of *De usu partium* into Latin dated from the beginning of the fourteenth century, and Galen's most important work, *De anatomicis administrationibus*, was translated in the sixteenth century.[104] Nicolo Leoniceno, professor of natural history (Padua), also translated works of Galen and corrected other translations.[105] By end of the sixteenth century, Aristotle had gradually replaced Galen and was linked to the anatomical projects of various anatomists.[106]

Mondino de Luzzi, in his *Anathomia corporis humani*, introduced the separation of classical anatomy (in particular, from Galen) and the physiological concept.[107] His book becomes very popular in European Universities. For instance, it arrived in Montpelier in 1320 and became the central book for anatomy in 1366.[108] The successive editions make it one of the most important books of the fifteenth and sixteenth centuries. Luzzi's work promoted the coordination of the theoretical lessons with demonstrations, new rules for

---

[103] Klestinec, 377; Siraisi, *The Clock and the Mirror*, 95.
[104] Siraisi, The Faculty of Medicine," 378.
[105] Romero, et al., 155.
[106] De Angelis, 207.
[107] Mondino de Luzzi was well known in Coimbra. When dissections on animals were performed at this University, the Mondino de Luzzi protocol was followed (Rodrigues and Fiolhais 2013, 441).
[108] Jole Agrimi and Chiara Crisciani, *Edocere Medicos: Medicina Scolastica nei Secoli XIII-XV* (Napoli: Guerini e associati, 1988).

dissections, and the necessity to begin the dissection through the parts that decompose earlier.

Because students and professors traveled regularly to the main centers for teaching anatomy, they promoted similar ideas that shaped many of the works on anatomy that were produced in the centuries to come (the University of Padua had a central role in this process). Two main ideas seem to be present in the new books: the combination of the information from the texts with the practice on cadavers (the professor described the situation and simultaneously demonstrated the knowledge from the texts) and that this new scientific production consolidated the teaching of anatomy and regulated its practice and methods.[109] This more practical approach (with the resource of experiments to create new knowledge of the human body), was present in the works of several anatomists. Before Vesalius, Jacopo Berengario[110] introduced new concepts about the importance of direct observation and the comparison with texts of main authorities. The result was the appearance of manuals accompanied by notes and illustrations.

Critical of the acceptance of the ideas of Galen without a comparison with direct observation on corpses, Vesalius describes the errors of Galen and criticizes the academic conservatism in his *De humani corporis fabrica*.[111] Unlike Galen, Vesalius prioritized dissection on human cadavers and not on animals; he prioritized dissections and direct demonstrations performed by himself and his students, and anatomical research started to be planned and systematized with the aim of achieving a more complete knowledge of human anatomy.[112] *De humani corporis fabrica* became the main work taught in European Universities.[113]

---

[109] Diana, "Anatomy between Public and Private in 14th-16th Century Europe," 352–53.

[110] Levi Robert Lind, *Studies in Pre-Vesalian Anatomy: Biography, Translations, Documents* (Philadelphia: American Philosophical Society, 1975).

[111] Diana, "Anatomy between Public and Private in 14th-16th Century Europe," 357; Siraisi, "Vesalius and the Reading of Galen's Teleology," 1–37.

[112] Romero et al., 156; Ruben Eriksson, *Andreas Vesalius' First Public Anatomy at Bologna: An Eyewitness Report by Baldassar Heseler* (Uppsala and Stockholm: Alqvist and Wiksells, 1959).

[113] John Bertrand Decusance Saunders and Charles D. O'Malley, *The Illustrations from the Works of Andreas Vesalius of Brussels* (New York: Dover: Dover Publications, 1973); Juan José Barcia Goyanes, *El mito de Vesalio* (Valencia: Real Academia de Medicina– Universitat de Valencia, 1994); Nancy G. Siraisi, "Vesalius and Human Diversity in *De humani corporis fabrica*," *Journal of the Warburg and Courtauld Institutes* 57 (1994): 60–88.

The many statutes of the University of Salamanca made Hippocrates, Avicenna,[114] Galen and, later, Andrea Vesalius, mandatory authors. Vesalius was well known in Spain for being King Filipe II's personal physician. Although, *De humani corporis fabrica* had an irregular presence in the statutes of the Spanish University. Since anatomy was taught in Coimbra and Salamanca earlier than the official date of the creation of its discipline,[115] it is possible to find books about this matter also earlier than the creation of the discipline.

The ancient authors (mainly Galen) remained at both Universities during and after the period under study. In Coimbra, in 1559, it is possible to identify the preference for the work of Galen divided over the various years of the course.[116] Equally, in 1594 in Salamanca, *De usu partium* is indicated as the central authority.[117] Later, the statutes of 1625 of Salamanca maintained the same idea.[118] The several volumes of this work were divided in the two first years in Salamanca.[119]

In a textbook of an unknown author used in the University of Coimbra (*Opus mixtum*), the preference for Galen is clear.[120] The textbook followed closely the book *De usu partium* with a double finality: describe every part of the human body and treat diseases that affect every part.[121] The work of Galen in Coimbra had a general and long acceptance. The main critics arrived only

---

[114] Biblioteca General Histórica, BGU, Avicena: *Codex... totius scientiae medicine principis ...* [Venetiis: Lucae Antonii de Giunta], 1523. BGU 12.237.

[115] In Salamanca, it possible that the teaching of anatomy existed since the thirteenth century and was included in other disciplines such as practical medicine (Romero, et al., 153). In Coimbra, not only is the authorization to do anatomies in human cadavers prior to the creation of the discipline but, the theorical component of this matter was taught in the discipline of prima.

[116] Leite, 299.

[117] Rodríguez-San Pedro Bezares, *La Universdiad Salamantina del Barroco. Período 1598-1625*, 2:364. In this period, Salamanca had a great influence on the University of Coimbra. This resulted from the fact that between 1581 and 1640 a dynastic union existed between Portugal and Spain. Portugal was ruled by three Spanish Monarchs (Filipe I, II and III). For this, the Spanish Monarch referred to the statutes of the University of Salamanca to reform the University of Coimbra.

[118] Fonseca, "A Medicina," 841.

[119] *Constituciones apostólicas, y Estatuos de la muy insigne Universidad de Salamanca, recopilados nuevamente por su Comisión*. En Salamanca: impreso en casa de Diego Cusio, 1626.

[120] Biblioteca Geral da Universidade de Coimbra, BGUC, *Opus mixtum ex fabrica corporis humani et singularum partium morbis*, ms. 2879, p.1. This book is a volume where various notebooks with annotations and notes are compiled.

[121] Fonseca, "A Medicina," 862.

in the eighteenth century. The professor Manuel dos Reis, in 1739, and in the line of criticism made by Vesalius, advocated that Galen never made dissections in human cadavers.[122] The same professor also understood that dissections were possible because people have lost their aversion to corpses.[123] Galen's stay (and also Hipocrates and Avicena) at the University of Coimbra was long because the various reforms limited the entry of other authors.[124] The main followers of Galen and critics of Vesalius were the professor António Luís and, mainly, the first professor of anatomy at Coimbra, Afonso Rodrigues de Guevara.

In his book, Guevara opposes some of Vesalius' criticisms of Galen; however, based on his personal observations, he also distances himself from some of Galen's and Vesalius' ideas.[125] Guevara probably doesn't understand the novelty of the ideas of Vesalius, and, in a way, it is possible to conclude that he compromised the dissemination of the pioneering ideas of Vesalius in Coimbra.[126] Despite the resistance, Vesalius become an obligatory author in both Universities (Table 3.1). Salamanca, at the end of the sixteenth century, had a considerable number of available works (in addition to those already described; see Table 3.2).[127]

Table 3.1: Works of Vesalius in Coimbra.[128]

Andreae Vesalii Bruxellensis, Scholae Medicorum Patavinae Professoris, De humani corporis fabrica libri septem	1543
Tabulae anatomicae sex	1538
Epistola, docens venam axillarem dextri cubiti in dolore laterali secandam	1544
Epistola rationem modumque propinandi radicis Chynae decocti	1546
Anatomicarum Gabrielis Fallopii observationum examen	1564

---

[122] In this line, he wrote, *Tractatus anatomicus de universa corporis humani fabrica*. Biblioteca Geral da Universidade de Coimbra, BGUC, Tractatus anatomicus de universa corporis humani fabrica, ms. 2856.

[123] Fonseca, "A Medicina," 872.

[124] Lemos, *História da Medicina em Portugal. Doutrinas e Instituições*, I:157.

[125] Fonseca, "A Medicina," 849. Alfonso Rodríguez de Guevara, *Alphonsi Rod. Da Guevara, In, Academia Conimbricensi rei medicae professori,*1559.

[126] Rodrigues and Fiolhais, 443. His disciple, John Bravo Chamiço, also mentions Veslius in his book, *De medendis corporis*.

[127] Becedas González, 11–15.

[128] Carlos Fiolhais, "Livros Médicos do Renascimento," 274–82.

Table 3.2: Books Available in Salamanca.[129]

Luis de Mercado	*Institutiones chirurgicae* (1594)
Andrés Laguna	*Anatomica methodus, seu de sectione humani corporis contemplatio* (1535)
Juan Valverde de Amusco	*Historia de la composicion del cuerpo humano* (1556)
Gabriele Fallopio	*Opera omnia* (1600)
Andrés de León	*Tratados de medicina, cirugia y anatomia* (1603)
Bartolomé Hidalgo	*Thesoro de la verdadera cirugia y via particular contra la comum* (1624)

One of the main differences between Coimbra and Salamanca is the number of national authors. In Salamanca, the number of Spanish authors was higher, and in Coimbra it was residual. But not all the authors were present in both Universities. Apart from the most representative authors in this matter, many others have only appeared in one University, as was the case with Ambroise Paré in the University of Coimbra.[130]

Salamanca and Coimbra made significant advances and were able to provide their students with important works in anatomy. Although they did not always share Vesalius' ideas, his main works became mandatory and were present at the University. Thus, it is possible to conclude that, as happened in other universities, the use of animals and books was a recurring practice in the teaching of anatomy.[131]

Conclusion

The questions that guided this work are interconnected (how the studies of anatomy appeared and evolved in Coimbra and Salamanca and how advanced was the study of anatomy in Coimbra and Salamanca in relation to the main Europeans centers). The Portuguese and Spanish authorities sought to modernize the teaching of anatomy in their countries based on European centers of reference, such as the Italian Universities. However, the limitations

---

[129] http://bibliotecahistorica.usal.es/es/salamanca-1598-lecturas-academicas/de-las-lecturas-de/medicina. The list was finalized in 1625 because the last statutes used in this work dated from this year.

[130] Biblioteca Joanina, BJ, Ambroise Paré, *Opera*. (Paris: apud Iacobum Du-Puys, 1582). 4 A-21-2-16. Baudry, 355–77.

[131] Siraisi, *The Clock and the Mirror*, 95.

that they eventually encountered, and their own realities led to their own unique developments.

The University of Coimbra had its first authorization for dissections as early as 1546, well before it had an anatomy discipline or even an anatomical theater. In the case of Salamanca, it was with the appointment of Cosme de Medina in 1552 that the most practical anatomy began to be taught.

Perhaps due to some excessive enthusiasm, the statutes suggested a rather high number of dissections. However, the reality was quite different, and the number of anatomies performed would have been quite low. From the sources consulted, it seems possible to affirm that the number of anatomies performed was higher in Salamanca than in Coimbra. The relationship with the Hospitals was not the easiest and, in both Universities, presented several limitations to accessing cadavers. The intervention of the central authorities seems to have been decisive in forcing the city hospitals to cede their cadavers.

The investment in the acquisition of new books was part of a calculated effort to modernize the teaching of anatomy at these Universities. The most resounding example was the acquisition of *De humani corporis* of Andreas Vesalius. Present in both Universities, it was met with criticism, especially in Coimbra.

By the end of the sixteenth century, both Universities already had many works available for the study of anatomy. The big difference between these institutions was in the adoption of works by national authors. In Salamanca, this number was higher. Nevertheless, some professors from the University of Coimbra left us some important works.

The construction of anatomical theaters was a reality in both Universities but was faced with more difficulties in Coimbra. Salamanca stood out for building a permanent structure relatively early in relation to other Universities. In 1560, the University of Coimbra starts the construction of the theater in the *Paço das Escolas* but did not allow for the dissection of corpses at the University. Those dissections took place in another structure closer to the Hospital that was built later. Closer proximity to the Hospital where the cadavers came from and to the cemetery where they were buried after the dissections was essential to decreasing the University's costs.

In this work, it was possible to demonstrate that anatomy occupied an important place in Coimbra and Salamanca in the fifteenth and much of the sixteenth century, 'the century of anatomy.'[132] Unfortunately, in both

---

[132] Domenico Laurenza, *Art and Anatomy in Renaissance Italy. Images from a Scientific Revolution* (New York: Metropolitan Museum of Art, 2012).

Universities, the decline begins to appear during the sixteenth century. However, it was not only in these institutions that problems occurred.[133]

This decline, which continued practically until the eighteenth-century reforms, had one of its main causes in the lack of stimulus from the central authorities. At the same time, the sources also show us that another of the causes was the relaxation of the teachers. This was because the anatomy chair did not have the same status, nor did they have the same salary as, other more senior chairs. This situation led to many professors not staying in charge of the anatomy chair for a long time, which could have caused some instability for the development of anatomy teaching in these Universities. Finally, another reason may relate to the expenses that the Universities incurred for dissections. The case of Coimbra is enlightening. This University was responsible for all expenses related to cadavers for the anatomies: transportation, burial, funeral ceremonies, and all expenses arising from dissection in the theater. The highest cost would be the construction of the anatomical theaters, but it was not the only cost. The acquisition of books and, mainly, the expenses with cadavers were recurrent.

In conclusion, we have seen a significant development of anatomical studies in Coimbra and Salamanca from the fifteenth century until much of the next, although it was marked by some problems. Both Universities, during this period, managed to modernize their teaching, getting it closer to the main European centers.

---

[133] For instance, in Padua at the end of the sixteenth century, students complained that public anatomies were better known as a public spectacle than as a class (Klestinec, 344–450).

Figure A: Frontispiece of Vesalius' *De Humani Corporis Fabrica*, 1543.

Chapter 4

"How sweetly then she on her death-bed lay": Edward May's Rhetorical Anatomization of a Woman Burned at the Stake

Jennifer Lodine-Chaffey

Southeastern Oklahoma State University

Abstract: Long recognized by scholars as a literary form of anatomy, the early modern blazon exhibits and metaphorically dissects the body of the other, typically a woman. The traditional blazon isolates female body parts, making no attempt to unify the physical form, instead subjecting isolated fragments to the male gaze. Yet, curiously, in a 1633 poem entitled, "On a Woman Burned in Smithfield the 20 of April 1632," Edward May uses the blazon form to initially eroticize and rhetorically dissect a female execution victim but ends by evoking symbols of spiritual unity. By employing the phoenix, the trinity, and the triple nature of the executed woman as "a wife, a widow, and a maide," May attempts to sanctify and unify her burning body even while vicariously seducing his immobile Muse. Part of the tension in May's poem involves his struggle to come to terms with the woman's guilt. Her death by immolation, of course, signifies the crime of husband murder, a type of petty treason. Judging such a fate unjust, May both elegies the woman and dismantles her body, imagining himself as the flames that brush against her sexualized form. Yet, more is at stake here than just the sexualization of a woman suffering a horrific execution. In his effort to resolve the paradox of a beautiful woman who killed her spouse May ultimately repositions the woman as a sacrifice, thus providing her with spiritual, if not physical, unity. Ultimately though, the juxtaposition between May's eroticization of the female execution victim's body and his decision to transform her into a symbol of spiritual renewal suggests that this literary anatomization, although it metaphorically fragments, silences, and exploits the female body, could be combined with religious rhetoric to assuage male guilt and sanctify sexually violent fantasies.

Keywords: Blazon, Edward May, Female Execution, Anatomization

***

Introduction

A woman, dressed in white and bound to a stake, stands before a group of onlookers. The faggots placed around her feet are lit and slowly, the woman burns to death. In the audience, a male observer looks on, mesmerized by the spectacle. He watches as the flames climb up her body; he watches as she dies. Later, he pens a poem about the event.

Edward May's Epigram: "On a woman burned in Smithfield the 20 of April 1632. who dyed a Wife, a Widdow, and a true maide, by her owne free confession":

> [When] all in white pure as her quiet thought
> She to her journies end was easly brought
> How sweetly then she on her death-bed lay,
> How cheerefully her eye did dart its raye,
> What crimson blushes in her cheekes were spread
> And how the snow strove gently with the red;
> All this I saw and thousands more beside,
> Whose Eyes flow'd over, twas so high a tyde,
> That had the fiers then bin kindled round,
> They had bin quenchd, and she in teares bin dround
> How quickly up the nimble flame did skip
> And like glad lovers, fed upon her lip;
> Kist her faire eyes and with such fervor strove,
> That they destroyd what they so much did love:
> Impartiall death thy skill is strange and great
> Thou wound'st with frost, but here thou kil'st with heate,
> And she like gold thou hast in fire tride,
> And her bright soule thou now hast purifide;
> For 'twas unfit the greedie wormes should tare
> Such daintie flesh, or such a banquet share,
> That was ordained by the destinies,
>
> For a burnt offering and a sacrifice.
> Yet with my selfe when I thy case doe trye,

Me thinkes it is injustice thou shouldst dye
A Wife, a Maide, a Widow, can this be?
The Law condemned onely one, not three,
And if the Wife the Jury guilty found,
Why was not shee alone with fires cround?
Or if the Widow did the offence commit,
Why was not then the innocent Maiden quit?
'Tis strange no drop of mercie could be showne,
But let three suffer for the fault of one;
Yet of that one this might be truly said,
She dide a Wife, a Widow, and a maide.
Thus did this Phoenix, Phoenix like Expire,
(Not three but one; not one but three) in fire.[1]

This poem by Edward May and included in his 1633 *Epigrams Divine and Morall* offers readers not just an elegiac commentary on the execution of a woman. Instead, in "On a Woman Burned in Smithfield the 20 of April 1632," May catalogues the condemned's body parts as she is burned at the stake and describes the flames stroking her flesh; May's interest is not in her crime and the horror of her execution, but rather in her death as an erotic moment.[2] For May, the body of the unnamed woman[3] functions as an object of desire, even

---

[1] May, "On a woman burned in Smithfield the 20 of April 1632," C2.

[2] May, "On a woman burned in Smithfield," C2

[3] The unnamed woman May writes about may be the same individual listed in Richard Smyth's list of early seventeenth-century deaths ("a woman burnt in Smithfield for poisoning her husband" on April 20, 1632). The probability of May's victim being the same individual as the woman mentioned by Smyth seems likely as Smyth also references the execution of Robert Cromwell that same year and May's poem on Cromwell's execution is included in his *Epigrams Divine and Morall*. See Richard Smyth, *The Obituary of Richard Smyth*, ed. Henry Ellis (London: Camden Society, 1849), 6-7 and May, "On Mr. *Robert Cromwell*, who for poysoning his Master, was executed at Tiburne, on Saturday, *June 2. 1632,*" in *Epigrams*, D3. Frances Dolan, in her insightful account of researching and assessing early modern accounts of petty treason, also notes that fragmentary evidence concerning a number of women executed for petty treason in the 1630s may have included one woman "whose execution Henrietta Maria supposedly 'labored earnestly' to prevent." Dolan also points out that Henry Goodcole, in his account of the crime and execution of husband-murderer Alice Clarke, mentions a woman burned at Smithfield around the same time who was "much commiserated, much lamented." It is possible that May's unnamed woman may be the petty traitor the queen sought to save, or the woman referenced by Goodcole. See Dolan, "Tracking the Petty Traitor Across Genres," in *Ballads*

as she is burned. He praises her conventional beauty, imagines that the flames caress her lips and eyes, and rejoices that her "daintie flesh" would never rot and become food for worms. May seemingly would agree with Edgar Allan Poe's statement that the "death of a beautiful woman is, unquestionably, the most poetical topic in the world."[4] Yet, May's elegy attests to more than his fascination with a dying woman's beauty. The imagery of the poem allows May metaphorically to become the fire that consumes her body. In his poem, May depicts the condemned woman, not as a suffering body, but instead as a spectacularly visualized and immobilized victim of seduction and rape. He mentally probes her body parts, envisions touching her skin as the flames do, and interprets her death as a moment of sexual consummation that she welcomes due to her cheerful gaze and flushed cheeks. In short, by cataloguing and blazoning the body parts of the condemned woman, May turns her into an object of imaginative consumption.

Despite his interest in the woman's body and its potential as an object of lustful fantasies, May cannot leave his readers only with his musings as a voyeur and blazoner. Instead, to sanctify and sanitize his poem, May ends by evoking symbols of spiritual unity. By employing the Phoenix, the trinity, and the triple nature of the executed woman as "a wife, a widow, and a maide," May provides religious significance to her burning body even while vicariously seducing his immobile Muse. The tension in May's poem involves his struggle to come to terms with the woman's guilt as well as his own desires. Her death by immolation suggests the woman is guilty of husband murder, a type of petty treason. Judging such a fate unjust and enchanted by her physical form even while she burns, May both elegizes the woman and dismantles her body, imagining himself as the flames that brush against her immobilized form. In his effort to resolve the paradox of a beautiful woman who killed her spouse and suffers for her crime May ultimately repositions the woman as a sacrificial victim through his use of the rhetoric of martyrdom, thus providing her with spiritual, if not physical unity. In the end, the juxtaposition between May's eroticization of the female execution victim's body and his decision to transform her into a symbol of spiritual renewal suggests that this literary anatomization, although it metaphorically fragments, silences, and exploits the female body, could be combined with religious rhetoric to assuage male guilt and sanctify sexually violent fantasies.

---

and Broadsides in Britain, 1500-1800, ed. Patricia Fumerton, Anita Guerrini, and Kris McAbee (Burlington, VT: Ashgate, 2010), 154.

[4] Poe, 201.

A relatively unknown author, Edward May seems to have borrowed nearly all of the epigrams in his collection from other sources, save this particular poem and a few others. While the title (*Epigrams Divine and Morall*) suggests the spiritual value of the poems, most of the pieces are actually, according to Hoyt Hudson, "witticisms, scurrilous anecdotes, imitations and translations."[5] The only other notable poem not closely paraphrased or copied from other sources is May's elegy to Robert Cromwell, who was executed for poisoning his master the same year as the female victim.[6] Although both poems share similarities due to subject matter and religious rhetoric, May's piece on Cromwell focuses on the executed man's spiritual redemption and crime rather than his physical demeanour and body. Indeed, May highlights the law's condemnation of Cromwell as just, characterizing the death sentence as "Astrea weigh'd thy crime with even hand," and the execution as a "Potion which may doe us good." Despite his belief in the young man's guilt, May expresses confidence in Cromwell's repentance, noting that "like the good Theef thou stoll'st heaven at thy death." Additionally, May attempts to imagine the victim's thoughts as he encounters death, proposing that in his final moments, Cromwell was attended by "legions of Angels" and heard "the chime of the Coelestiall spheares."[7] May's elegy to Cromwell, therefore, includes similar elements to his piece addressed to the unnamed woman burned on a pyre. Yet, unlike his approach to Cromwell's death, May's poem to the female victim focuses less on her crime and repentance than on her body parts and their value as a text that he controls.

The opening of May's poem could be usefully categorized as an anatomical blazon, although his poem is an anomaly. Most blazons typically consider imaginary or living women rather than female execution victims in the midst of their deaths. Medieval and early modern writers often used the anatomical

---

[5] See Hoyt H. Hudson, "Edward May's Borrowings from Timothe Kendall and Others," *The Huntington Library Bulletin*, no. 11 (April 1937): 28. According to James Doelman, "the volume's title and the presentable pious poems with which it opens stand as a thin veneer over a more typically disreputable collection." (508).

[6] May, "On Mr. *Robert Cromwell*, who for poysoning his Master, was executed at Tiburne, on Saturday, June 2. 1632," in Epigrams, D3.

[7] May, "On Mr. Robert Cromwell," D3. The death of Cromwell's master, Joseph Lane, although suspected to be caused by poison, was not clear cut. Charles I actually initiated an inquiry and asked the College of Physicians to examine the case. Tasked with finding out whether Lane died from poison or accidental use of an apothecary's medicine, the Fellows could not reach a consensus with 18 contending that Lane was poisoned and four believing poorly prepared medicine was to blame. See Charles Goodall, *The Royal College of Physicians of London* (London: Walter Kettilby, 1684).

blazon to praise female beauty, metaphorically dissecting the woman's physical attributes by focusing on her constituent parts.[8] Perhaps the most well-known example of the anatomical blazon is Thomas Campion's 1601 piece, "Cherry-Ripe," better known as "There is a Garden in Her Face," which catalogues the features of the woman's face, comparing her teeth to pearls, her lips to rosebuds, and her cheeks to lilies.[9] Philip Sidney's sonnet sequence *Astrophil and Stella* likewise presents readers with fragmented descriptions of the beloved, focusing not only on her face, but also on her breasts, legs, and skin.

Indeed, in Sonnet, 29, Stella's physical attributes belong to erotic love, signifying the male author's desire and attesting to his position as her thrall:

> So Stella's heart, finding what power Love brings,
> To keep itself in life and liberty,
> Doth willing grant that in the frontiers he
> Use all to help his other conquerings.
> And thus her heart escapes, but thus her eyes
> Serve him with shot, her lips his heralds are,
> Her breasts his tents, legs his triumphal car,
> Her flesh his food, her skin his armour brave.[10]

Here, Stella, despite the speaker's insistence that she remains aloof and her heart free from affection, becomes a tool of erotic love. The speaker, while recognizing his own bondage to desire, in turn linguistically objectifies the woman causing these feelings. As Ann Rosalind Jones and Peter Stallybrass note, Sidney's lust for the woman "unites him to a male world in which language can become an instrument of domination and women the naïve

---

[8] The anatomical blazon and the anti-blazon were used by a number of medieval and early modern writers. In addition to well-known verses by Francesco Petrarch, poems by Thomas Campion, Philip Sidney's *Astrophil and Stella*, and William Shakespeare's sonnets, Fulke Greville's "Caelica" and Robert Herrick's "Hesperides" highlight fragmented descriptions of female body parts, which scholars argue strip women of their subjectivity and assert male control over both the written word and women in general. For further context, see Moira P. Baker, "'The Uncanny Stranger on Display:' The Female body in Sixteenth- and Seventeenth-Century Love Poetry," *South Atlantic Review* 56, no. 2 (1991): 7-25 and Christine Suki, "'Stella is Not Here:' Sidney's Acts of Writing as Acts of Erasing," *Etudes Epistémè: revue de littérature et de civilisation* 21 (2012) http://journals. openedition.org/episteme/411.

[9] Campion, 162.

[10] Sidney, *Astrophil and Stella*, 179.

subjects (that is, objects) of men's desire."[11] Sidney's Stella, then, is a woman made of diverse parts that serve to induce the speaker's desire and inspire his imaginative dissection of her physical form.[12]

The use of this technique often, then, functioned as a fragmentation of the female body, both expressing male sexual desire and fetishizing the woman's body parts by comparing them to desirable objects like cherries, pearls, or golden wires.[13] Although many of these poems celebrate the female body as beautiful and sought after, Nancy J. Vickers posits that this strategy, first popularized by Francesco Petrarch's cataloguing of Laura's body parts, served as a way for the poet to neutralize the threat of female sexuality to his masculine identity.[14] Thus, by blazoning the female body as parts rather than a whole, the male poet silences the woman and refashions her as his own textual creation. Jonathan Sawday argues that poetic blazons reflect the theaters of dissection present in most early modern European cities and highlight a contemporary obsession with the female body. Noting that during this time period, "a strange fantasy of anatomical surrender seems to have, briefly, flourished," Sawday posits that the English blazon served to metaphorically dismember the female form, thereby bolstering patriarchal control.[15]

The majority of anatomical blazons written during the sixteenth and seventeenth century describe the body parts of living women or women imagined as alive. The gaze of the poet and of the reader, while figuratively

---

[11] Jones and Stallybrass, 59.

[12] Colin Yeo interprets the references to the body parts of Stella in Sidney's Sonnet 29 as creating "a grotesque and disturbing vision of a cannibalistic individual devouring a woman and dressing up in parts of her body" (139).

[13] See Hillary Nunn, *Staging Anatomies, Dissection and Spectacle in Early Stuart Tragedy* (Aldershot: Ashgate, 2005),29-30; Jonathan Sawday, *The Body Emblazoned*, 193-196; Grant Williams, "Early Modern Blazons and the Rhetoric of Wonder: Turning Towards an Ethics of Sexual Difference," in *Luce Irigaray and Premodern Culture: Thresholds of History*, ed. Elizabeth D. Harvey and Theresa Krier (Taylor and France, 2004), 126-137; Nancy J. Vickers, "Diana Described: Scattered Women and Scattered Rhyme," Critical Inquiry 8 (1981): 265-279; and Vickers, "Members Only: Marot's Anatomical Blazons," in David Hillman and Carla Mazzio, ed. *The Body in Parts: Fantasies of Corporeality in Early Modern Europe* (New York: 1997), 3-21. In addition to fragmenting the woman's body, anatomical blazons also invite the reader to reimagine the female form as comprised of other objects and life forms, which, according to Patricia Parker, "makes explicit an aspect of the rhetorical tradition's own relation to natural plenitude" and constructs the woman as "a passive commodity in a homosocial discourse or male exchange in which the woman herself, traditionally absent, does not speak" (131).

[14] Vickers, "Diana Described," 277-278.

[15] Sawday, *The Body Emblazoned*, 191.

dissecting the subject, does not typically conceptualize the body as dead or dying. Yet, recently, a number of scholars have noted that the early modern stage often created spectacles of dismemberment that employed the conventions of the blazon and that the verbal components of the genre were often combined with the body of an actor perceived as dead by the audience.[16] Sara Morrison observes that the theater frequently drew "on Petrarchan conventions that display the female body, express desire, and convey the inherently visual nature of the blazon."[17] By providing the audience with access to verbal and visual representations of female dismemberment, playwrights involved those watching plays in a new way—the audience became complicit in acts of violence. Thus, the use of the theatrical blazon often dehumanized the human actors, reducing them or their body parts to props in the audience's imagination.[18] May, on the other hand, asks his audience to consider an actual death; as readers, we act as witnesses not to an actor's simulation of death or dismemberment nor to a poet's appropriation of the female form for creative purposes, but to the suffering and death of a once-living woman.

Anatomizing the Female Figure

May's poem begins with the image of the female execution victim "easly brought" to the site of execution. While the woman still breathes, the poet attempts to bestow a passive persona on the victim through his use of the anatomical blazon. Noticeably, this woman is never provided with a name, suggesting that she is merely a cipher on which May pens his erotic and possibly sadistic longings. Instead of supplying a clear image of the whole woman, her crime, or her suffering, May catalogues and interprets her body parts, creating for himself a willing victim not only of execution, but also of his lustful desires:

> [When] all in white pure as her quiet thought
> She to her journies end was easly brought
> How sweetly then she on her death-bed lay,
> How cheerefully her eye did dart its raye,
> What crimson blushes in her cheekes were spread
> And how the snow strove gently with the red;

---

[16] See Deborah Uman and Sara Morrison, *Staging the Blazon in Early Modern English Theater*. Studies in Performance and Early Modern Drama (London: Routledge, 2016).
[17] Uman and Morrison, 67.
[18] Marchesi, 93.

All this I saw and thousands more beside . . .
How quickly up the nimble flame did skip
And like glad lovers, fed upon her lip;
Kist her faire eyes and with such fervor strove,
That they destroyd what they so much did love.

Here May uses the conventional language of the blazon, moving from the woman's eyes to her cheeks, then her lips, cataloguing her features even as they burn. Patricia Parker notes that such an "'inventory' of parts becomes a way of taking possession by the very act of naming or accounting."[19] By naming the woman's parts, May takes ownership of her body; he also, though, renders her physical fragments as signs of her affective response, thereby possessing not only her body, but also her mind. May paints his victim as an ideal woman, noting the traditional markers of beauty in her cheeks, as "the snow strove gently with the red."[20] Her blush can be interpreted as a sign of her sexual desire, at least according to May's reading of her face, even though readers may assume that the redness of her face denotes the heat of the fire and the pain she suffers while undergoing immolation. The adjectives May employs denote the female victim's willingness to die (and to figuratively give herself to the flames just as May imagines she gives herself to him). Not only does the woman "sweetly" lie upon her "death-bed," she also gazes about "cheerefully," blushes, and cries. Much of May's language here implicates the woman in the violence against her body both literally and figuratively, thus erasing her subjectivity by imposing his own interpretation of her physical responses.

While May employs traditional wording used by many early modern poets in order to claim ownership of the woman's body, his piece works not just to linguistically dismember her, but serves to recount the real destruction of her body by fire, thereby doubly erasing her subjectivity. Usually, anatomical blazons reduce the woman into a number of cherished items or foods that suggest her value as an object of exchange and her passive and silent position within this patriarchal economy.[21] May, though, offers up the woman's parts as objects of consumption and exchange only to then report on their complete destruction. His dismantling of her body, therefore, becomes not simply a partitioning that implies ownership, but instead a complete

---

[19] Parker, 131.

[20] Romana Sammern notes that "The ideal Renaissance face was a composition of white and red: a high forehead free from hair and wrinkles, and skin, even and whitened, accentuated by a blush on the cheeks and the red of the lips" (398).

[21] See Parker, 131.

obliteration of her personhood through both the textual blazoning of his work and the annihilation of her body by fire.

After establishing the beauty of the execution victim as well as her acquiescence to her upcoming death and metaphorical rape, May details her burning by again blazoning her. The body parts described in this section of the poem, though, are no longer used to provide the woman with an emotional response to her upcoming death. Instead, the poet itemizes her body parts as the embers move to devour each constituent part "like glad lovers." May traces the movement of the flames as they skipped up her body, "fed upon her lip," "kist her faire eyes," and at last "destroyd what they so much did love." These images position May as vicariously assaulting the condemned woman, imagining his own hands and lips as the flames that touch and kiss her burning body, eventually extinguishing her life. By envisioning the victim as lying down upon a bed, May also figuratively rapes the woman, "devouring" her "daintie flesh" like the fire that caresses and penetrates her body.[22]

While recognizing that the unnamed woman becomes, for May, a symbol of sexuality, we must consider his poem not only in terms of its reaction to the theatrical spectacle of her death, but also in relation to its understanding of the execution ritual. There are, of course, a number of other poems written in the early modern period that respond to the executions of individuals. Andrew Marvell's "Horatian Ode" (1650) famously laments the beheading of Charles I, while John Taylor, the "Water Poet," penned the "Description of Tyburne" (1630), which describes the famous gallows used for London's commoners. Thomas Wyatt also mourns the execution of Thomas Cromwell in his translation of a Petrarch sonnet ("The Pillar Perished Is"). None of these poems, though, combine elegy with anatomical blazon. One exception is a poem written by John Cheke that commemorates the poet, Henry Howard, Earl of Surrey, following his decapitation in 1547. In a recent article, Joel Grossman explores this elegy, contending that Cheke, who labored "to reconcile the contradictions inherent in a man simultaneously worthy of great praise and great blame," used the anatomical blazon in order to symbolize his conflicted attitude towards Surrey. [23] In short, Grossman argues that Cheke uses fragmented images and language to represent Surrey's divided nature as both gifted writer and treasonous subject. Something similar, I argue, occurs in May's poem. Rather than May simply struggling to resolve his own erotic impulses when gazing on the executed woman, he also contends with the issue of her guilt.

---

[22] May, "On a Woman Burned in Smithfield," C2.
[23] Grossman, 2, 20.

May's poem and the historical record suggest that the woman burned at the stake was condemned for petty treason and most likely poisoned her husband ("the Wife the Jury guilty found").[24] Originally defined by the Treason Act of 1351, petty or petit treason was "an inferior form of treason which consisted of the slaying of a person to whom the killer 'oweth faith and obedience.'"[25] In his 1632 examination of laws relating to women, lawyer Thomas Edgar explained that petty treason occurred "if any servant kill his Master, any woman kill her husband, or any man secular or religious person kill his Prelate to whom he owes obedience."[26] Thus, early modern English people viewed the crime of petty treason as a rebellion against the social order. While the law, however, included three different varieties of petty treason, in practice married women were most frequently charged with and suffered for this crime. The punishment of female petty traitors reflected not only the unequal legal position of women in early modern society, but also, as Frances Dolan points out, "collapsed the distinction between the two kinds of treason"— petty and high.[27] Thus, the punishment for petty treason differed for men and women. For men, the punishment was less severe than that of high treason. Rather than being hanged, drawn, and quartered, as most non-noble men convicted of treason were, men found guilty of petty treason were simply hanged. For women, though, the punishment for both high and petty treason remained the same: burning at the stake.[28]

The law, therefore, punished women in a more violent manner than men convicted of petty treason.[29] Burning was also the penalty for a number of

---

[24] May, "On a Woman Burned in Smithfield," C2. For historical documents relating to this case, see Smyth, *The Obituary of Richard Smyth,* 6-7 and *Seventh Report of the Royal Commission on Historical Manuscripts,* Part 1, Appendix, "The Manuscripts of Geo. Alan Lowndes, Esq., of Barrington Hall, Co. Essex," ed. Alfred J. Horwood (London, 1879), 548. In his personal records (entries nos. 420 and 421), George Alan Lowndes states that in April of 1632, "another wife has given her husband a poison of melted lead, but it was because he came home drunk." He later notes that "This day was the poor woman burnt in Smithfield that poisoned her husband, which is wondered at the cruelty, since there was so much excuse of mercy to her."

[25] Lockwood, 33.

[26] Edgar, 208.

[27] Frances Dolan, *Dangerous Familiars,* 23-24.

[28] Ruth Campbell points out that "this whole area of punishment smacks of discrimination." See Campbell, "Sentence of Death by Burning for Women," 22-23.

[29] For the history of petty treason laws see Ruth Campbell, "Sentence of Death by Burning," 44-59 and Sheely A. M. Gavigan, "Petit Treason in Eighteenth Century England: Women's Inequality Before the Law," *Canadian Journal of Women and the Law* 3, no. 2 (1989-1990): 335-374. For discussion of the punishment of death by burning and

other crimes in this period, including heresy and sodomy, suggesting that burning was reserved for crimes deemed particularly heinous and unnatural by early modern people. As Marisha Caswell points out, execution by burning functioned as more than merely a symbolic remainder of hell fire; instead, she interprets immolation as the reflection of "a need to destroy the body of the offender and in doing so to purify society from the harm caused by the offender's actions."[30] Women who killed their husbands, according to contemporary understandings of the divine hierarchy, were analogous to individuals who sought to kill the monarch and should pay for their extreme rebellion by having their bodies utterly destroyed. The goal in staging the burnings of women was not only to punish the offender, but also to dissuade other wives from choosing the penultimate form of rebellion against their earthly lords.

In an attempt to mitigate the victim's crime and assuage his own guilt over his lustful fantasies about a woman undergoing immolation, May strives to reframe the execution itself:

> And she like gold thou hast in fire tride,
> And her bright soule thou now hast purifide;
> For 'twas unfit the greedie wormes should tare
> Such daintie flesh, or such a banquet share,
> That was ordained by the destinies,
> For a burnt offering and a sacrifice.

Rather than delve into the woman's crime, May chooses to reimagine her as a holy martyr— "a burnt offering and a sacrifice."[31] Burning at the stake, of course, was not just used in cases of high or petty treason; instead, perhaps the most well-known contemporary accounts of individuals burned at the stake were the Marian martyrs, who were executed for their refusal to practice Catholicism and their embrace of English Protestantism. Hagiographies, including John Foxe's famed *Acts and Monuments*, sought not only to provide a history of martyrdom, but also to offer readers examples of how to live and die for their faith. Such works, especially Foxe's hagiographies, were widely circulated and influenced religious thought in England and in the British

---

its connection to early modern cultural understanding of Indian sati, see Pompa Banerjee, *Burning Women: Widows, Witches, and Early Modern European Travelers in India* (Basingstoke: Palgrave Macmillan, 2003).

[30] Caswell, 198.

[31] May, "On a Woman Burned in Smithfield," C2.

colonies.[32] Foxe notably celebrates not only men who were burned at the stake for their beliefs, but also provides graphic accounts of female executions, which highlighted God's ability to work through the weak and suffering female body.[33] Contemporary understandings of immolation as not just a punishment for crime, but also as a signifier of martyrdom, come into play in May's poem as he attempts to rewrite the unnamed victim's death as a holy event.

In order to reframe the victim's burning as a type of martyrdom, May employs terminology frequently used in early modern accounts of martyrdom. Echoing popular publications of sermons and hagiographies, May asserts that the woman has been consecrated via the method of her death: "and like gold thou hast in fire tride, / And her bright soule thou now hast purified."[34] For May, this process of purification ends only when the woman expires, suggesting that her sins are expunged. Additionally, by reframing the unnamed victim as a martyr, May replaces his conception of her as an eroticized figure with an image of her as a holy victim "with fires cround." May, then, in order to suppress (or transcend) his own desire for the sexualized body of the woman burning at the stake, must offer her as a sacrifice. It is only by sanctifying the violence of the execution and destroying the object of his desire, that May is able to constrain his own lusts and assuage his guilt.[35]

May's shift from thinking of the woman as an erotic victim to a holy martyr, though, is complicated by his textual struggle to cease thinking of her body. Even as the speaker rejoices that "the greedie worms" cannot "tare / Such

---

[32] John King notes the *Acts and Monuments* was "revered by many Protestants as a 'holy' book" and was often "chained alongside the Bible for reading by ordinary people at many public places including cathedrals, churches, schools, libraries, guildhalls, and at least one inn" (1). Megan Hickerson described Foxe's work as "one of the most widely disseminated and influential texts of the sixteenth century and beyond, surpassed in importance only by the Tyndale Bible as a formative text of English Reformation" (6).

[33] See Susannah Brietz Monta, *Martyrdom and Literature in Early Modern England* (Cambridge: Cambridge University Press, 2005), 220-221.

[34] May, "On a Woman Burned in Smithfield," C2. This particular phrasing, found in a number of early modern works and referenced in Foxe's *Acts and Monuments*, is based on 1 Peter 1:7, which in the 1611 King James Version states, "That the triall of your faith, being much more precious then of golde that perisheth, though it bee tryed with fire, might be found unto praise, and honor, and glory, at the appearing of Iesus Christ." John R. Knott notes that John Bradford interpreted suffering itself as a "a purifying fire to burn the dross away of our dirtiness and sin" (*Discourses of Martyrdom*, 96).

[35] For a similar reading of the use of staging violence against sexualized women in early modern drama, see Huston Diehl, *Staging Reform, Reforming the Stage: Protestantism and Popular Theater in Early Modern England* (Ithaca: Cornell University Press, 1997), 156-181.

daintie flesh, or such a banquet share," he continues to focus on her physical form by imagining the penetration and consumption of her body. In these lines, May expresses his reluctance to share the body of the unnamed woman with anyone else (even the worms) and rejoices that her flesh will never rot, but instead, will turn to ash and become, in words that echo the language of Foxe's *Acts and Monuments*: "a burnt offering and a sacrifice."[36]

By comparing two differing ways of consuming the woman's body, May elevates the fires of martyrdom above the destruction of her corpse by vermin. The suggestion here, which shares similarities with Andrew Marvell's "To His Coy Mistress," is that death by fire is preferable to the woman's posthumous rape by necrophilic worms because it not only allows the woman to subvert the ravages of time, but also allows the poet to participate in the consumption of her body.[37] Dying on the pyre ensures that the victim will never decay, never lose her beauty through death or old age, and never become a "banquet" for "greedie worms." What perhaps is more important to the speaker, though, is the protection of his position as a vicarious lover whose lustful thoughts, like the literal fire, devour and penetrate the woman's body.

Sexualized images of female martyrs, while less prevalent during the early modern period, were common in medieval hagiographies and artwork and might, as Madeline H. Caviness argues, have elicited a "sado-erotic" response from readers in a way not unlike May's own engagement with the unnamed victim.[38] Medieval depictions of the suffering of female martyrs often included naked bodies and sexual torture, which could be interpreted and responded to differently. Indeed, as Martha Easton notes in her study of numerous images of Saint Agatha's mastectomy, the mutilation of martyred women "creates a simultaneously empathetic and voyeuristic response," which worked to visually purify sexual violence inflicted on female bodies.[39] What is noteworthy about May's amalgamation of the sexual and the holy, however, is his return to medieval renderings of female martyrdom. Protestant hagiographies, like Foxe's famed *Acts and Monuments*, presented suffering

---

[36] May's words here share similarities with the final words of the martyr, John Bland, who was burned in 1555. According to Foxe, Bland's last speech included the following: "Accept thys burnt offering and sacrifice, O Lorde, not for the sacrifice it selfe, but for thy deare sonnes sake my Sauiour: for whose testimony I offer this free wil offering with all my hart and with al my soule" (Book 11, 1697).

[37] The speaker of Marvell's poem famously reminds the beloved of her mortality by noting the possibility that "worms shall try" her "long preserved virginity" (lines 27-28).

[38] Caviness, 84.

[39] Easton, 109.

and graphic violence as a realistic outcome of martyrdom and the martyrs' ability to withstand such pain as proof of their faith. Medieval hagiographies, in contrast, highlighted the martyrs' ability to transcend pain through the miraculous assistance of God and the saints.[40] May's poem, drawing on the traditional representations of virgin martyrs and their experiences of sexualized torture, tries to combine the erotic with the religious, but erases the victim's experiences of pain. The unnamed woman, a passive victim of the law and of May's narrative rewriting of her story, responds to her execution more like a medieval than an early modern martyr by exhibiting a "quiet thought," laying "sweetly" upon her deathbed, "cheerefully" looking about, and seemingly showing no physical reactions beyond a blush and tears. May's depiction of the victim, I suggest, reveals his conflicting emotions about the victim and his attempt to rhetorically repress his own desires by envisioning her as a martyr, but as a medieval martyr that remains erotic object rather than a contemporary martyr that proves her faithfulness to the divine by withstanding torture and death.

Despite his attempts to reframe the woman's execution as martyrdom, May still labors to come to terms with the woman's transgressions. How can he justify his construction of a husband-murderer as a martyr? Sympathetic and laudatory accounts of the executions of husband-murders typically highlighted the woman's repentance, willingness to die, and active role in the ritual.[41] Minister Henry Goodcole's account of the 1635 burning of Alice Clarke for the murder of her husband is a case in point. According to Goodcole, the victim wept tears of contrition, offered a moving speech to the gathered crowd, and presented herself as a changed woman. Yet, May's unnamed victim's voice remains eerily absent from the poem and her physical responses to the pain she endures are rewritten as erotic desire and docile acceptance. She never offers a statement of repentance and never gives a final prayer. Instead, May depicts her as a passive figure, smiling and crying by turn, and peacefully allowing the fires to consume her body. In a sense, then, May depicts and interprets the body of the condemned woman according to his purposes; he does not allow her to fashion herself because he never provides readers with her words on the scaffold nor does he acknowledge the

---

[40] For more on the differences between Protestant hagiographies and the medieval variants, see John R. Knott, "John Foxe and the Joy of Suffering," *The Sixteenth Century Journal* 27, no. 3 (Autumn 1996): 721-734 and James C. W. Truman, "John Foxe and the Desires of Reformation Martyrology," *ELH* 70, no. 1 (Spring 2003): 35-66.

[41] See Henry Goodcole, *The Adultresses Funerall Day in Flaming, Scorching, and Consuming Fire* (London: N. and I. Okes, 1635).

possibility that her blushes may be more accurately read as a physical response to pain. By presenting her as a sacrificial victim, May wipes away her crime, just as he had reframed her suffering as acquiescence to seduction at the start of his poem.

To further his fashioning of her as a martyr, May employs a well-known contemporary riddle that divides the woman into three separate identities — "A Wife, a Maide, a Widow":

> Yet with my selfe when I thy case doe trye,
> Me thinkes it is injustice thou shouldst dye
> A Wife, a Maide, a Widow, can this be?
> The Law condemned onely one, not three,
> And if the Wife the Jury guilty found,
> Why was not shee alone with fires cround?
> Or if the Widow did the offence commit,
> Why was not then the innocent Maiden quit?
> 'Tis strange no drop of mercie could be showne,
> But let three suffer for the fault of one;
> Yet of that one this might be truly said,
> She dide a Wife, a Widow, and a maide.[42]

While at first glance, May's use of this threefold identification is confusing, his intention here is to equate the unnamed victim with the trinity and to inscribe on her an identity that encompasses all acceptable female designations. Found in a number of early modern literary works and even engraved on a seventeenth-century memorial to a young aristocrat, this three-part designation of conventional female identity referenced by May was often used to categorize the traditional heteronormative movement of women through life — from unwed virgin, to wedded wife, to widow.[43] These terms, though,

---

[42] May, "On a Woman Burned in Smithfield," C2.

[43] Textual uses of this triple designation for virtuous women can be found in Shakespeare's *Measure for Measure*, Sir John Davies' "A Contention betwixt a Wife, a Widow and a Maid" (1602), and Ester Sowerman's *Ester Hath Hang'd Haman* (1617). Additionally, a monument to Elizabeth Dutton in Little Gaddesden Church, Herts, includes a plaque commemorating the deceased as one who died "a wife, a widow, and a maid in the year 1611, aged 16." Apparently, Elizabeth's husband was thrown from his horse directly following their wedding and she died shortly afterward of grief. As the marriage was not consummated, the triple description of Dutton can be readily explained. See *Memorials of the Duttons of Dutton in Cheshire: With Notes Respecting the Sherborne Branch of the Family* (London: Henry Sotheran & Co., 1901), 29.

always relate to the woman's marital status, reproductive body, and sexual identity. Jo Carruthers, in her analysis of this terminology, points out that, for early modern readers, the only designation for women not deemed maid, widow, or wife was a wanton.[44] Yet, according to Carruthers, the early modern proto-feminist Ester Sowernam, by employing this phrase in her pamphlet upholding the worth of women (*Ester Hath Hang'd Haman*), offers a more nuanced definition of womanhood. In her pamphlet, Sowerman toys with her readers, announcing herself as simultaneously a woman of ill-repute and a virtuous woman in order to transcend the two different designations of female identity.[45] Indeed, Linda Woodbridge suggests that Sowernam's claim to be "neither Maide, Wife or Widow, yet really all," offers readers "a paradox implying that marital status is irrelevant, that a woman possesses an indestructible self, unalterable by sexual or marital experience."[46]

Edward May applies a similar paradox, thereby allowing his readers an interpretation of his executed muse as more than simply a wanton. Evoking the three different categorizations of a virtuous woman, though, initially disrupts the unity of the female victim May seeks to reframe as a martyr. Rather than viewing the unnamed woman as a singular individual, May asks which of her three personas was found guilty of the crime. Did the jury condemn the wife? Did the widow commit the murder? Was the maiden persona innocent of husband-murder? May seems unsure. He can instead

---

[44] Carruthers, 323. The contemporary understanding of a woman who could not claim to be maid, wife, or widow, as wanton or whore is clearly defined by the poem "What is shee?" by Robert Armin and included in his collection of poetic dialogues:

What is that Woman: Sir she was a Mayde.
O, but she is not now. How happens this?
Yes sir she is, but therewith ill apayde:
Mayde is she, no Mayde by one deede amisse.
In deede, one deede which lately for she did,
From Maydes estate I must her needes forbid.

Is she a Wife? neither, not so blessed,
That honour last leape yeere escapt her too.
What, is sh'a Widdow, late by death distressed?
O no, nor that way wrongde: I know not how,
Onely thus much I say, and talke no more,
Nor mayde, wife, widdow, but a common whore.

See Armin, *Quips upon Questions, or, a Clownes Conceite on Occasion Offered Bewraying a Morrallised Metamorphoses of Changes Upon Interrogatories* (London: W. Ferbrand, 1600), n.p.
[45] Carruthers, 335.
[46] Woodbridge, 93.

only lament that all "three suffer for the fault of one" and conclude that the woman burned at Smithfield "died a Wife, a Widow, and a maide."[47] Perhaps for May, the woman now symbolizes all women and becomes yet again another cipher on which May emblazons a new identity.

In order to further envision a new persona for the unnamed woman May connects his description of her as "a Wife, a Widow, and a maide" to common language about the Trinity. The flames of execution, he writes, consumed "Not three but one; not one but three." Using nearly identical language to a number of contemporary biblical commentaries and spiritual guides, May positions the victim as not only a holy martyr, but also a quasi-divine figure.[48] Her body, identified as containing all acceptable versions of female sexuality, is reconstructed as encompassing not sin, but godliness. Furthermore, the destruction of this body, rather than erasing the woman, enhances this identity by equating her immolation as sacrificial and her execution as a necessary route towards holiness. In the end, by imagining the woman as a sanctified vessel containing not one but all three elements of virtuous womanhood, May attempts to negate his metaphorical erotic consumption of her body. Although he imagines himself as flames that caress her skin, kiss her eyes, and eventually devour her body, May works to rewrite her narrative and purify his own desires.

Perhaps, though, the most noteworthy symbol May employs in an attempt to repudiate his desire for the victim and sanitize his suggestive anatomical dissection of her as she burns is his evocation of the Phoenix. Widely used by early modern writers, the mythological bird was believed to self-immolate on its own nest and then regenerate from the ashes. Images of the Phoenix typically "appear as religious symbols of resurrection and immortality," or "as a metaphor of the secular immortality to be gained through one's progeny."[49] Yet, May's Phoenix only expires; it is not granted a religious or secular rebirth, suggesting that for the poet, a differing concept of the well-known bird may be at work. Petrarch, the originator of the anatomical blazon, employs the

---

[47] May, "On a Woman Burned in Smithfield," C2.

[48] The phrase, "not three, but one," is found in a number of late sixteenth- and early seventeenth-century religious works, including the following: Joseph Fletcher, *The Historie of the Perfect-Cursed-Blessed Man* (London: M. Flesher, 1628); John Keltridge, *Two Godlie and Learned Sermons Appointed and Preached, Before the Jesuites, Seminaries, and Other Adversaries to the Gospell of Christ in the Tower of London* (London: J. Charlewood and Richard Ihones, 1581); and John Carpenter, *The Plaine Man's Spirituall Plough Containing the Godly and Spirituall Husbandrie* (London: Thoams Creede, 1607).

[49] Hill, 64.

Phoenix not only to reference immortality, but also to signify Laura herself "as a dead phoenix who will never be reborn."[50] May's poem similarly ends not with the resurrection of the bird/woman, but instead suggests the annihilation of the victim: "Thus did this Phoenix, Phoenix like Expire, / (Not three but one; not one but three) in fire."[51] Nevertheless, by using the symbol of the Phoenix, May does provide his dying muse with spiritual significance. Although the body of the woman has been reduced to ashes, May's references to the Phoenix and to the triad nature of the victim connect her to Christ and reinforce an allegorical reading of the woman as martyr rather than criminal.

Conclusion

Ultimately, though, despite his attempts to sanitize his eroticization of the female victim, May engages in a type of necrophiliac fantasy that strips her of identity in order that he might possess her.[52] By partitioning her body, interpreting her physical reactions, and employing her corpse as an emblem of martyrdom, May silences the condemned woman. Bound to the stake and set on fire, the female victim cannot resist May's gaze and has no say in his attempts to provide her with a crown of martyrdom. "On a Woman Burned in Smithfield," though, speaks to May's unease with his desire for the dying victim. Like the body of the woman, which is metaphorically dismembered, the poem itself becomes bifurcated, split between the virtual rape of an immobile woman and May's attempt to provide her death with spiritual meaning. If May's purpose is to lament the death of a beautiful woman burned to death for the murder of her husband, his first impulse involves an erotic rather than religious commemoration. The addition of language drawn from the martyrdom literature seems tacked on, serving mainly to diminish May's violent and sadistic fantasies. Ultimately, despite his attempts to provide spiritual meaning to the unnamed victim, May represents her execution as a sexual fantasy that involves the destruction of her body and a reimagining of her reactions to her own immolation. The woman's death at the stake progressively strips her of her identity, just as May's representations

---

[50] Bednarz, 119.

[51] May, "On a Woman Burned in Smithfield," C2. Usually the term "phoenix-like" is used to describe the reconstitution of the bird and its ability to rise again. May follows the phrase "phoenix-like," though, with the word, "expire," which suggests that focusing on the victim's method of death rather than her ability to resurrect is the poet's intention.

[52] Although May's poem cannot technically be described as necrophilia, Linda Neiberg, in her study of necrophilia in early modern literature, explains that the term can mean more than just sex with dead bodies and instead encompasses "all eroticism that occurs within the vicinity of death and dead bodies in English Renaissance drama" (iv).

of the event articulate his control over her physical and spiritual being. While the blazon tradition reveals the attempts of many male authors to dominate and display the female body in "On a Woman Burned in Smithfield" May extends the blazon's erasure of the woman by tracing her literal anatomization and consumption.

Chapter 5

Her Body, His Evidence: Female Subjugation in the Early Modern Anatomy Theaters

Leslie R. Malland

University of Texas Permian Basin

Abstract: Parallel to the emerging science of anatomy, women were gradually being excluded from practicing medicine. Though women were once considered physicians, they were limited to a handful of procedures after the late fifteenth century. Women were systematically suppressed and forbidden to participate as equals in the English patriarchal social order, and men found justification for their suppression of women in the bodies of women within the space of the anatomy theater. This chapter offers a biopolitical reading of England's anatomy theaters and their approach to the female cadaver, arguing that within the biopolitical space of the anatomy theater, anatomists and corpses engage in embodied, rhetorical practices to convey knowledge; the anatomists then disseminate that knowledge to a wider audience through publications. In turn, those publications, and the evidence they cite, further enforce the patriarchal society and the suppression of the female body in early modern society. Thus, I argue that anatomical texts produced from anatomy theaters are not just documentation of knowledge but are also examples of contributors to the biopolitical culture of early modern England.

Keywords: Anatomy, Biopower, Feminism, Foucault, Generation

***

Introduction

Lay her I'th' earth/and from her fair and unpolluted flesh/may violets spring.

(Hamlet 5.1.235-237)

The context that the Renaissance anatomy theater places the female body within extends beyond the physical space of the theater itself outward to the virtual space of its culture. For example, some take for granted the normalization of the value of perceived chastity, often because its roots predate early modern writing. However, we must pause to consider the implications of this normalization when it is supported from the sovereign down the hierarchical ladder to the bedrooms of citizens. Normalizing chastity is one symptom of a culture concerned with surveilling the human body through the subjugation of women and their bodies.

An aspect of surveilling the body includes *biopower,* the term *biopower,* put simply, is state control over the biological: "a number of phenomena that seem to me to be quite significant, namely, the set of mechanisms through which the basic biological features of the human species became the object of a political strategy."[1] When control over the biological is used for political purposes and regulated by state-sponsored agents, it is *biopolitical* — governing by and through displays of biopower.[2] Since death and decay are "basic biological feature[s] of the human species," their regulation constitutes biopower; additionally, the use of the dead to enforce modes of behavior for the living — such as female chastity — makes the dead body itself a tool for implementing biopower. This chapter considers the space of Renaissance anatomy theater as a biopolitical space that mediates sovereign authority by and through the study of the human body as representative of its species.

My critical approach considers that Foucault's biopower applies not only to the living body, but also to the deceased body and its parts — the corpse and cadaver created and regulated by the state, bodies and their parts, and so forth. Many scholars provide a valuable structure that supports my

---

[1] Foucault, *Security, Territory, Population,* 1.
[2] Foucault, "From the Power of Sovereignty to Power over Life," 239-263.

investigation into the roles that corpses play "in the affairs of this world."[3] State-sponsored anatomies serve as examples of "the sovereign power arrogating to itself the right to establish the truth."[4] In fact, all power endowed upon English anatomists stems from the sovereign.[5] We see the relationship between monarch and anatomy depicted in Thomas Geminus' translation of Vesalius' *Fabria*. Geminus rearranged the frontispiece to depict his monarch, which emphasizes "the king's enforcement of cultural production - and essentially the redistribution of knowledge - in England."[6] He continues that tradition in subsequent editions dedicated to Edward VI and Elizabeth I, though none dedicated to Mary I. Monarchs continually approved and supported the dissection of criminal corpses and the subsequent publications of anatomical knowledge.

By sponsoring anatomies, the sovereign vicariously establishes the "truth" about the human body that anatomists discover. That "truth" has social repercussions for still-living members of society, especially women. While

---

[3] As Thomas W. Laqueur asserts, "the dead, in short, are a powerful category of the imagination, and the corpse is their token, then and now. And, as such, they—the corpse and whatever the dead are or are not—play an important role in the affairs of this world" (79). Jonathan Sawday's *The Body Emblazoned* recognizes early modern England's interest in death and the dead as an example of what Michel Foucault has analyzed as the "'surveillance' of the body within regimes of judgement and punishment" (4). Modern scholars, such as Vernon W. Cisney and Nicolae Morar, continue to extrapolate upon Foucault's concept of biopower, arguing, "we can use the term 'biopolitics' to embrace all the specific strategies and contestations over problematizations of collective human vitality, morbidity, and mortality; over the forms of knowledge, regimes of authority, and practices of intervention that are desirable, legitimate, and efficacious" (298). These scholars build upon Foucault's theories on biopower to analyze how it continues to manifest within society.

[4] Foucault, *Discipline and Punish*, 225.

[5] Public dissections were the direct result of Henry VIII's 1540 Act of Parliament. Anatomists were state sponsored to perform four public dissections per year. For a full history, see Florike Egmond's "Execution, Dissection, Pain and Infamy- A Morphological Investigation," in *Bodily Extremities: Preoccupations with the Human Body in Early Modern European Culture*, edited by Florike Egmond and Robert Zwijnenberg. Ashgate, 2003, pp. 92-127. While the Barber-Surgeons were established as a guild in 1540 and began anatomies, the College of Physicians was established by a Charter of 1518, but it did not receive bodies for dissection until 1565 through an order by Queen Elizabeth. As the translators of William Harvey's *Lectures on the Whole of Anatomy* note, the lectures of the College of Physicians were a direct result of an endowment from Queen Elizabeth in 1581. For more on the history of England's Company of Barbers and Surgeons, see their website at barberscompany.org.

[6] Lo, 239.

anatomists were acting as agents of the sovereign in a public and political deployment of punishment, they were actively researching the bodies granted to them to discover knowledge of the human body and define its parts.[7] Defining a body part is an act of biopower that assigns meaning to living and dead bodies. As Kenny Fountain observes, "the discourse of anatomical terms has real material effects both in renaming the body and in authorizing certain ways of knowing that body."[8] Thus, anatomical discourse and its texts contribute to societal knowledge and control of the body. Anatomical research, public dissections, and the dissemination of anatomical knowledge were all attempts "to appropriate the dead for the regime of life. The dead body thus became ground zero of what Foucault called biopower, a 'technology' of power that governed subjects through the regulation of live bodies, individually, and, more importantly, collectively."[9] The biopower exhibited by many early modern anatomists continues to manifest today as we continue to use the terminology they assigned to bodies and their parts.[10]

Only through dissection can anatomists learn to use their body as a tool for understanding another body, and touching the body is key. Early modern anatomists touched their specimens without surgical gloves (that would be anachronistically impossible) or any barriers to prevent the interaction of their hands with the corpses. Because the anatomists are learning from the cadaver, it is communicating knowledge: "anatomical knowledge is *discourse made flesh or enacted in the flesh* through practices that are embodied and

---

[7] The hypervisibility of the punishment seemingly contrasts with the panopticon notion of invisible power of discipline; however, it is the visibility of punishment itself that creates this atmosphere of societal acceptance that invisibly upholds sovereign authority. Direct authority hides in the shadows within a perfect system of discipline, so a body does not exactly know from where the power originates. A panoptic society "assures the automatic functioning of power" (Foucault, *Discipline* 201). Society itself becomes self-regulated when power has infiltrated all other aspects of a disciplined society. Because "a normalizing society is the historical outcome of a technology of power centered on life," the internalization of knowledge found at scenes of state-sponsored death and the anatomy theater contributes to the power of the sovereign over life (Foucault, *History of Sexuality*, vol. 3, 144). The visual displays of power at a public execution or anatomy act as a threat, a show of power that promotes the internalization of sovereign authority within members of a disciplined society, rendering the source of power and its mechanisms invisible.

[8] Fountain, 27.

[9] Lacqueur, 184-5.

[10] Control over the knowledge of the body is controlling the body as "medicine was expected to propose, in the form of regimen, a voluntary and rational structure of conduct" (Foucault, *History*, vol. 3 100).

rhetorical simultaneously."[11] Not only is it communicating knowledge about its own species body, but it is shaping the actions of the anatomist's body.[12] Only this inter-corporeal interaction — bodies touching bodies — can facilitate the embodied practice of learning. This learning produces scientific truths that, when further communicated to society, work to discipline living bodies through "a rational structure of conduct."[13]

Because anatomy manuals tell culturally driven stories about bodies and corpses, they are clearly literary expressions, akin to oral traditions that are eventually consigned to a text and fixed by it. By reading and analyzing these texts, I find that these writers translated knowledge and disperse that knowledge to their society through anatomical publications. In turn, those publications, and the evidence they cite, further enforce the patriarchal society and the suppression of the female body in early modern society beyond the physical spaces of the Renaissance anatomy theater. Thus, the *space* of the anatomy theaters encompasses the social and private lives of citizens and the gender roles they must play. Though an analysis of anatomical literature, this chapter looks specifically at how the emerging knowledge of "generation" has consequences for early modern women.

Women and the Space of Anatomy Theaters

Parallel to the emerging science of anatomy, women were gradually being excluded from practicing medicine. Though women were once considered physicians, they were limited to a handful of procedures after the late fifteenth century. Women were systematically suppressed and forbidden to participate as equals in the English patriarchal social order, and men found justification for their suppression of women in the bodies of women within the space of the anatomy theater.

Though notions of patriarchal superiority existed long before the publication of anatomy manuals, those anatomy manuals offer substantial "evidence" that supports Biblical and social claims for "the superiority of men over women."[14] Women are disciplined throughout history, and disciplining the body is just one example. This new public space gets folded into existing discourses. The corpses that "speak with most miraculous organ," their literal

---

[11] Fountain, 30, emphasis mine.

[12] As Diana Coole and Samantha Frost note, "all bodies...evince certain capacities for agency" (20). The corpse as biomaterial exhibits its unique agency when it communicates with the anatomist.

[13] Foucault, *History, vol. 3,* 100.

[14] Margócsy, et. al, 112.

organs, in turn contribute to the disciplining of women within their society; thus, the action of the anatomists becomes argumentative as it produces physical evidence to support the ongoing discourses of female subjugation, especially concerning female sexuality.[15]

Anatomy itself was a practice of inserting parts of the male body (fingers, hands, arms) into another, disrupting the autonomy of the corpse and wielding power over it. This initial intervention into a female body leads to further interventions, such as prescribed methods of treatment for women, some of which require further intervention by male body parts. Such dialogues include the political relationship between men and women, which was analogous to a subject's relationship to the sovereign. Early modern practices of regulating bodies based upon anatomical findings is just one example of how, as Kathryn Schwarz notes, "the female body imposes a causality of acts as women play the social parts to which their body parts confine them.[16] And, especially since anatomists were men studying women, these actions consequently increase and enrich the patriarchal structures in which their society functions. While still-living women were excluded from the anatomy theater, many anatomists (including Andreas Vesalius) actively sought to include deceased women in those same theaters.

---

[15] *Hamlet* 2.2.588-9. Foucault identifies how early anatomists and their ancient influences connected care of the body to sexuality. For Galen, desire "was most certainly planned as an integral consequence of the mechanisms of the body. Desire and pleasure are direct effects of anatomical dispositions and physical processes" (*History, vol. 3*, 107): "Sexual acts must therefore be placed under an extremely careful regimen" (*History, vol. 3*, 124). These regimens include care of the body, care of the self, daily routine, best practices when it comes to sex, and the best schedule for sex. There is special attention to what the state of the body should be at the time of sex: i.e., not hungry, but not full, empty bowls, energized, not tired. Thus, early modern anatomists continue the tradition of viewing sex as a physical action. Katherine Usher Henderson and Barbara F. McManus find that "woman suffered more emotional shame and community disapproval" for charges of unchastity than their male counterparts. Thus, women were more likely to bring lawsuits for slander against such charges (59). Female sexuality was considered a bodily action that could be regulated, disciplined, and punished. Mary E. Fissell's work, *Vernacular Bodies: The Politics of Reproduction in Early Modern England*, connects the female body to politics, arguing that gender relations "were the hinge that connected body and politics" (2). She builds upon the theories of Foucault and Laqueur to reveal how early modern culture influenced "people's ideas about women's reproductive bodies" (1). Her first chapter notes, "writing about women's reproductive bodies was a politically charged act" in early modern England (14). To write about women's bodies is to participate in a biopolitical conversation.
[16] Schwarz, "Missing the Breast," 148.

Dissecting the Female Cadaver

Andreas Vesalius was one of the few anatomists who sought female cadavers to expand anatomical knowledge of women. His audience was intrigued and demanded more information on women's bodies for future editions of his *De Humani Corporis Fabrica,* which was the most popular and influential anatomy book for centuries. He goes as far as to feature a female corpse on the dissection table in the frontispiece of his *Fabrica* (Figure A). That frontispiece exemplifies the argument that anatomical studies were methods of biopolitical discipline because the featured female cadaver was used as evidence against a woman. Vesalius says the corpse is of a woman who had "falsely decarled herself pregnant" to escape hanging: "However, by order of the judge she was interrogated by midwives who declared her not at all pregnant."[17] After her execution, the woman's body was used for anatomical research that verified the lack of a viable fetus. Vesalius' notes on the anatomy confirm the midwife's diagnosis. Thus, Vesalius' frontispiece shows women that their internal organs will expose their bodily actions just as it exposes this woman's lie about pregnancy. It also shows that a midwife's assessment requires further "proof" or verification by a male authority.

In their expansive study of the 314 publicly owned copies of Vesalius' 1543 and 1555 *Fabrica,* Dániel Margócsy, Mark Somos, and Stephen N. Joffe find that for...

...early modern students of Vesalius, generation was the key question of human anatomy. They annotated the chapters dealing with the reproductory organs in great detail. For these readers, the key problem was how to understand and interpret sexual differences between men and women in a society that aimed to maintain the dominance of men. They examined carefully how the uterine muscles, the hymen, and the labia contributed to tempering or arousing the passions of women, and how the overall structure of the genitalia revealed the divine plan that supported the propagation of the species without disturbing social order. As male members of urban elites, they studied Vesalius to find an anatomical justification for the hierarchical gender relationships of their contemporary societies.[18]

---

[17] qtd. in O'Malley, Andreas Vesalius of Brussels, 143.
[18] Margócsy, et. al, 132. In her study of the influence anatomical research had on women's societal roles, Katharine Park finds a "complexity of themes [surrounding the clitoris] was connected with certain specific mid-sixteenth-century changes in medical

Thus, readers of anatomical publications actively sought information that could "maintain the dominance of men."

Though rarer than anatomies performed on male corpses, anatomies of female bodies were not unknown in England and became more popular after Vesalius' initial 1543 *Fabrica* due to "an active demand" for information on human generation, which is why Vesalius revised that section the most for his 1555 edition.[19] While some anatomists, such as John Banister, writing in 1578, refuse to discuss "womens shapes" for fear of committing "indecencie agaynst the office of decorum," other anatomists dissected female corpses to better understand reproduction.[20] Even when anatomists refuse to discuss the female corpse, they still participate in the regulation of the female body by labeling it as an indecent object whose mere mention goes "against the office of decorum."

James Cooke hoped his "labour might be spared" from having to study women's bodies for "operations belonging to their Privities, as in Child-births."[21] In their search for female reproductive organs, anatomists brave enough to dissect a female cadaver actively sought information on propagation: "Generation, sexual intercourse, and erotic pleasure mattered so much to readers of the *Fabrica* not simply because of their pornographic potential, but rather because of the threat they may have posed to the established social and divine order. Such concerns were key issues for Vesalius' main audience."[22] In fact, in the 314 studied copies of the *Fabrica*, the pages on generation were the second most popular, behind only the frontispiece. Humoral theory and medical knowledge work to define and regulate the female reproductive organs associated with generation, especially the womb.

---

and anatomical thought concerning sex and difference" ("The Rediscovery of the Clitoris: French Medicine and the Tribade, 1570-1620," in *The Body in Parts: Fantasies of Corporeality in Early Modern Europe*. Edited by David Hillman and Carla Mazzio. Routledge, 1997, 173). The rediscovery of the clitoris is one example of how anatomical research spurred cultural conversations concerning female sexuality and its regulation.

[19] Margócsy, et al., 8.

[20] Banister, 88. Though he spends seven pages of his anatomy giving details about the testicles and "yard," or penis, John Banister, like some anatomists of his day, refuses to discuss "womens shapes" (88). He does, however, point out that an area of man's brain "very elegantly expresseth the shape of privye part of a woman" (100). Though, he dares not give more details on that shape for sake of propriety.

[21] Cooke, 18.

[22] Margócsy, et al., 112.

Menstruation

One aspect of generation includes menstruation. The passages on menstruation were "most heavily underlined and commented upon by early modern readers."[23] Humoral theory informed the early modern man's assumption that women menstruated due to inferior blood. Anatomists believed that if the female body were colder, then the blood of women was colder and lesser quality than the warmer man's blood. They often used dissections as opportunities to prove humoral theory to be correct. The notion that women are colder was "verified" by observing that the female corpse had more fat than the typical male corpse; for example, William Harvey bases his theory of cooler blood on Vesalius's conviction that women are inherently fatter than men.[24] The extra fat was meant to insulate the female body. Through early modern logic, if women needed more fat, then their bodies must be colder. Humoral theory dictates that colder bodies meant colder temperament. These observations of female corpses contributed to the early modern treatment of women as colder, shrewder, and weaker individuals whose chastity must be closely guarded by men. One can find these sorts of descriptions of women throughout early modern texts: "No/mates for you unless you were of gentler, milder mold"; "This is my comfort, gentlemen, and I joy/in this one happiness above the rest, /which will be called a miracle at last, /that, being an old man, I'd a wife so chaste."[25]

Because men perceived that female blood was of lower quality, women must need more of it than men. This causes a buildup of too much blood, which is why women menstruate. The menses is the overflow from the overfilled uterus. Since menstruation is involuntary, it proves again that women are weaker because they are unable to control that bodily function.[26] While men control their bloodletting for when it is necessary to purge their bodies of foul humours, women could not control their body's letting of blood. This is one example of how "menstruation functions in the Renaissance as another sign of the open

---

[23] Ibid., 108-109.

[24] Harvey, William. *Lectures on the Whole of Anatomy.* Translated by C.D. O'Malley, F.N.L. Poynter, and K.F. Russell, (University of California Press, 1961).

[25] *The Taming of the Shrew* 1.1.59-60; *The Revengers Tragedy* 1.4.74-77.

[26] For an in-depth conversation surrounding the feminine perceptions of blood, see Gail Kern Paster, "'In the Spirit of Men There Is No Blood:' Blood as Trope of Gender in Julius Caesar." *Shakespeare Quarterly,* vol. 40, no. 3, 1989, pp. 284–298. In her book, *The Body Embarrassed,* Paster explains how many child births could cause involuntary bladder release in mature women, which was argued by early modern physicians as evidence that women were even more out-of-control of their own bodies. As the weaker gender, women were more likely to suffer confinement than men.

and leaky female body" that must be controlled and disciplined.[27] The study of female anatomy built upon long-imagined theories of menstruation that further reinforced the necessity for female confinement. These theories "keep women from their more obvious role as man's partner and fellow human."[28]

Theories on women's menses also contributed to theories of gestation. According to Vesalius and his contemporaries (based upon Galenic medicine mixed with humoral theory), menstrual blood is reappropriated to the child during pregnancy, then to the breasts after childbirth. Based upon the early modern belief that the uterus was connected to the mammary glands, blood from the uterus rises up to the breasts to make breast milk. For this reason, one should not let blood from a pregnant woman. Instead, physicians would cup the breasts in an effort to massage the blood upward.[29] Thus, early modern theories on women's blood led to prescribed medical treatments for women.

In addition to prescribing medical treatment to menstruating and breastfeeding women, Vesalius also invented serums to assist women in the overall health of their reproductive system. Vesalius' cure-all oils attempted to aid "against the grene sicknes in wemen, and the stopping or staieng of ther natural course, as also to dispose them the better to conception, whether it be druncken, or with conuenient meanes (as weme and phisitios do knou) couaied to the priui places, it hath ben found alwais a thing of greate aad readi success."[30] This green sickness occurred in young, malnourished, mid and post-pubescent women. Early moderns believed that a woman undergoing puberty who ceased menstruation or had irregular cycles, became lethargic and pale, and had what we might call "anemia, anorexia nervosa, or simply adolescent depression," were actually suffering from a lack of male intervention.[31] Many understood those symptoms as a female's body suffering and, in some cases, ceasing menstruation for lack of sex.

---

[27] Dawson, 202. Dawson continues by noting, "Although there is evidence to suggest that more positive and human approaches to menstruation existed in the early modern period, physiological accounts of women's monthly bleeding served on a whole to reinforce traditional notions about female inferiority, justifying women's subordinate position in society" (200).

[28] Ibid., 195.

[29] Vesalius, *The Bloodletting Letter of 1539.*

[30] Vesalius and Raynalde. 35.

[31] Hillary M. Nunn observes how early modern authors used plant-like descriptions and depictions of women's reproductive organs in connection with greensickness to blur the boundary of human and plant ("On Vegetating Virgins," 161).

The cure for greensickness is marriage, which means heterosexual vaginal intercourse meant to open and loosen the female's body to allow for the flow of menstruation.[32] Here, the prescribed treatment of the female body calls for male intervention. Such theories on menstruation serve to "produce a 'natural' justification for woman's relegation to the home and exclusion from public office."[33] By studying and intervening into the female corpse's reproductive organs, anatomists like Vesalius could suggest treatments for women in order to ensure their productive participation in society.

Virginity

In addition to their concerns for women's menstrual health, anatomists paid special attention to the overall effects intercourse had upon female bodies. According to early modern thought, a post-mortem anatomy could verify a woman's virginity based upon an analysis of her corpse. In order to define "virginity," anatomists had to locate evidence that it could physically exist.[34] In pure Foucauldian panopticon fashion, early moderns attested that they could verify a woman's sexual purity by examining her body.[35] This suggests that a sexually active female can be caught, even postmortem, just as the woman on the frontispiece of the *Fabria* was "caught" lying about pregnancy. Thomas

---

[32] It is interesting to note that, as Katharine Park points out, heterosexual intercourse actually occurs *within* the female body (*Secrets of Women*). For this project, unless otherwise stated, when I refer to *sex* or *intercourse*, I am referring to heterosexual vaginal intercourse. For many early moderns, female homosexuality was considered an exaggerated form of masturbation, not sex. See, Merry E. Wiesner-Hank's *Women and Gender in Early Modern Europe*, Third Edition. (Cambridge University Press, 2008).

[33] Maclean, 46.

[34] Susan Scholz and Mary E. Fissell connect the early modern idea of a chaste female body to larger societal issues in their respected works. Scholz approaches the body symbolically whereas my argument approaches the body more literally. Though sound and valid, Scholz's argument does not produce the same evidence as mine. While she claims, "there is no positive evidence of the existence of a membrane that signified the closure of an untouched female body before the mid-seventeenth century," I have found several instances in sixteenth-century manuals that suggest otherwise (81). She even states in her footnote four to that same chapter that "Vesalius did not mention the hymen at all" (182). However, my research finds that Vesalius was very much interested in the hymen, though he may have referred to it as "panicle."

[35] A panoptic society "assures the automatic functioning of power" (Foucault, *Discipline* 201). Society itself becomes self-regulated when power has infiltrated all other aspects of a disciplined society. By suggesting that women's very bodies could expose their behavior postmortem, anatomical rhetoric contributes to the early modern panoptic society by disciplining women and implying that their actions will always be seen.

Raynalde's translations of Eucharius Rösslin's *Der Rosengarten*, *The Birth of Mankynde Otherwyse Named the Womans Booke*, describes the "inner partes" of the female body so that "it is nowe so playnely set forth that the simplest mydwyfe which can reade, may both understand for her better instruction, and also other women that have neede of her helpe."[36] This "guide for women" includes a "Prologue to the Women Readers" that clarifies his intentions of instructing midwives (Figure 5.1)[37] He even suggests that women who cannot read should have his book read to them. Hence, his goal was to instruct women about their own bodies and instruct midwives how to care for those bodies, echoing biopolitical sentiments of the societal role women must play.

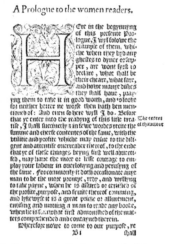

Figure 5.1: Raynalde's *Prologue to the Women Readers*.

Further, Raynalde's work represents the systematic efforts to exclude women from the professional realm, which included replacing licensed midwives with male physicians. Prior to the mid-fifteenth century, midwifery was the one realm where women held a hierarchical order like their male counterparts. Midwives were the authority on matters related to women; they were often called to inspect women for fornication, testify in court, and examine female prisoners.[38] With the

---

[36] Raynalde and Rösslin, 3.

[37] Ibid., 5.

[38] See, Merry E. Wiesner-Hank's *Women and Gender in Early Modern Europe*, Third Edition. (Cambridge: Cambridge University Press, 2008).

growing popularity of anatomical research, male physicians — like Raynalde — strove to present their own findings to further instruct midwives and women, sometimes countering the centuries-old wisdom of midwives.

Even though midwives had a reputation for being able to discern virginity, Raynalde insisted there was a need for an anatomy manual to teach midwives about the female body. In his description of the cadavers featured in the 1565 publication, Raynalde clarifies not once, but *twice* that the matrix and womb are intact: "as in this woman it is seene, no part of the sayde matrix or wombe beying moved. For here is as yet to pannicle pluckt away from the matrix or wombe, but that all thinges are here yet whollye seene" (Figure 5.2)[39] His note to "L" corresponding to the figure is, "The former seate of y bottome of the Matrix, from whence is nothing perceyved pluct away" (Figure 5.3).[40] Though this "to some seem incredible," Raynalde assures us that "by Anathomie yee may see it to bee true."[41] As Raynalde clarifies, according to early modern understanding, the "matrix" or "wombe" is forever visibly altered after the "pannicle," which we might think of as a hymen, has been "pluckt away." Raynalde's interest in this pannicle reflects the overall interest in the effect of sex upon a woman's body. Because her "panicle" was intact, Raynalde concludes that this corpse is virginal.

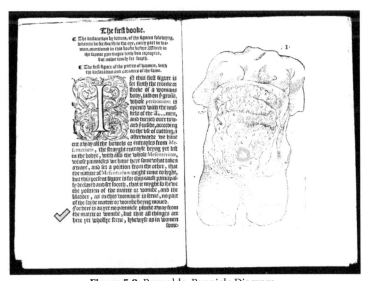

Figure 5.2: Raynalde, Pannicle Diagram.

39 Raynalde, 62.
40 Ibid., 63.
41 Ibid., 26

The firſt booke.　　　　Fol.rliiii.

ſomewhat fat they do appeare to the cutter, the bowels beyng taken away. For women are ſo fatte, that when they be bexed and kylled with long ſickneſſe, and become moſte leaneſt, then they ſhewe no kynde of proceſſe of beſſels, vnleſſe the pannicles or thinne couerynges be ſepera=ted a ſunder.

A,B,C,D. The inner face or part of the former ſeate of Peritonium.

E E A part of Meſenterium, knitting the thinne intrayles to the backe.

FF Here is noted another pannicle of Meſenteri-um, plucked from the other which we haue mar=ked with G and G. But both the pannicles do ſhew the order of the beſſels of Meſenterium, and order of the karnelles put betweene the diſtribu=tions of the beſſels.

H H In this part of Meſenterium, the entraile Colon was committed and ſc' to, where it was nyeſt to the ſtraight gut.

I And in this part of Meſenterium, did conſiſt and ſtande the beginning of the intrayle Colon, or his continuaunce with the thinne intrailes, and alſo the blynde gut.

K The ſtraight gutte beyng there cut of where Colon dyd ende, whiche ſeate or place is ryght a=gaynſt the place of the knitting together of the hockle bone with the loweſt turnyng ioynte of the loynes.

L The former ſeate of y bottome of the Matrix, from whence is nothing percepued pluct away.

M The right ſtone or teſticle in a woman.

　　　　　　　　　　　　　　　　　　　　　　N The

Figure 5.3: Raynalde, Corresponding Note to Pannicle Diagram.

Thomas Vicary also asserts that there are noticeable changes in the body of a woman who have had sex.[42] Using the corpse as evidence, anatomists cultivate medical knowledge aimed to protect the female body by providing unequivocally that heterosexual intercourse alters the female body. The theory was that a body without the appropriate panicle could not be virginal. Thus, anatomical studies served as a quest for the virginal female body, something Kathryn Schwarz calls "early modernity's great escape artist[s]."[43] Though these notions were not new to early moderns, anatomical research provides the evidence that supports long-held notions of female virginity and sex.

Raynalde and Vesalius argued they could not only assess a woman's virginity, but also if she had ever been pregnant. Many anatomists believed that the uterus in childbearing women looked different than the uterus of one who had not carried a child. According to early modern theory, a female uterus is permanently altered upon bearing children; and those alterations are also thought to be clearly visible to an early modern anatomist. In a pointed effort to obtain female reproductive organs from a sexually active woman, Vesalius stole the "body of a woman who had been the mistress of a certain monk...expressly to examine the female organs."[44] He describes that uterus from "a woman of very tall stature who had often given birth" as extremely large: "in dimensions it greatly exceeded the normal."[45] The consensus among leading anatomists was that a woman's body was permanently physically altered by intercourse and childbearing, so much so that the changes were perceivable postmortem.

The uterus becomes proof of a female's sexual and reproductive activity, and by extension, corruption, and must be regulated by men, especially husbands and fathers. Arguably, it is the uterus (womb) that holds the most cultural significance of all the female body parts. Vesalius found the uterus to be "rich in oblique fibres."[46] He suggests the uterus is composed of such strong fibers because it "retains the genital seed for a long time, harboured for the renewal

---

[42] See, Thomas Vicary's *The Anatomie of The Bodie of Man*, 1548. Edited by Fredk J. Furnivall, M.A., Hon. Dr. Phil, and Percy Furnivall. (Oxford University Press, 1888). And his *The Englishemans Treasure*, 1587. Imprinted by George Robinson for John Perin.

[43] Schwarz, "Death and Theory," 54.

[44] "Vesalius and his pupils, hearing of her death, snatched the body from the tomb, but, unfortunately, the monk together with the parents of the girl complained of the outrage to the city magistrates so that the anatomist and his students were compelled to dismember and free the body from all skin as rapidly as possible to prevent its being recognized" (Saunders and O'Malley, 170).

[45] Vesalius qtd. In Saunders and O'Malley, 170.

[46] Vesalius, *The Bloodletting Letter,* 57.

of the race; and it must either attract this [seed] or expel the foetus at birth."[47] This definition of the uterus endows it with substantial power, using active verbs such as *retains* and *expel*. However, six pages later, Vesalius says this amount of strength is no more extraordinary than other organs with the same fibres, such as the bladder.

Further, these definitions of female reproductive organs, "established from dissection of bodies," provided evidence of long-held notions of male superiority.[48] Vesalius assures early modern men that God did not grant "circular muscles" to "the walls of the vagina...because such muscles would have provided them [women] with too much control over the penis."[49] He makes a similar argument for the involuntary muscles of the uterus that could not fully close, arguing that without these muscles, women could somehow "prevent[ed] conception by closing off the uterus when the semen was about to enter. Thanks to divine design, however, women were unable to give free rein to their passions as the danger of pregnancy served as a sufficient deterrent to them."[50] Vesalius notes that while the uterus is endowed with powerful fibres, male bodies (and all bodies) have similar fibres in "the heart, stomach and both bladders with three types of fibres, since they need to possess in almost equal amounts the powers of attraction, expulsion and retention."[51] This analogy suggests that pregnancy and childbirth are just as rigorous as a male holding his bladder and bowels until he can expel their contents. Unlike men's bodies, female bodies were involuntarily open. They were unable to close against a man, so they must be guarded to prevent unwanted pregnancies and, after marriage, to force pregnancies upon women. They were strong, but not more so than their male counterparts.

By suggesting that women's bodies could expose their infidelity, virginity, or reproduction, anatomist fuel a panopticon-like culture. A woman's actions were watched and judged by society, even after her death. Regulation of a woman's body meant regulating not only her sexuality, but also her role in serving the sovereign. All relationships were viewed as power dynamics and political, thus, female virginity and sexuality "are now being examined politically, in both their internal power relationships and their connections with more formal institutions of political power or the public sphere."[52]

---

[47] Ibid., 57.
[48] Ibid., 63.
[49] Margócsy, et al., 111.
[50] Ibid., 112.
[51] Vesalius, *The Bloodletting Letter*, 63.
[52] Wiesner-Hanks, 277.

Through anatomical research, men can verify the virginity of a female postmortem without depending upon a midwife's wisdom; this "evidence" reminds females that their sexual actions can be caught, so they are never free from their disciplined society and its gaze. Such anatomical evidence produced by agents of the sovereign upheld the woman's role as subservient in early modern society.

Many early modern plays capitalize upon this idea of a subservient female. Shakespeare and Middleton often explore notions of subverting the female role. Their comedic tropes depend upon the preexisting concept that women are supposed to behave a certain way. Then, the writers introduce female characters who do not "play by the rules," such as Beatrice, Olivia, or Moll Cutpurse.

By arguing that virginity can be verified, these early modern anatomical texts echo the biopolitical messages found at the gallows, suggesting that a member of society should consider how their sexual cleanliness relates to their "Christian brethren."[53] Audiences are reminded that offences like premarital sex are detectable; thus, women are inspired to behave a different way, a way that better contributes to "the bettering of thy state."[54] Medical knowledge, such as defining the uterus and virginity, worked to (re)enforce the patriarchal society. Indeed, it was men who were defining and interpreting the body parts of women. The sovereign — through the extension of the anatomists — defines the woman's role as one in charge of protecting the uterus for the clean propagation of the sovereign's subjects at the discretion of men.

Conclusion

Inherent to the discussions surrounding female bodies are notions of power. Anatomists exhibit power over the female corpse. Through inter-corporeal communication, anatomists gain embodied knowledge from the corpse that subsequently supports the suppression of women in society. In this biopolitical society, adhering to a societal role equates to serving the sovereign. Any participation in society directly correlates to one's loyalty to king and country. To succinctly summarize, early modern England witnesses state-authorized agents collecting knowledge from female cadavers that they codify into medical terminology in a new regime of knowledge whose audience is educated, wealthy men. In turn, those men (many members of court) use this knowledge to uphold beliefs about women's inferiority. Those

---

[53] Golding, 8.
[54] Ibid., 8.

beliefs are then internalized by women, so they self-discipline by adhering to the very stereotypes the study of female cadavers suggest. Women's very bodies were used against them as "evidence" to justify male supervision over the female body, which women internalized and repeated. Thus, they were disciplined by the sovereign, the anatomists as extensions of the sovereign, men, even the men in their lives, such as fathers, brothers, and husbands, and by themselves through "infinitesimal distribution[s]" of biopower.[55] The space of the Renaissance anatomy theater encompasses the space of such gender roles in society and even finds a space upon the stage when writers capitalize upon medical theories concerning the female body.

---

[55] Foucault, *Discipline and Punish*, 216.

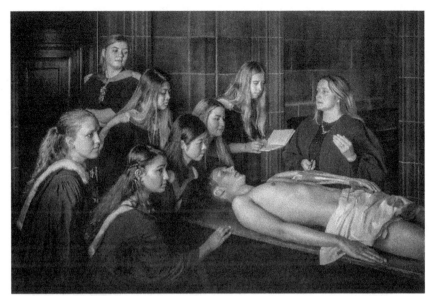

Figure B: Modern Remake of Rembrandt's *The Anatomy Lesson of Nicolaes Tulp.*

Chapter 6

"Into the Bowels of Ungrateful Rome": Anatomizing the Body-Politic of Shakespeare's *Coriolanus*

Gilad Gutman

Tel-Aviv University

Abstract: This chapter anatomizes the body-politic metaphor in early modern England and its contested status in Shakespeare's *Coriolanus*, analyzing the metaphor in relation to the anatomy theatre as a part of a network of social spaces. By examining spatial conflicts in early modern England, their relation to *Coriolanus* and the body-politic discourse at the time, the chapter traces the role of the anatomy theatre in the metaphor's decline. Shakespeare's *Coriolanus* enacts the conflicts in the anatomy theatre and their implications on the body-politic metaphor, such as the confrontation over authority in which traditional medical models found themselves under the anatomist's scalpel. Beginning with the enclosures of land and the depopulations of the English countryside, the chapter examines the increase of spatial division in England, its articulation as a disease of the body politic and the discovery of new internal anatomical divisions in the public dissections. Although the enclosures and the Midland Revolt of 1607 are a pertinent historical context of *Coriolanus*, this chapter takes into account a broader context that include London's expansion and population growth, the plague quarantines and the execution site, thus considering the relation between these social spaces as parts of a whole and reconstructing their relation through the body-politic metaphor. The idea of the body politic as a whole unified autonomy finds itself under attack in *Coriolanus*, as internal division grows and the borders between the inside and the outside become unstable. Placing Shakespeare's *Coriolanus* in the space of the anatomy theatre opens up a passage into the dead body politic of ancient Rome, a passage through which Shakespeare explores the living social fabric of early modern England and the implications that the body-politic metaphor has on the collective and the individual.

Keywords: Body Politic, Boundaries, Midland Revolt, *Coriolanus*

***

Introduction: Laying out the Body

Space, but you cannot even conceive the horrible inside-outside that real space is.

– Henry Michaux, *Shade-Haunted Space.*[*]

In 1597 the Dean of Durham Cathedral, William James, wrote a grievance letter to Robert Cecil, the Secretary of State, recounting the delipidated state to which the county had fallen into in the past 50 years. According to William James:

> The decay of tillage and dispeopling of villages offends God by spoiling the Church, dishonours the prince, weakens the commonwealth, &c., … The inhabitants' arms were wont to be the strength walls, but now there are open gaps… Of 8,000 acres lately in tillage, now not eight score are tilled;…In the bishopric 500 ploughs have decayed…; villages are dispeopled, and no man to stop the enemy's attempt.[1]

Although the depopulation of villages was mainly taking place in the Midlands, almost all over England, and as far north as Durham, the rise in the enclosures of arable lands had brought with it a landscape of deserted villages. The relation between Shakespeare's *Coriolanus* and the Midland Revolts of 1607, whose cause was the enclosures and the dearth of corn, has been critically studied by scholars ever since E. C. Pettet's article in 1950.[2] This chapter, however, considers the enclosures as a long-standing phenomenon and their relation to the social space of the dissected body in the anatomical demonstrations, situating this relation within a network of spatial relations in early modern England, through which *Coriolanus* constructs the Roman body politic. As in an anatomy of a body, beginning with an incision to the skin, to the outermost layer, then making its way deeper into the body's interior, this

---

[*] *Nouvelles de l'étranger*, Mercure de France, Paris, 1952, qtd. in Gaston Bachelard, *The Poetics of Space*, trans. Maria Jolas, (Beacon Press, Boston, 1994), pp. 216-217.

[1] Green, *Calendar of State Papers, Domestic Affairs, Elizabeth, 1595-97*, 347-8.

[2] See Lee Bliss's "What Hath a Quarter-Century of Coriolanus Criticism Wrought." *The Shakespearean International Yearbook 2: Where are We Now in Shakespearean Studies.* Ed. W. R. Elton and John M. Mucciolo. (New York: Routledge Press, 2018).

chapter structurally begins with the border of England's body politic (Durham county), makes its way inward through the enclosures in the Midlands, advances towards London — the heart and seat of power — through its plague-stricken streets, quarantined spaces and execution sites, finally arriving to the circular closed spaces of the anatomy and entertainment theaters, to the corpse and the actor's body.

The Enclosures: Into the Divided Body

Throughout the sixteenth century, new barriers erected mostly by land owners in the form of hedges and fences were spreading over the English landscape in increasing numbers, by and large in order to transform arable lands into pasture and thus boost profits.[3] These enclosures did not only bring the extinction of the open-field system and a redefinition of property rights, but altogether contributed to the process of capitalist reconceptualization of space itself.[4] The development of capitalism brought about a new spatiality, one in which social space underwent various paradoxical changes, such as, according to Poulantzas, "separation and division in order to unify; parcelling out in order to encompass; ...[and] closure in order to homogenize."[5] Enclosing lands meant recreating the geographical relation between part and whole, as for example, in certain enclosures the land that had been previously one whole turned into two separate parts, altering in the process the function of these parts, i.e., utilizing the land for new purposes.

As early as 1517, the effects of enclosures gave rise to an Inquisition of Depopulations, a royal commission in charge of investigating the matter and gathering evidence as to the decay of husbandry.[6] For Thomas Starkey, in *A Dialogue Between Reginald Pole and Thomas Lupset,* published in 1532, such a state of affairs is nothing less than a disease, "for like as in a consumption, when the body is brought to a great sklenderness, there is lack of power and strength to maintain the health...so in a country, city or town, where there is lack of people there wanteth power to maintain the flourishing state of the

---

[3] See Robert S. Duplessis's *Transitions to Capitalism in Early Modern Europe,* (Cambridge University Press, 1997), 63-70.

[4] This process has been discussed by several theorists, such as Henri Lefebvre, Edward W. Soja and others (See Lefebvre's *The Production of Space.* Trans. Donald Nicholson-Smith. (Basil Blackwell, 1991); and Soja's *Postmodern Geographies.* [Verso Press, 1989]).

[5] Poulantzas, 107.

[6] R. H. Tawney notes that "investigations were made by Royal Commissioners in the years 1517-1519, 1548, 1566, 1607, 1632, 1635, and 1636" (*The Agrarian Problem in the Sixteenth Century,* 261).

politic body."[7] In Starkey's analogy between depopulation and consumption, the body politic is not merely metaphorically associated with the human body, rather there is a necessary connection between the prosperity of the body politic and the actual flesh and blood presence of the people. And yet, the individual's body remains here for Starkey only as a part in service of the body politic as a whole, not as an autonomous entity in its own right. During Shakespeare's time, however, the metaphor of the body politic was already losing its power,[8] putting into question the subjugation of the natural body to the body politic, a process in which both the space of the anatomical theater and the presence of the cadaver played a role.

Although by the time Shakespeare writes *Coriolanus* the body politic metaphor had already begun to crack, it still held relative sway over people's minds. Throughout the play, this contested status of the body-politic analogy undergoes an inspection. At the beginning of *Coriolanus*, the poor state of the natural bodies of the Roman plebeians appears initially as analogous to the consumptive "sklenderness" described by Starkey regarding the body politic, and yet we quickly discover that as far as the Roman patricians see it, the plebeians in this bodily state serve their proper function for the whole. For the patricians, as for Starkey, what matters is not the individual bodies of the people, but that they will collectively keep to their allotted space in society within the body politic. Like the peasants in the Midland Revolts, rising in arms and destroying enclosures, transgressing their social space, so does the hungry mob in *Coriolanus* revolt against the patricians, announcing that they are "resolved rather to die than to famish,"[9] echoing explicitly the words of the English rebels in *The Declaration of the Diggers of Warwickshire*.[10]

The partition of the land brought an internal imbalance in the spread of the people, deepening social divisions to the extent of threatening to split the English body politic. Hence, applying Starkey's medical analogy requires a combination between his notion of consumption and that of pestilence of the

---

[7] Starkey, 78.

[8] See David Hale, *The Body Politic*, 8, (Mouton & CO. N.V. Publishers, 1971), 68-9. According to Hale, "while the organic analogy was being used more widely and more artistically than ever before, the challenges to its validity increased in number and importance" (69). Hale argues that the metaphor was questioned by the rising materialistic explanation of the universe, the discourse of covenant theology and that of economic individualism.

[9] Shakespeare, *Coriolanus*, 1.1.3-4.

[10] From *The Declaration of the Diggers of Warwickshire* of 1607: "better it were in such case wee manfully dye, then hereafter to be pined to death for want." (British Library, Harley MS 787, f. 9v, Papers found in William Dell's study, Laud's secretary. 1607).

body politic, the latter being a state of division between the parts in which "the head agreeth not to the feet, nor feet to the hands; no one part agreeth to other; …they parts of this body be not knit togidder as it were with spirit and life, in concord and unity, but dissevered asunder, as they were in no case parts of one body."[11] Although in *Coriolanus*, for the most part, the distinction between Rome and the outside is a clear one, the internal Roman body politic comprises rather of two distinct parts, the plebeians and the patricians, between which there seems to be no permeability, thus putting into question the very idea that it is one body at all. For Coriolanus, the ideal of the masculine body as well as of the body politic dictates that permeability be excluded in order to fashion a self-sufficient and autonomous identity, one that does not depend on the mercy or whimsy of another;[12] hence, in the play's political situation of growing division, Coriolanus struggles to maintain an image of a harmonious body politic. From the plebeians' perspective, this division entails that their suffering equals Rome's sick body, since "the people are the city," whereas in the eyes of Coriolanus, the patricians are "the fundamental part of state" and the plebeians are but a "musty superfluity" to be excreted.[13] However, this neat division of the Roman body politic only works to a certain extent, a division that throughout the play proves more convoluted than first meets the eye.

Underlying the metaphor of the body politic is the notion that society is a natural phenomenon and not a contractual entity, only thus can it be analogous to the natural body. According to Aristotle, "the state is by nature clearly prior to the family and to the individual, since the whole is of necessity prior to the part; for example, if the whole body be destroyed, there will be no foot or hand…; But he who is unable to live in society, or who has no need because he is sufficient for himself, must be either a beast or a god."[14] And according to the early modern thinker Edward Forset, in "the bodie politique each part is to know and administer his owne proper worke, without entermixing or entermedling in the offices of any other. Shall the foot be

---

[11] Starkey, 83-4.

[12] See Joo Young Dittmann's "'Tear him to pieces:' De-Suturing Masculinity in Coriolanus." Following the work of Gail Kern Paster, Dittmann observes that "in medical discourses, the self-sufficient masculine body functioned as a regulatory ideal that must be sustained by differentiating itself from the open, disorderly female body" (*English Studies*, Vol. 90, No 6, [December 2009], 653-72, 654).

[13] Shakespeare, *Coriolanus*, 3.1.198, 150: 1.1.225.

[14] Aristotle, *The Politics of Aristotle*. Trans. B. Jowett. (London: Oxford University Press, 1885). (1253a), 4-5.

permitted to partake in the point of preeminence with the head?"[15] Edward
Forset's argument, similarly to Aristotle's, entails that hierarchy and
immobility must abide in order to produce a unified image of the body politic,
one in which the value of the parts is conditioned upon the whole since the
parts lack autonomy.

The body-politic metaphor, hence, regards the very idea of partition as
foreign, as a notion of autonomy that could only be accepted as external to it,
and yet, is an enemy from within. Forset illustrates this problem by imagining "a
bodie so monstrous, as whereunto two heads were at once affixed" and
rhetorically asking, "shall not that bodie receiue much damage by the diuision
and confusion of those two heads?"[16] To cure the body politic, Forset prescribes
that the "confused and all disturbing Anarchie," as he calls the disease of
division, "is to be exiled."[17] Although the partition of the body politic is
inevitable, the body politic must exclude the partition's potential for becoming a
determining force. In the anatomy theaters, the newly discovered bodily
structures made it ever more difficult to resolve this conflict between the body
as a whole and its inevitable partition, asserting on the one hand that "the body
mirrored the harmonious orchestration of the universe," yet on the other hand,
exposing a labyrinth of "bewildering complexity…, a confusion of function and
organic integrity."[18]

Just as Coriolanus ruthlessly guards the borders of Rome's body politic from
the Volscian threat, so does he keep at bay the border between Rome's two
body parts, the plebeians and the patricians — the rulers and the subjects.
However, for Coriolanus, such a division does not entail a dissolution of the
body politic as long as there is an exclusion of the subjects' inevitable
partition, as long as the "common fools" do not grow heads of their own and
rule themselves, spawning thus a monstrous body politic, a "beast / With
many heads," as Coriolanus calls them.[19] In Langis's interpretation of the play,
"Coriolanus's opinion regarding the plebeians is that their condition is static,"
and she argues that "such a naturalized view of hierarchical classes is clearly
antithetical to the very definition and existence of a republic."[20] The
supposedly well-defined border of Rome entails an inside and an outside,
constituting the former as a static space of unity while the latter as a space of

---

[15] Forset, *A Comparative Discourse of the Bodies Natural and Polituque,* 50.
[16] Forset, 57, 58.
[17] Ibid., 49-50.
[18] Sawday, *The Body Emblazoned,* 88.
[19] Shakespeare, *Coriolanus,* 3.1.99: 4.1.1-2.
[20] Langis, 5-6.

partition; and yet since division runs amok in Rome's interior as well, the separate spaces within it generate new insides and outsides. Thus, the Roman body politic as a whole comes to include that which should be external to it, resulting in a threat to its hierarchical stability. Likewise, throughout England, the enclosures demarcated insides and outsides where previously there had been none, producing new boundary violations and turning the body politic inside out, creating a situation in which the part rises above the whole as though it is bigger than the sum total of which it is supposedly merely a part.

According to the plebeians at the beginning of the play, the patricians are to blame for the "leanness that afflicts" them, since they keep the stores of grain only for themselves and to such extent that "authority surfeits;" thus, one part of the body politic is deficient while the other is in excess.[21] Such an imbalance between the parts, as the imbalanced population due to the enclosures in England, parallels the humoral pathophysiology of Galen, the Greek physician who was one of the most influential medical theorist on the early modern period and according to whom "all illness was imagined to be the product of a lack or excess of some bodily fluid."[22] The Galenic physiology, however, also sees the healthy functioning body as producing excesses, such as in the digestive process, conflating sickness with health and placing bodies "perpetually in danger of poisoning themselves on their own nutritive material."[23] Due to this conflation, the plebeians can hold on to the view that the Roman body politic is sick, whereas in the patricians' eyes, the imbalance does not entail a disease but is merely a temporary imbalance and a part of healthy physiology, as Menenius's fable of the belly aims at showing, though unconvincingly. As a double-edged sword, a rhetoric of infections and disease is prevalent throughout the play as each social group both appropriates that rhetoric and suffers from it, generating an atmosphere of constant fear of being infected by the other as well as producing an otherness. The plebeians regard Coriolanus as "a disease that must be cut away," "Lest his infection, being of catching nature, / Spread further";[24] hence, only his death can secure the health of Rome. Whereas the patricians, though they too use a rhetoric of disease, regard the whole as healthy, making Coriolanus but a part that can be maintained, "a limb that has but a disease: / Mortal, to cut it off; to cure it, easy."[25]

---

21 Ibid., 1.1.19, 15.
22 Schoenfeldt, 244.
23 Ibid., 244.
24 Shakespeare, *Coriolanus* 3.1.292, 307-8.
25 Ibid., 3.2.293-4.

Although in Livy's *History of Rome*, one of Shakespeare's historical sources, Menenius successfully disperses the rebellious mob by telling them the fable of the belly, in *Coriolanus* the fable ironically fails.[26] According to Shakespeare's Menenius, the belly is neither in excess nor idle, but rather healthily stores the nutrients for the entire body in order to distribute them to all the parts, "even to the court, the heart, to th'seat o'th'brain."[27] This version of the body politic places the distributive system, represented by the belly, above a strict concept of hierarchy in which the head is the sovereign. Furthermore, the belly metaphor underlines the spatial relations between a center of power and the periphery, the poor laboring limbs. While the plebeians may accept Menenius's analogy between the patricians and the belly as "the store-house and the shop / Of the whole body," what Menenius misses or perhaps conceals, but the mob implicitly senses and cannot accept, is that the gates of the storehouse containing the food are closed and Coriolanus is the one who controls whether or not to "send it through the rivers of your blood."[28] Although the plebeians recognize the patricians' hand in their misery, the mob directs its violence especially towards Coriolanus since, they argue, although he serves his country against the Volsces, "he pays himself with being proud."[29] As the head of Rome's executive power, Coriolanus controls and safeguards the border between the plebeians and the patricians, turning inward on Rome the violence he directs outward in order to preserve the autonomy of the Roman body politic. Between the two parts of the Roman body stands Coriolanus as the very embodiment of borders, barring the permeability of resources. Likewise, a recurring complaint by the English commoners was that the enclosures led to blocked roads, hence interrupting the distribution of resources,[30] an issue that also served as an argument by Francis Trigge in his petition to King James against enclosures (1604) in which he tried to persuade James by pointing out that even "your Maiestie cannot passe in their waies and lanes, vnlesse they throwe open their hedges."[31] Underlying this invocation by Trigge is the notion that the head of

---

[26] See Philip Brockbank's introduction in *Coriolanus*, p. 29. The Arden Shakespeare, 2007.

[27] Shakespeare, *Coriolanus*, 1.1.131.

[28] Ibid., 1.1.132-3, 134. Zvi Jagendorf argues that Coriolanus's death reveals the triumph "of the limbs over the belly, of the spread of power over its concentration" ("*Coriolanus*: Body Politic and Private Parts," 467).

[29] Ibid., 1.1.32-3.

[30] See three instances mentioned by Edwin F. Gay in *The Midland Revolt and the Inquisitions of Depopulation of 1607*, (Royal Historical Society, 1904), pp. 212, 216, 221.

[31] Trigge, 83.

the body politic, which is the version of the metaphor repeatedly used by King James,[32] loses its superiority to those who control distribution.

Following Leah Marcus's reading of *Coriolanus*, which locates the play's crux in the "jurisdictional disputes between the London corporation and the crown, which led to the new city charter in 1608," Nate Eastman argues that the importance of the Midland Revolt in reading *Coriolanus* requires a reexamination and that there are "clearer correspondences between the play and essentially urban anxieties."[33] A one-to-one correspondence between the different parties in *Coriolanus* and those involved in the Midland Revolt is, to say the least, difficult to sustain through and through, starting with the simple fact that the plebeians reside inside Rome's city walls and are not rural peasants, and complicated by the fact that Coriolanus goes to battle with the cowardly plebeians against the Volsces. As the embodiment of borders, Coriolanus occupies a liminal space, simultaneously inside and outside, standing even between the divine and the earthly, as Volumnia notes in her plea for Rome, telling him: "thou barr'st us / Our prayers to the gods."[34] Coriolanus is both a part of the patricians and yet not one of them, both a part of the plebeians and their antagonist, and finally, he is both a Roman and yet an exile, joining forces with the Volscian enemy for whom he remains a threat. Hence, my reading of *Coriolanus* focuses neither on the Midland Revolt nor on the enclosures in isolation, but on the relations between the various social spaces that chart the layout of the play's power dynamics.

The City: Plaguing the Borders of the Body

Penetrating deeper into the anatomy of the body politic, we leave behind the enclosures and step into London and its inner divisions. In 1608, the year when *Coriolanus* was most likely composed, the plague once again ran wild in the streets of London, bringing city life to a standstill with the cancelling of pageants and fairs, the shutting down of bearbaiting and theaters, as well as

---

[32] The head version of the body-politic metaphor was used by King James on many occasions, such as in *The Trewe Lawe of Free Monarchies* and in his parliament speeches (see Hale, *The Body Politic*, 111-3; Jonathan Gill Harris, *Foreign Bodies and the Body Politic: Discourses of Social Pathology in Early Modern England*. [UK: Cambridge University Press, 1998], 32; and Eastman, "The Rumbling Belly Politic: Metaphorical Location and Metaphorical Government in Coriolanus." *Early Modern Literary Studies* 13, no. 1 [May 2007] 1-39).

[33] Eastman, 18, 1.

[34] Shakespeare, *Coriolanus*, 5.3.104-5.

the prohibiting of any sort of public assemblies.[35] According to Ian Munro, the "plague is a spatial disease; it refigures the livid and symbolic space of the city, altering and transforming the urban aspect."[36] On the one hand, in order to suppress the plague, the state deployed a strategy of divide and rule, which controlled the spaces of London in the form of house arrests and street regulations. Yet on the other hand, the divisions and subdivisions of London's aristocratic buildings, accommodating the growing population of the city,[37] prompted royal proclamations against such practices due to fear that overly crowded tenements would increase the spread of the plague.[38] Absurdly, spatial division was both a cure for the plague and a potential cause. For Coriolanus, the multiplicity of the mind-changing mob is itself a disease of the body politic as well as of the self-sufficient, autonomous individual whose aim is to rise above the biological demands of the body. Again and again, Coriolanus reminds the plebeians of their inherent partition, calling them a "Hydra," "bosom multiplied," and exhorting them, "get you home, you fragments!"[39] And yet, when dispersing their mutiny, Coriolanus divides them into supposedly controllable parts, dissolving their collective amorphic whole; thus, he ends up nourishing the very thing he despises about them – their multiplicity and growing autonomy. Unwittingly, he implicates himself in the same ruinous outcome he reproaches certain patricians for causing by their consent to give the plebeians corn for free, that by doing so they "nourish'd disobedience, fed / The ruin of the state."[40]

The massive growth of London's population during that period makes London appear as the surfeiting patricians of *Coriolanus*, being the belly of England, but instead of distributing its resources it distributes sickness as its nutrients transform into poison. Like the overgrown self-poisoning belly, London had "surfeit[ed] out of action" due to its plague-stricken excessive population spilling out of the city walls, increasing, on the one hand, the permeability between the inside and the outside, blurring this line as though expanding the city, yet on the other hand, placing the transgressors outside

---

[35] See Ian Munro. *The Figure of the Crowd in Early Modern London: The City and its Double,* (Palgrave Macmillan, 2005), 176.

[36] Ibid., 179.

[37] Estimations are that London's population, including the suburbs, "quadrupled from 50,000 (or fewer) inhabitants in 1500 to approximately 200,000 in 1600" (Hopkins, 34).

[38] See Leonard Tennenhouse, "Family Rites: City Comedy and the Strategies of Patriarchalism," *New Historicism & Renaissance Drama.* Eds. Richard Wilson and Richard Dutton. (UK: Logman Publishing, 1992), 197.

[39] Shakespeare, Coriolanus, 3.1.92, 130: 1.1.221.

[40] Ibid., 3.1.116-7.

the reach of London's authorities since suburban divisions had jurisdictions of their own.[41] Hence, taking measures within the walls, such as expelling all the beggars,[42] did not ensure the city's isolation from the plague. Quarantining infected houses or even the entire city by dividing and isolating social spaces had failed to cut off the spread of the plague.[43] According to Munro, "like the official processions through the streets of London, plague is both inside and outside the city: at once alien and…inherent to urban experience";[44] thus, he regards Coriolanus as the plague itself, simultaneously "a conquering invader and as a corruption internal and inherent to the city."[45]

Understood thus, the disease of Rome's body politic adheres both to Galen's conception of disease as an internal imbalance,[46] as well as to the Paracelsan model in which disease "is an entity in its own right, whose origins lie outside the body in a foreign invader."[47] According to Hippocrates, an external cause of infectious disease is miasma, or polluted bad air, thus escaping London to the clean air of the countryside and its open spaces appeared as a viable solution.[48] However, John Stow in his *A Survey of London* (1603) describes how the open fields outside the walls of London in which citizens would "recreate and refresh their dulled spirites in the sweete and wholesome ayre"[49] transformed in a few years into an urban landscape of buildings. Escaping became less and less possible as the city was spreading and with it, the miasmic air. Imagery of polluted air appears throughout the play in relation to

---

[41] Ibid., 1.3.25. James Shapiro notes that due to the plague the Mayor of London begged the Privy Council "to press authorities in the suburbs to enact precautions as strict as those in the city;" Moreover, "with suburbanites resorting to London to shop," the inside/outside division was instable (*The Year of Lear: Shakespeare in 1606.* [Simon & Schuster, 2015], 278). Regarding suburban jurisdictions, see Joseph P. Ward's *Metropolitan Communities: Trade Guilds, Identity, and Change in Early Modern London.* (Stanford University Press, 1997).

[42] Shapiro, 279.

[43] See Paul Slack's "The Response to Plague in Early Modern England: Public Policies and their Consequences," in *Famine, Disease and the Social Order in Early Modern Society.* Eds. John Walter and Roger Schofield. (Cambridge University Press, 1989), 167.

[44] Munro, 177.

[45] Ibid., 197.

[46] For more on Galen's theory of disease as an internal imbalance see Paster's *The Body Embarrassed*, esp. 69-75.

[47] Harris, *Foreign Bodies and the Body Politic*, 23.

[48] See Holly Dugan's *The Ephemeral History of Perfume*, (The John Hopkins University Press, 2011), 107-9.

[49] John Stow. *A Survey of London by John Stow Vol 1*, Ed. Charles Lethbridge Kingsford. (UK, Oxford: Clarendon Press, 1908), 127.

the plebeians, not only from Coriolanus who portrays them as the "rank-scented meinie" infecting one another "Against the wind a mile" or as "carcasses of unburied men / That do corrupt my air,"[50] but even from the tribunes, their own representatives, who refer to them as having "stinking breaths."[51] Upon Coriolanus's banishment, the city comes back to life; the "tradesmen sing[ing] in their shops," productive members of the commonweal once again, instead of "Dissentious numbers pest'ring streets," violating the lockdowns, and infecting one another and the body politic as a whole.[52] However, the resurrection of the city is premature as rumors that Coriolanus had joined forces with the Volsces against Rome are quickly spread by the plebeians and, just as quickly, the rumors are verified by the patricians. In an instant the singing turns into infectious rumors that are "spoke freely out of many mouths," the mouths of those who exiled Coriolanus and "made the air unwholesome."[53]

The fear of depopulation as an illness of the body politic went hand in hand with the plagued city, sweeping the streets of London in a silent pageant, a fear that in the play the tribunes and plebeians project onto Coriolanus, referring to him as the "viper / That would depopulate the city."[54] Although the depopulation of the English countryside is distinct from that of the plagued city, in both cases, spatial division and regulations function as severe measures for controlling the population. However, the Roman historical context provides a third reading for this reference to the depopulations, one in which the subjects resist the rulers' spatial control. The tribunes' accusation that Coriolanus depopulates the city is, on the one hand, for bringing to the death of citizens, whether through wars, hunger or disease; but on the other hand, through this accusation, the tribunes remind the patricians of the historical event known as the first secession in which the plebeians left the city of Rome in protest.[55] Thus, this accusation also serves as a threat that if Coriolanus does not change his ways, they will again depopulate the city. The power of this threat derives from two distinct definitions of the word city as noted by Isidore of Seville in *The Etymologies*: "a city (*civitas*) is a multitude of people united by a bond of community, named for its 'citizens' (*civis*)... Now *urbs* (also 'city') is the name of the actual buildings, while *civitas* is not the

---

[50] Shakespeare, *Coriolanus*, 3.1.65: 1.4.43: 3.3.122-3.

[51] Ibid., 2.1.234.

[52] Ibid., 4.6.8,7.

[53] Ibid., 4.6.65, 131.

[54] See Munro, 185; Shakespeare, *Coriolanus*, 3.1.261-2.

[55] See Titus Livy, *The History of Rome, Books 1-5*, Trans. Valerie M. Warrior. (Hackett Publishing Company, 2006), 122-3.

stones, but the inhabitants."[56] Since the "people are the city," the tribunes can threaten to depopulate the *urbs* and lead the *civitas* somewhere beyond the reach of the patricians.[57] Interestingly, Shakespeare does not mention the first secession in the play, without which the plebeians appear as having no real power to make such threats at all. The plague lockdowns in London and Coriolanus are both a threat to the city as *civitas* because they reduce the citizens to the *urbs*, since by controlling their mobility and depopulating the streets and other public spaces, the only resort becomes the private space of the house, which severs the bond of community but ties the individual to the state's restrictions. Coriolanus as the very border of Rome, however, turns the tables when upon his banishment he raves "I banish you;"[58] thus, in leaving Rome Coriolanus takes the *urbs* with him wherever he goes and without him the *civitas* remains defenseless, an open body prone to invasions and dissolution.

As the very idea of borders, Coriolanus functions as an absolute marker for those he stands between, signifying for each group a limit and a place that encloses and defines them against the other, but Coriolanus, as the line itself, belongs to neither. According to Henri Lefebvre, the notion of the closure applies to "both natural and social life," but in contrast to the biological organism in which the boundaries "generally remain permeable," in the social organism, "closures tend to become absolute."[59] The relation between *Coriolanus* and King James's absolutist monarchy has yielded copious critical analysis, whether critics interpret the play as pro patricians and absolutism or as advocating republican values, or even as advocating for liberal democratic participation,[60] either way, Coriolanus himself mostly remains a figurehead of absolutism. Peter Cefalu, however, argues that interpretations that "have described Coriolanus as either absolutist or bourgeois-individualist…do not accurately reflect the politics of the play."[61] Following Glenn Burgess and other critics who debunk the "assumption that early seventeenth-century monarchy was either absolutist or arbitrary in nature,"[62] Cefalu considers Coriolanus as having certain ideological commonalities with the plebeians and others with

---

[56] Isidore of Seville, *The Etymologies of Isidore of Seville*, 305.
[57] Shakespeare, Coriolanus, 3.1.198.
[58] Ibid., 3.3.123.
[59] Lefebvre, 176.
[60] See Lee Bliss's Introduction in *Coriolanus*, (Cambridge University Press, 2000), 99.
[61] Cefalu, 54.
[62] Ibid., 56.

the patricians, as well as incongruencies with both.[63] Langis, as well, interprets Coriolanus as following an inherently flawed Roman virtue that dictates "to be both uncommon and common, to rise above the herd and to be co-operative within it."[64] For all of Cefalu's resistance to absolutist arguments, he does concede that Coriolanus has an "absolutist personality," albeit irrelevant to the play's political tensions since they "are not characterologically caused."[65] Coriolanus, hence, has a dual relation to absolutism, as on the one hand, he signifies an absolute relation for others, being a boundary, but on the other hand, he is bifurcated, a mere biological organism unable to uphold an absolute position himself, a member and yet not a member, until finally he is dismembered by the oppositions he marks with his own body.

The tribunes brand Coriolanus as a "viperous traitor," "A foe to th'public weal," and demand that he shall be executed, purging thus the body politic of the disease, sacrificing him in order to position partition outside and reconstitute a unified image of the people.[66] Notably, in Shakespeare's England, public dismemberment was the punishment for traitors, excluding in this way the body politic's partition and healing the injured sovereignty.[67] The sweetening of Coriolanus's sentence, in the end, neither erases the mark of a traitor, as demonstrated when Aufidius again rebukes him after signing the peace treaty with Rome, calling Coriolanus a "traitor in the highest degree," nor does it save Coriolanus from the same fate suffered by traitors in England.[68] Like a microcosm of the overflowing city transgressing its own boundaries, London's execution sites were social spaces of excess, both revolving around the grotesque spectacle of the executed and vivisected body, whose insides would be pulled outside, as well as giving way to public disorders as "chaos and misrule governed the proceedings."[69] As a body of people, the crowd at the executions was itself grotesque and unbridled, or as Bakhtin notes, connecting the carnival, the marketplace, and the body, "the grotesque body is not separated from the rest of the world. It is not a closed,

---

[63] Cefalu argues that Coriolanus is, on the one hand, "governed by negative libertarianism" (60), which Cefalu associates also with the plebeians (65), yet on the other that Coriolanus's "militant antipaternalism" (62) opposes the paternalistic ideal voiced by the patricians, the tribunes, and the citizens (63-4).

[64] Langis, 4.

[65] Cefalu, 70.

[66] Shakespeare, *Coriolanus,* 3.1.284,174.

[67] Sawday, *The Body Emblazoned,* 55.

[68] Shakespeare, *Coriolanus,* 5.6.85.

[69] Sawday, The Body Emblazoned, 84.

completed unit; it is unfinished, outgrows itself."[70] In contrast to the grotesque body, Bakhtin places a body associated with the artistic tradition of classical antiquity, which the Renaissance regarded as a "finished product..., isolated, alone, fenced off from all other bodies."[71]

The conflict between Coriolanus and the plebeians over the unveiling of his wounds, as "custom wills," enacts the opposition between the grotesque and the classical, both in relation to Coriolanus's body and in terms of social spaces.[72] The plebeians know that if Coriolanus will follow custom, they must comply and give him their voices, which hence renders their voices empty, as one of the citizens astutely expresses regarding their ability to deny Coriolanus: "it is a power that we have no power to do."[73] Thus, doing so, withholding their voices, will mark them as a grotesque body, since "for the multitude to be ingrateful, were to make a monster of the multitude."[74] Coriolanus is unwilling to appear in the marketplace in front of the plebeians, to wear the gown of humility and expose his wounds in order to receive their voices for the consulship. But after he relents to Menenius and goes to the market, Coriolanus does confide with one of the citizens, saying that he will show the wounds "in private," which ultimately Coriolanus manages to avoid as well.[75] In order to preserve his distinction from the incoherent multitude, Coriolanus invokes a private space in which the classical standards of the body can be upheld, a space akin to that of the anatomy theaters.

The Anatomy Theatres: Probing the Wounded Soul

The classical world was part and parcel of the anatomy theaters, as their very design was after the fashion of Vitruvius, the Roman architect, and his secular theaters of entertainment.[76] But it was not only the ancients' architecture that enjoyed a renaissance, as the anatomical spectacle itself gave life to the classical writings on anatomy, both reaffirming the old models of Galen and Aristotle as well as criticizing them.[77] Sawday argues that "the confrontation which had taken place outside the anatomy theater, on the gallows, was

---

[70] Bakhtin, 26.

[71] Ibid., 29.

[72] Shakespeare, *Coriolanus,* 2.3.117.

[73] Ibid., 2.3.4-5.

[74] Ibid., 2.3.10-1.

[75] Ibid., 2.3.77.

[76] See Andrew Cunningham. *The Anatomical Renaissance: The Resurrection of the Anatomical Projects of the Ancients.* (England: Aldershot. Scolar Press, 1997), 65-7.

[77] Ibid., esp. chapters 4 & 6.

transformed once the body had been taken inside the theater,"[78] a transformation of the grotesque body, of social disorder, into a classical structure in which "a new regime came into being."[79] Through the seating arrangements in accordance with social rank,[80] the anatomy theaters reified spatially the hierarchical model of the body politic. Furthermore, in contrast to the chaotic disembowelment at the execution site, the corporeal order of the anatomical process and the discovered inner structures reaffirmed the status of the body politic as a natural phenomenon. And yet, the anatomy theaters provided plenty of space for confusion as well, since the inner body was producing more and more spaces of exploration "bereft of reliable maps" in the dissections.[81] Sawday notes how "the confrontation between the body and the anatomist came to replace the tripartite division of textual authority, living authority, and the passive authority of the body";[82] thus, prevalent medical models found themselves under the anatomist's scalpel, undermined by the authority of God's book of nature, the human body, and, by extension, the anatomies asserted and exercised the sovereign's authority over the living bodies of the subjects.

Coriolanus's wounds incite a struggle over their meaning among the patricians, the plebeians, and Coriolanus — a struggle that mirrors the authorial confrontation in the anatomy theaters. Like a medieval anatomist for whom the cadaver held no authority but to verify the professor's lecture and the ancient texts,[83] Coriolanus advocates the authority of the patricians and his own words as sufficient proofs for the existence of his wounds. Moreover, in the anatomies of the late Middle Ages after the fashion of Mundinus, it is likely that the body was not even present during the lecture, as the dissection took place separately;[84] thus, Coriolanus's desire to reveal the wounds privately serves to separate their meaning from the possible interpretations of the crowd. In Coriolanus's eyes, it is not by hiding his wounds that they might "fester 'gainst ingratitude, / And tent themselves with death,"[85] but rather by revealing them that it might happen, for they will be exposed to the subjective interpretations of anyone in Rome and any meaning could infect them with lies. Coriolanus stands in contrast to the principles of

---

[78] Sawday, *The Body Emblazoned*, 75.

[79] Ibid., 84.

[80] Ibid., 75.

[81] Ibid., 129.

[82] Ibid., 65.

[83] Cunningham, *The Anatomical Renaissance*, 44.

[84] Ibid., 44.

[85] Shakespeare, *Coriolanus*, 1.9.30-1.

Vesalius's new anatomy in which the eyes were the ultimate authority, suggesting that anyone who witnesses the ocular evidence has the ability to judge and thus promoting a decentralized notion of power and dissolving the unity of the body politic and the sovereign's image.[86] Although England only saw the construction of the first anatomy theater in 1636 in London, the Barber-Surgeon guild and the College of Physicians "had rights for the regular dissection of corpses prescribed by civil legislation dating from the mid-sixteenth century,"[87] and the work of Vesalius was well known to English practitioners.[88] Towards the end of the sixteenth century, the visibility of public dissections in London was increasing,[89] and since demand was rising as well, the design of the anatomy halls in England set out "to ensure that as many people as possible could see what was happening."[90] Coriolanus's private space is hence neither that of the anatomy theater nor that of the English anatomy hall, but rather the space of the old medieval anatomies in which seeing is inconsequential. The new anatomy theaters are the public space of the plebeians, making it impossible for Coriolanus to claim the classical body for himself. Moreover, the grotesque space of the marketplace, the space of the plebeians, absurdly appears as the enclosed private space, as though residing within the grotesque space and turning it inside out, like the divided body in the anatomy theater.

Advances in the study of anatomy gave rise to reexaminations of the relationship between body and soul, a relation that produced an analogous debate in the body politic discourse. Just as competing models regarding the soul's relation to the body coexisted, so did different perspectives as to the soul of the body politic. Cunningham observes that three main models were prevalent at the time: "the tri-partite soul of Plato, the unitary distributed soul of Aristotle, and the immortal soul of Christianity."[91] Concerning the body

---

[86] See Rafael Mandressi's "Of the Eye and the Hand: Performance in Early Modern Anatomy," The Drama Review. Trans. Elizabeth Claire. (Massachusetts Institute of Technology Press [MIT Press], Fall 2015), 59 (3), pp. 60-76. Mandressi refers to many primary sources by 16th century anatomists who stress the salient role of the eyes. See also Cunningham, *The Anatomical Renaissance*, 102.

[87] Billing, 10.

[88] Mitchell, Perry. *The Purple Island*, 294.

[89] Sawday, *The Body Emblazoned*, 56.

[90] Billing, 10.

[91] Cunningham, *The Anatomical Renaissance*, 207. These models found different advocates amongst the anatomists, from Vesalius' general adherence to Plato in his three-venter approach, to Fabricius regarding the soul as the various bodily operations in the Aristotelian manner (92, 110, 171-3).

politic discourse, Edward Forset argued that "like the soul, the king is not a part of the body,"[92] paralleling the Christian concept regarding the soul's absence from the flesh, an argument through which, according to Harris, Forset aims to reassert the body politic metaphor as an absolutist model of sovereignty. Starkey, on the other hand, regards the relation between body and soul as corresponding respectively to that between society and its laws,[93] whereas a third view advocated by Keckermann and Hooker is a version of the Aristotelian *homonoia*, translated as "like-mindedness,"[94] according to which the soul of the body politic lies in the bond between people and the voluntary participation in communal life.[95] As Sawday notes, the body in the anatomy theaters functioned as a passage "into THE body, but not My body," a passage into a shared universal body, and yet one's own experience of inwardness was nowhere to be found in THE other's body.[96] By concealing his wounds, Coriolanus blocks the passage into this universal body and safeguards not merely his body but his very soul; thus, he is unwilling to turn MY soul into THE soul of the body politic. The body holds no communal value for Coriolanus and so he resists being turned into a passive participant laid out on the anatomist table, subjected to the scrutinizing gaze of the common rabble. At the same time, he resists being incorporated into the living body of the actor on the Shakespearean stage, giving his soul to the theatrical event, to the manipulations of the text, the props, the other actors, the performing body, and to the audience. It is a reversal of what is supposedly the natural order in which the mind holds the reins of the body, thus leading inevitably to depravity and corrupting the soul. For Coriolanus, to "perform a part," as Volumnia puts it, and to kneel to the plebeians is possible only through this abhorrent reversal:

> I will not do't,
> Lest I surcease to honour mine own truth,

---

[92] Harris, 58.

[93] Hale, 63.

[94] Bejan, 21.

[95] See Hale, 19, 21, 83-4; See Debora Shuger's "'Society Supernatural:' The Imagined Community of Hooker's Laws." *Religion and Culture in Renaissance England.* Eds. Claire McEachern and Debora Shuger. (Cambridge University Press, 1997), 127-8; and Noah Dauber's *State and Commonwealth: The Theory of the State in Early Modern England 1549-1640.* (Princeton, New Jersey: Princeton University Press, 2016), 217.

[96] Sawday, *The Body Emblazoned*, 7.

> And by my body's action teach my mind
> A most inherent baseness.[97]

In *Coriolanus* Shakespeare explores the body politic of England through the dead body politic of ancient Rome, resurrecting Coriolanus only to find him unwilling to yield his soul. Like an anatomist, Shakespeare dissects Roman history, starting chronologically from the layer closest to his own time, with *Titus Andronicus*, then he penetrates deeper into the bowels of the historical body with *Julius Caesar* and *Antony and Cleopatra*, as though in search of the body's internal truth; and finally, Shakespeare reaches *Coriolanus*. Reading Shakespeare's Roman history plays in the order they were written and not in their historical chronology could potentially reveal the anatomical character of Shakespeare's historical project into the body politic. That analysis, however, is beyond the scope of this essay and so is a thorough inquiry into the relation among the theatrical space, the actor's body and the anatomy theaters.

At the end of *Coriolanus*, the Roman body politic appears to have been healed by Volumnia as she persuades her son to break off the attack on Rome, but this victory leaves the city without defense, reunited in its survival but open to the uncertainties of the external world. Coriolanus's unparalleled vitality, his inhuman health, and ability to ward off so many wounds without suffering infection make him desirable as a sacrifice, as these characteristics indicate that he is an extremely potent medicine for healing the body politic. Yet, as Cavell notes, Coriolanus "dies in a place irrelevant to his sacrifice."[98] Sacrificing Coriolanus does not heal the body politic, in a sense, but rather brings to a new social order that cannot sustain the metaphor of the body politic. For Coriolanus, belonging to the Roman body politic is a transcendent state independent of locality, which is possible in so far as the borders of Rome are its people, a requirement that enables the *civitas* to rise above the *urbs*. Coriolanus brings together the threefold figure of the medieval anatomist, the executioner, and the sovereign,[99] which aligns him with the idea that in executions, the public partakes in the executed body as a ritualistic formation and reaffirmation of the body politic. Unlike the inclusive open space of the public executions in which the executed body and the body of the people stretch far and wide, encompassing within the body politic even those who are not literally there, the closed space of the anatomy theaters means that partaking in the anatomized body and belonging to this body of

---

[97] Shakespeare, *Coriolanus*, 3.2.120-3.
[98] Stanley Cavell. *"Who Does the Wolf Love?" Reading Coriolanus, Representations*, No. 3, Summer, 1983, 14.
[99] See Sawday, *The Body Emblazoned*, 79-82.

participants is only a temporary state conditioned by one's physical presence within the structure of the theater. In persuading Coriolanus not to attack Rome, Volumnia transforms the fable of the belly into a version that centers on her womb, telling him "thou shalt no sooner / March to assault thy country than to tread— / Trust to't, thou shalt not—on thy mother's womb."[100] Volumnia's body does not permit Coriolanus to be a Roman wherever he goes, but rather binds him to a localized space, to the city borders of Rome where she resides. The womb fable thus creates both a literalization and a localization of the body politic, emptying out the transcendent state of belonging, as though turning Rome into an anatomy theater in which even blood relations appear to be conditioned and temporal as Volumnia is willing to deny kinship with her son, saying he "had a Volscian to his mother."[101]

Although Coriolanus wishes to take revenge on Rome, shunning his Roman identity in the process, it does not entail for him severing the bond with his mother, since he does not equate the Roman body politic with the literal body of Volumnia. Hence, once he faces the implications of the womb fable in the presence of his mother, he gives in to the literal body, revealing himself as inconstant as the flesh and just as fickle as the plebeians. In the body politic discourse, the whole must be prior to the part, hence the individual's literal body cannot be a metonymy for the entire society, otherwise it would render the body politic metaphor absurd. Seemingly, Volumnia does place Rome above the family, being but a part of the body politic, however, what she does is rather to equate kinship with the state and in doing so she also localizes familial relations, conditioning them to Rome's borders. The body-politic metaphor does not allow Coriolanus to be a self-sufficient individual, and yet he defines his god-like autonomy in relation to it, thus once the metaphor becomes unsustainable, he turns into "a kind of nothing,"[102] neither self-sufficient nor a part of the social world. Ultimately, it is Coriolanus who turns into a grotesque, monstrous body whose inside cannot be contained by the whole, his "heart / Too great for what contains it."[103] Rome survives to live another day, but in the new social order, leaving the *urbs* negates one's identity as a Roman, turning the body politic into a tenuous community of seemingly free individuals like those participating in the dissection of a body at the anatomy theater. Setting aside the body-politic metaphor transforms the social order, enabling the individuals a limited version of self-sufficiency, and yet, as social members, the subjects become dispensable just like Coriolanus is at the end.

---

[100] Shakespeare, *Coriolanus*, 5.3.122-4.
[101] Ibid., 5.3.178.
[102] Ibid., 5.1.13.
[103] Ibid., 5.6.103-4.

Chapter 7

'*Nous ne scavons distinguer la peau de la chemise*': Perceiving the Naked Skin in Montaigne's *Essais* and Titian's "Flaying of Marsyas"

Elizabeth Anne Kirby

New York University

Abstract: Towards the end of the note to his reader, Montaigne confesses that the *Essais* are unsuccessful attempts to depict himself naked. Taking Montaigne at his word, this chapter investigates Montaigne's engagement with bare skin — the surface at which nakedness appears and is felt. In examining Montaigne's descriptions of skin in conversation with Titian's late sixteenth-century painting of Marsyas, my readings of Montaigne's chapter "De la vanité" and of Titian's painting demonstrate that each depicts a dismantling gaze that upsets the concept of body and disturbs apparent demarcations between form and ground. Beginning with Montaigne's meditation on the Oracle at Delphi, the chapter shows that, for Montaigne, human physiology and sense perception facilitate the dissolution of apparent bodily boundaries. A particularly locomotive and appetitive orientation to her surroundings prevents the human being from looking inward. The human, Montaigne argues, spills into her surroundings and reaches too far outward. The resulting perceptive difficulties, Montaigne suggests, threaten to collapse ontological distinctions in addition to preventing proper introspection. Titian's rendition of the flaying of Marsyas (c. 1570-76) depicts this very way of looking that Montaigne describes. Not only does he manage to render the confusion between the skin and flesh Montaigne argues is a common human mistake, but Titian invites the viewer of the painting to see a *way of looking* that ruptures apparent demarcations between bodies. Montaigne's and Titian's depictions of skin reveal that the confusion between interior and exterior, between what is ours and what is other, is an effect of the very fabric of naked skin. The porous, fragile integument conditions a way of looking by which the boundedness of body is continuously dismantled and reformed.

Keywords: Titian, Montaigne, perception, body

***

Introduction

In the note to his reader, Montaigne confesses that the *Essais* are unsuccessful attempts to depict himself naked: "I would most willingly have portrayed myself whole, and wholly naked."[1] Montaigne's project of naked self-portraiture, this chapter will show, leads him to confront the messy motion of embodiment. In attempting to render himself fully naked, Montaigne grapples with the liminal porosity of exposed skin, ultimately dismantling the body and displacing the nakedness he aims to depict. Montaigne's engagement with naked skin as a porous, fragile, and multifunctional organ facilitates his depiction of the human body as an entangled network of integuments and demonstrates that, as Didier Anzieu beautifully observes, "*tout être vivant, tout organe, toute cellule, a une peau ou une écorce.*"[2] By disrupting the apparent relationship between integument, interior, and exterior, Montaigne's attempts at naked self-depiction lead to an introspective self-exposure that upsets the concept of body as a formal organization of matter and interrogates the material consubstantiality between organism and environment.

This chapter begins by looking at Montaigne's treatment of bare skin in the *Essais*—the surface at which nakedness appears and is felt. Drawing on Didier Anzieu's concept of *le Moi-peau*, I examine Montaigne's engagement with naked skin as a porous, fragile, and multifunctional organ. Taking seriously Montaigne's painting metaphor for his own writing— "*je m'y fusse peint tout entier et tout nud*"— and his question "Why is it not equally permissible to

---

[1] "…je m'y fusse tres-volontiers peint tout entier et tout nud" (Montaigne, "Au lecteur"); Michel de Montaigne. 2004. *Les Essais* edited by Pierre Villey. (Paris: Presses Universitaires de France; Michel de Montaigne. 2003). *The Complete Essays*. Translated by M.A. Screech. (London: Penguin Books). Henceforth all parenthetical text references will be to these editions.

[2] "Every living being, every organ, every cell, has a skin or carapace" (Anzieu, 12). All English translations are mine unless otherwise indicated.

portray yourself with your pen as he did with his brush?"[3] I read Montaigne's meditation on—and reconfiguration of—*nosce te ipsum* (or, to use Montaigne's version, "look back into yourself") in "De la vanité" alongside Titian's "Flaying of Marsyas." Reading "De la vanité" alongside a late sixteenth-century painting that, like the *Essais*, revisits and reinterprets classical text, I aim to demonstrate how description and depiction of nakedness ultimately reveal the difficulty in perceiving the surfaces of skin and flesh and to show that the boundary between interior and exterior is dismantled in both Montaigne's writing and in Titian's painting. It follows, I argue, that perceiving the marginal and the liminal—and the distinction between body and ground—is integral to the capacity to feel naked.

Introspection and Montaigne's Dismantling of Body

Introspection, which is essential to Montaigne's naked self-portraiture, presupposes a bounded, hidden interior separate from an organism's surroundings. Montaigne's analysis of *nosce te ipsum*[4] at the end of "De la vanité" reworks—and problematizes—introspection by depicting the human as a porous and mutating organism. The end of "De la vanité" portrays the integration of human matter into the environment and demonstrates how introspection, in attempting to look inside the body, dismantles it. Montaigne explains to his reader that if others looked at themselves as attentively as he does, they would see that they, like Montaigne, are full of vapid nonsense.[5] The following sentence shows that this vapidity is the stuff of Montaigne's essence and that to extricate himself from his own nonsense would be to unravel his whole being. Montaigne explains that he cannot undo himself from his own inanities without undoing himself: "*De m'en deffaire, je ne puis sans me deffaire moy-mesmes*" (III, 9, 1000) (I cannot rid myself of them without getting rid of myself [1132]).

---

[3] "pourquoy n'est-il loisible de mesme à un chacun de *se peindre* de la plume comme il se peignoit d'un creon?" (II, 17, 653). All English citations are from M.A. Screech's translation of the *Essais* unless otherwise indicated and all French citations are from the Villey-Saulnier edition of the *Essais*.

[4] This injunction is also examined in Sir John Davies' 1599 poem *Nosce Teipsum* (Anderson 83).

[5] "Si les autres se regardoient attentivement, comme je fay, ils se trouveroient, comme je fay, pleins d'inanité et de fadaise" (III, 9, 1000) ("If others were to look attentively into themselves as I do, they would find themselves, as I do, full of emptiness and tomfoolery" [1132]).

This careful turning inward is conspicuously visual. By looking at his insides, Montaigne is able to perceive his own foolishness while the custom continues to be to look outwards and elsewhere.[6] Looking, Montaigne notices, is always directed towards space and motion outside of the embodied observer and is a transitive action we do to an *other.* The tendency to look at the motion of other bodies distracts human organisms from confronting their own being.[7] Our physiology, Montaigne explains, makes introspection uncomfortable and we tend to resist such intimate self-examining.[8] He then compares our reluctance to confronting our own *intimus* with the churning of the ocean, integrating this individual human reaction into the motion of other, vaster bodies, and thus preemptively dissolving the apparent material otherness between his body and theirs.[9]

The natural tendency to look outward, Montaigne explains, makes introspection a paradox with which he has to wrestle in the *Essais*: "*C'estoit un commandement paradoxe que nous faisoit anciennement ce Dieu à Delphes: Regardez **dans vous**, reconnoissez vous, tenez vous à vous*" (III, 9, 1001, italics mine) ("That commandment given us in ancient times by that god at Delphi was contrary to all expectation: 'Look back into your self; get to know your self; hold on to your self'" [1132]).[10] Nakedness—and naked self-portraiture—

---

[6] "Cette opinion et usance commune de regarder ailleurs qu'à nous a bien pourveu à nostre affaire" (III, 9, 1000). ("That commonly approved practice of looking elsewhere than at our own self has served our affairs well!" [1132]).

[7] "Regardez, dict chacun, les branles du ciel, regardez au public, à la querelle de cettuy-là, au pouls d'un tel, au testament de cet autre: somme regardez tousjours haut ou bas, ou à costé, ou devant, ou derriere vous" (III, 9, 1001). ("Everyone says: 'Look at the motions of the heavens, look at society, at this man's quarrel, this other man's pulse, this other man's will and testament'—in other words always look upwards or downwards or sideways, or before or behind you" [1132]).

[8] "Pour ne nous desconforter, nature a rejetté bien à propos l'action de nostre veuë au dehors" (III, 9, 1000) ("So as not to dishearten us, Nature has very conveniently cast the action of our sight outwards" [1132]).

[9] "...de rebrousser vers nous nostre course c'est un mouvement pénible: la mer se brouille et s'empesche ainsi quand elle est repoussée en soi" (III, 9, 1000) ("to struggle back towards our self against the current is a painful movement; thus does the sea, when driven against itself, swirl back in confusion" [1132]).

[10] This difficulty of distinguishing—and orientating—interior and exterior that I investigate in Montaigne's writing and Titian's painting is also essential to Miranda Anderson's work on Renaissance subjectivity. See, for example, *The Renaissance Extended Mind*, in which Anderson examines "Renaissance notions of cognitive and subject extensions" (Anderson, 5), "the embodied, embedded, and extended nature of the

presuppose an exposed outer surface that both the self-portraitist and the reader/viewer scrutinize. Yet in attempting his own naked self-portrait, Montaigne is forced to reckon with the liminal position of exposed skin, and with the difficulty of extricating his gaze from his surroundings. Montaigne's oracle commands that humans look inside themselves and, at the same time, recognize their embodied existence as already dissipated, and in-cohesive: "your mind and your will which are being squandered elsewhere; you are draining and frittering your self away."[11] Where, Montaigne wonders, is inside, if humans already tend to be consumed by the exterior? He suggests that it is impossible to wholly grasp oneself ("*se tenir à soi*") because the human organism is not a cohesive entity.[12] The reflexive verbs *se tenir, se reconnaître, s'écouler, se répandre* die out mid-sentence and are replaced with the impersonal "on," suggesting that without cohesion, reflexive, subjective actions are impossible: "*appilez vous, soutenez vous, **on** vous trahit, **on** vous dissipe, **on** vous desrobe à vous*" (III, 9, 1001, italics mine) ("Consolidate yourself; rein yourself back. They are cheating you, distracting you, robbing you of your self" [1132]). In this way, Montaigne takes advantage of his linguistic medium to illustrate the fragility of subjective embodiment.[13] Introspection, integral to Montaigne's naked self-portraiture, reveals the fragility of cohesive, organic embodiment—which, in turn, threatens to dismantle the nakedness Montaigne would like to depict.

In the following question, the entire world becomes introspective: "Can you not see that this world of ours keeps its gaze bent ever inwards and its eyes ever open to contemplate itself?"[14] The beginning of the question continues the motif of looking but suggests the human being is relatively blind to the contemplative gaze of her environment. By means of the oracle at Delphi, Montaigne argues that human *looking* inward does not facilitate *seeing*. He writes that both interior and exterior amount to vanity but stipulates that the less spread out and separated is less vain: "It is always vanity in your case, within

---

Renaissance subject" and engages Renaissance texts in conversation with contemporary psychoanalysis and phenomenology (Anderson, 177).

[11] "vostre esprit et vostre volonté, qui se consomme ailleurs, ramenez la en soy; vous vous escoulez, vous vous rependez" (III, 9, 1001).

[12] See Anderson, p. 7: "nor does [the self] top at the skull or skin boundary."

[13] On the fragility of subjectivity, see Cynthia Marshall's *The Shattering of the Self: Violence, Subjectivity, and Early Modern Texts* in which she describes "the early modern experience of the self as fluid, volatile, and vulnerable to outside influence" (9).

[14] "Voy tu pas que ce monde tient toutes ses veues contraintes au dedans et ses yeux ouverts à se contempler soy-mesme?" (III, 9, 1001).

and without, but a vanity which is less, the less it extends."[15] The human is the least cohesive organism. All beings except for the human, Montaigne explains, are naturally absorbed in their embodied experiences, and their relation to their environment is more bounded than the human: "Except you...each creature first studies its own self, and, according to its needs, has limits to its labours and desires."[16] This human lack of boundedness in relation to the environment renders human desire equally unbounded: no creature is as empty and needy and, at the same time, no creature embraces its environment to the same degree: "No one is as empty and needy as you, who embrace the universe."[17] Human emptiness is, for Montaigne, an unfocussed way of perceiving the world, by which we look avidly without seeing or understanding: "you are the seeker with no knowledge, the judge with no jurisdiction and, when all is done, the jester of the farce."[18] Montaigne's description of humans' empty, unfocussed, and avid looking, moreover, questions the ontological cohesiveness of the human being. In an earlier chapter, Montaigne writes: "We are all patchwork, and so shapeless and diverse in composition that each bit, each moment, plays its own game" (Montaigne 296).[19] The way Montaigne conveys a dissolution of boundary between body and environment by means of an open embrace resembles Merleau-Ponty's description of phenomenology as revelation of world in *Phénoménologie de la Perception*—world being "*non pas ce que je pense, mais ce que je vis, **je suis ouvert au monde**, je communique indubitablement avec lui*" (Merleau-Ponty 1945, 17, emphasis mine). I am not suggesting a reading of Montaigne—or of Titian—through Merleau-Ponty. Rather, I propose that both Montaigne and Titian depict a *way of looking* that is lively and open.

---

[15] "C'est tousjours vanité pour toy, dedans et dehors, mais elle est moins vanité quand elle est moins estendue" (III, 9, 1001).

[16] "sauf toy...chaque chose s'estudie la premiere et a, selon son besoin, des limites à ses travaux et desirs" (III, 9, 1001).

[17] "Il n'en est une seule si vuide et necessiteuse que toy, qui embrasses l'univers" (III, 9, 1001).

[18] "tu es le scrutateur sans connoissance, le magistrate sans jurisdiction et apres tout le badin de la farce" (III, 9, 1001).

[19] Here I use Donald Frame's translation of the *Essais* – "Nous sommes tous de lopins, et d'une contexture si informe et diverse, que chaque piece, chaque moment, faict son jeu" (II, 1, 337). Anderson sets this and other passages of Montaigne in conversation with Judith Butler, showing how each question "the metaphysical given of the separateness and singularity of a person" (Anderson, 146). In this chapter, I investigate similar stakes for perception in Montaigne's writing and Titian's painting by looking specifically at nakedness.

Throughout his conclusion to "De la vanité" Montaigne intertwines human porosity with human motion and desire: we desire and embrace our environment *because* we spill and overflow our own boundaries. Human sense perception of environment facilitates the dissolution of apparent bodily boundaries. This dissolution, Montaigne demonstrates, conditions a particularly locomotive and appetitive orientation to our surroundings. In "De l'expérience," moreover, Montaigne explains that although his sole aim is to study himself—to follow the imperative "*regardez dans vous*"—he discovers an infinite multiplicity that ultimately impedes complete self-knowledge. He argues that the warning to know oneself is essential,[20] but confesses that he is overwhelmed by this task: "I who make no other profession but getting to know myself find in me such boundless depths and variety that my apprenticeship bears no other fruit than to make me know how much there remains to learn."[21] The variety and overflow of his insides makes Montaigne feel a visceral self-othering.[22] It is the process of stripping and spreading embodied material in his writing, moreover, that forces Montaigne to confront the depth and infinite variation of his body's movement in his written self-portrait. Being empty and needy constitutes an orientation towards the outside that disintegrates the material division between body and environment. In *Michel de Montaigne: Accidental Philosopher*, Ann Hartle demonstrates that Montaigne "collapses the ancient hierarchy" of ontological categories and shows how Montaigne "lowers" philosophical terms from their metaphysical heights to the accidental particular.[23] This collapse of ontological hierarchy is enabled by Montaigne's project of naked self-portraiture, but also threatens to dismantle the apparent integrity of bare skin, and the demarcation of the naked body.

In attempting to portray himself wholly naked, Montaigne is forced to confront the porosity, fragility, and multifunctionality of his bare skin. As Elizabeth Guild argues, he depicts his skin as "a porous membrane linking

---

[20] "L'advertissement à chacun de se cognoistre doibt estre d'un important effect" (Montaigne 1075) ("It must be important to put into effect the counsel that each man should know himself" [1219]).

[21] "Moy qui ne faicts autre profession, y trouve une profondeur et varieté si infinie, que mon apprentissage n'a autre fruict que de me faire sentir combien il me reste à apprendre" (III, 13, 1075).

[22] In *The Renaissance Extended Mind*, Anderson shows how a "sense of fissure and uncanniness" (Anderson, 155) underlies (in part) Renaissance self-consciousness—in her reading of another passage from the *Essais*, she argues that "the subject is presented as a soft assembled coalition, which is constantly being modified" (Anderson, 147).

[23] Hartle 164, 40.

'inside' and 'outside' rather than demarcating them," particularly in "Des senteurs."[24] Guild examines the moment in "Des senteurs" in which Montaigne describes smell as something his skin drinks—that it physically absorbs: "Whatever the smell, it is wonderful how it clings to me and how my skin is simply made to drink it in."[25] This description of Montaigne's skin destabilizes his project of naked self-portraiture: if his clean, exposed skin is already a porous membrane that can drink in substance from the outside, what does it really mean to strip away clothing or to open the integument? The very orientation of inside to outside seems suddenly dismantled. Montaigne depicts his naked skin as a living organ that, as Didier Anzieu describes, "*respire et perspire, elle secrète et élimine, elle entretient le tonus, elle stimule la respiration, la circulation, la digestion, l'excrétion et bien sûr la reproduction.*"[26] The lively, diverse functions of naked skin enable Montaigne to dismantle his body in essaying his naked self-portrait.

Montaigne's project of naked self-portraiture and consequent contemplation of exposed skin diverges conspicuously from sixteenth-century French fashions. Late sixteenth-century decadence in France leads to an exaggerated cultural focus on clothing so that, as Pierre de Lancre laments, the portrait of a sixteenth-century Frenchman is a naked man standing by a pile of cloth, scissors in hand, fashioning a new outfit.[27] Nakedness, in de Lancre's depiction of a typical Frenchman, is an interim state in a process of superficial self-fashioning.[28] Whereas de Lancre is scornful of the piles of *estoffe* used to cover and adorn the naked body, Montaigne shrewdly observes in "De mesnager sa volonté" that the distinction between clothes and the skin beneath the clothes has been lost: "*nous ne scavons pas distinguer la peau de la chemise*" ("We cannot tell our skin from our shimmy!")[29] Montaigne uses

---

[24] Guild 2014, 173.

[25] "Quelque odeur que ce soit, c'est merveille combien elle s'attache à moy, et combien j'ai la peau propre à s'en abreuver" (I, 55, 315) Montaigne, 353.

[26] "...breathes and perspires, secretes and eliminates, maintains energy, stimulates breath, circulation, digestion, excretion, and of course reproduction" (Anzieu, 14).

[27] "It is a general calumny (o courageous and warlike nation) paraded throughout Europe that the picture of a naked man with cloth by his side and scissors in his hand to make a garment after his fashion is the picture of a Frenchman" (de Lancre, cit. O'Brien 2009, 55).

[28] On fashion and self-fashioning in Montaigne, see John O'Brien's chapter "Fashion" in *Montaigne after Theory/ Theory after Montaigne*, ed. Zahi Zalloua. On the materiality of Renaissance clothing, see *Renaissance Clothing and the Materials of Memory* ed. Jones and Stallybrass. On self-fashioning in the Renaissance, see Stephen Greenblatt, *Renaissance Self-fashioning: from More to Shakespeare.*

[29] Montaigne, III, 10, 1011.

this confusion in order to illustrate how private identity becomes eclipsed by public façade so that they are indistinguishable. He first observes, "We should play our role properly, but as the role of a character which we have adopted. We must not turn masks and semblances into essential realities, nor adopted qualities into attributes of our self."[30] The confusion between shirt and skin is, for Montaigne, a confusion between *le propre* and *l'emprunté*—between what is ours and what is other. At this point, this confusion appears to be a symptom of the superficial decadence Pierre de Lancre criticizes.[31] Yet for Montaigne, the distinction between *le propre* and *l'emprunté* is muddied by the very fabric of naked skin rather than by a misguided perception of the importance of costume.

Montaigne begins "De mesnager sa volonté" by thinking about the degree to which phenomena can touch him, and to what extent he can grasp them.[32] His tactile verbs and adjectives at the opening of the chapter demonstrate Montaigne's phenomenological engagement with his bare skin and make the later confusion between skin and shirt a phenomenological problem as much as—perhaps more than—a cultural one. Montaigne uses the verb *toucher* twice in the first sentence, alongside *tenir* and *posséder*: "*Au pris du commun des hommes, peu de choses me touchent, ou, pour mieux dire, me tiennent; car c'est raison qu'elles touchent, pourveu qu'elles ne nous possedent*" ("Compared with the common run of men, few things touch me or, to speak more correctly, get a hold on me (it being reasonable for things to touch us provided that they do not take us over)."[33] In the following sentence, whereas touching is inevitable, Montaigne seems wary of being held, or grasped, by other things: "*J'ay grand soin d'augmenter par estude et par discours ce privilege d'insensibilité, qui est naturellement bien avancé en moy*" ("I exercise great care to extend by reason and reflection this privileged lack of emotion, which is by nature well advanced in me.")[34] Insensibility requires diligence and

---

30 "Il faut jouer deuement nostre rolle, mais comme rolle d'un personnage emprunté. Du masque et de l'apparence il n'en faut pas faire une essence réelle, ny de l'estranger le propre" (III, 10, 1011) (Montaigne, 1144).

31 Ben Jonson satirizes superficial decadence possibly even further in 'XLII An Elegy,' 53-4: "an officer there did make most solemn love, / to every petticoat he brushed, and glove" (cit. Anderson, 160). Whereas Montaigne wonders how the confusion of exterior surface with interior warps one's sense of self, Jonson's satirical poetry transposes that misperception onto the object of sexual desire.

32 The tactility of the opening of "De mesnager sa volonté" appears to branch out directly from the spreading and commingling of organic embodiment at the end of "De la vanité".

33 Montaigne, III, 10, 1003, emphasis mine.

34 Ibid., III, 10, 1003, emphasis mine.

practice: Montaigne is immune to many things because he has cultivated a degree of separation from surrounding phenomena. Just as few things touch or grasp Montaigne, he restrains himself from becoming overly attached to them. Although Montaigne depicts his own separation from his surroundings, he describes this separation in terms of tactility, and even embrace: "I am wedded to a few things and so am passionate about few."[35] His vision has the capacity to touch objects, the verb *attacher* suggesting a kind of tactile contact between vision and object[36]: "*J'ay la veue clere, mais je l'attache à peu d'objects; le sens delicat et mol*" ("My sight is clear but I fix it on only a few objectives.")[37] Montaigne's distinction between his senses and his employment of his senses (*l'apprehension et l'application*), moreover, is described in tactile language: "*Mais l'apprehension et l'application je l'ay dure et sourde: je m'engage difficilement*" ("my perception is scrupulous and receptive…I do not easily get involved.")[38] In this opening passage, the reader is invited to envisage Montaigne's self-depiction in terms of her own sense of touch.

Montaigne depicts human skin as both transparent and reactive. For example, in "De la force de l'imagination" Montaigne notices how the skin often betrays more than we would like and shows how our skin testifies against us—that it moves in reaction to outer stimuli more than in obedience to our desire to conceal our own reactivity.[39] Though we might wish to hide certain thoughts or emotions, our skin is a reactive surface that—precisely because it is as sensitive to its surroundings as it protects our inner organs—exposes us in its momentary reactions. Our inability to control our own skin's motion, moreover, reveals a division between the immediate reaction at its surface and how we would wish our reaction to be perceived. In this way, Montaigne depicts a kind of fragmentation of the self, happening—and perceptible—at the surface of naked skin. In "Des vaines subtilitez," a later chapter, Montaigne describes the king of Navarre articulating how certain emotions are more immediately apparent at

---

[35] "J'espouse, et me passionne par consequant, de peu de choses" (III, 10, 1003).

[36] Book IV of Lucretius' *De rerum natura* describes sight in similarly tactile terms. See also Deleuze's concept of "la vue haptique" in *Francis Bacon : logique de la Sensation* (1981).

[37] Montaigne, III, 10, 1003.

[38] Ibid., emphasis mine.

[39] "A quant de fois tesmoignent les mouvemens forcez de nostre visage les pensées que nous tenions secretes, et nous trahissent aus assistans…Nous ne commandons pas à nos cheveux de se herisser, et à nostre peau, de fremir de desir ou de crainte. La main se porte souvent où nous ne l'envoyons pas" (I, 21, 102).

the surface of the skin than others.[40] In this moment, the man's skin betrays fear in spite of his courage—the surface of his skin visibly reacts to his armor before his courage can master it.

By portraying the skin as a reactive organ we have to master, Montaigne suggests that just as our bare skin is fashioned to be more sensitive by the custom of wearing clothing,[41] so too can our bare skin be habituated and accustomed to exhibit stoic resilience. Whether the gladiator's impassive, motionless countenance or the *gémissements* of pain and desire are more authentic is not at issue. Montaigne is primarily interested in how the surface of human skin can exhibit both vulnerability and resilience—how our habits fashion the interpretability of our bare integument. Citing Cicero, he shows how the gladiator's skin exhibits resilience of character by remaining impassive.[42] Unlike the layers of clothing Pierre de Lancre describes, easily cut and refashioned, the motionlessness of the gladiator's face is the result of difficult practice. Instead of borrowing external layers to portray a borrowed character, the gladiator fashions an impassive façade of courage and valor out of his own skin. If, as Montaigne suggests in "De mesnager sa volonté," borrowed vestments confuse what is ours and what is other, then mastering the movement—the legibility—of the skin's surface is a more intimate self-

---

[40] "… Et celuy à qui ses gens qui l'armoient, *voïant frissoner la peau*, s'essayoient de le rasseurer en apetissant le hasard auquel il s'alloit presanter, leur dict: Vous me connoissez mal. Si ma chair sçavoit où mon courage la portera tantost, elle s'en transiroit tout à plat" (I, 54, 312, emphasis mine) ("…as they helped him into his armour and saw his flesh a-quiver said to them: 'You know me badly: if my skin realized where my heart was soon to take it, it would fall flat on the ground in a faint" [349]).

[41] "Ainsi je tiens que, comme les plantes, arbres, animaux et tout ce qui vit, se treuve naturellement equippé de suffisante couverture, pour se deffendre de l'injure du temps, *Proptereáque ferè res omnes aut corio sunt, / Aut seta, aut conchis, aut callo, aut cortice tectae* (Lucretius IV.936-37) aussi estions nous; mais comme ceux qui esteignent par artificielle lumiere celle du jour, nous avons esteint nos propres moyens par les moyens empruntez" (I, 36, 225) ("I therefore hold that just as plants, trees, animals and all living things are naturally equipped with adequate protection from the rigour of the weather—*Proptereáque ferè res omnes aut corio sunt, / Aut seta, aut conchis, aut callo, aut cortice tectae*—so too were we; but like those who drown the light of day with artificial light, we have drowned our natural means with borrowed ones" [253-54]).

[42] "*Quis mediocris gladiator ingemuit; quis vultum mutavit unquam? Quis non modo stetit, verum etiam decubuit turpiter? Quis cum decubuisset, ferrum recipere jussus, collum contraxit?* (I, 14, 59) ("What quite ordinary gladiator has ever made a groan? Which has ever changed his expression? Which has ever behaved shamefully whether still on his feet or beaten to the ground? And having fallen, which of them ever withdrew his neck when ordered to receive the sword?" [63]).

fashioning that ultimately penetrates more deeply. The Parisian women's practice of flaying[43] their skin to uncover a new, more beautifully complexioned layer is similarly a more superficial self-fashioning than the woman Montaigne describes piercing her skin with a sharp hairpin in order to exhibit the ardor of her promises.[44] Montaigne shows how virtue is made into a spectacle at the surface of the naked skin: either the bare skin is fashioned into a kind of armor against betrayal of fear or cowardice, or it is ruptured in order to expose strength of character. Both the skin and the shirt are used for human self-fashioning, but Montaigne suggests that the naked skin is a better material since it is unborrowed.

The porosity and transparency of bare skin in Montaigne's writing give it the pliability ideal for self-fashioning but at the same time problematize the intactness of an embodied self. Because nakedness is seen and felt at the surface of the skin, writing a naked self-portrait compels Montaigne to confront naked skin's organic motion and, as a result, to depict the gradual dismantling of his body into scattered matter. Nakedness—the driving *telos* of the *Essais*—is contingent on a transient, material surface: the exposed skin.[45] The integrity of the human organism is bound by its outer integument, yet as Montaigne examines the material surface of his own nakedness, he exposes its multifunctional capacity to breathe, absorb, excrete, and feel. In this way, Montaigne's naked self-portraiture demonstrates that the unclothed human integument is as integral to cohesive, organismal existence as it is to maintaining the consubstantial relationship between body and environment.

---

[43] "Qui n'a ouy parler à Paris de celle qui se fit escorcher pour seulement en acquerir le teint plus frais d'une nouvelle peau?" (I, 14, 59) ("Who has not heard of that woman of Paris who had her self flayed alive merely to acquire a fresh colour from a new skin?" [63]). Montaigne's use of the verb *escorcher* recalls the *écorchés* in sixteenth-century anatomy books.

[44] "…j'ay veu une fille, pour tesmoigner l'ardeur de ses promesses, et aussi sa constance, se donner du poinçon qu'elle portoit en son poil, quatre ou cinq bons coups dans le bras, qui luy faisoient craquetter la peau, et la saignoient bien en bon escient" (I, 14, 60) ("I personally saw a girl who, to prove the earnestness of her promises as well as her constancy, took the pin she wore in her hair and jabbed herself four or five times in the arm, breaking the skin and bleeding herself in good earnest" [63]).

[45] Montaigne's depiction of bare skin in the *Essais* has a kind of plasticity – see Catherine Malabou's work on plasticity in *L'avenir de Hegel*: "La plasticité caractérise encore la souplesse (plasticité du cerveau), ainsi que la capacité à évoluer et à s'adapter. C'est ainsi qu'on parle de la "vertu plastique" des animaux, des végétaux, et du vivant en général" (Malabou 1998, 21) ("Plasticity characterizes flexibility (plasticity of the brain), as well as the capacity to evolve and to adapt. Thus, one talks about the "plastic quality" of animals, of plants, and of living beings in general").

Titian: No Distinction between Skin and Flesh

Just as Montaigne's written self-portraiture willingly confronts the liminal nature of naked skin and mixes the optic and the haptic in perceiving and representing nakedness, so does Titian's late painting. Looking closely at Titian's "Flaying of Marsyas" (c. 1570-76) alongside Montaigne's written dismantling of body reveals the commingling of the visual and the tactile in both sixteenth century written and painted representations of skin and flesh. Both Montaigne and Titian demonstrate that organic integument makes definite distinctions between interior and exterior impossible. Titian captures pictorially in "Flaying of Marsyas" what Montaigne depicts in writing: environment becoming skin, and skin becoming flesh. Instead of establishing the naked skin as an intact surface, Montaigne and Titian show their reader/viewer how to see the disintegration of bare integument. Whereas, as Sarah Kay demonstrates in "Original Skin: Flaying, Reading, and Thinking in the Legend of Saint Bartholomew and Other Works," both Anzieu and Deleuze "see the self as produced through the establishment of a surface which is originally supported on the individual's skin."[46] Montaigne depicts himself naked by portraying the motion, porosity, and disintegration of skin surface and bodily interior. In looking at Titian's Marsyas alongside the *Essais*, this chapter aims to show how late sixteenth-century writing and painting reveal a dismantling gaze that, in rupturing bodies' integuments, disturbs the apparent demarcations between body and environment, and between form and ground.[47] Instead of suggesting that Titian and Montaigne are in direct conversation, this approach takes Montaigne's metaphorical link between writing and painting[48] seriously and examines how both writing and painting are capable of depicting a *way of looking* at bodies in space that upsets their integrity. In doing so, both Titian and Montaigne each appear to undertake a phenomenological project—both *"l'effort de retrouver ce contact naïf avec le monde"* (the effort of rediscovering this naïve contact with the world) and *"l'essai d'une description directe de notre experience"* (the attempt at a direct description of our experience) that Merleau-Ponty argues is the essence of

---

[46] Kay, 57.

[47] See Merleau-Ponty's *Phénoménologie de la perception*. In his chapter on "La sensation" he describes perception as distinguishing between "figure" et "fond" (form and ground) and shows how the self-organization of what we perceive is echoed by the way our body is oriented to the world.

[48] In the note to his reader Montaigne writes, "Je me *peins* tout entier et tout nud" (Montaigne 3). See also in "De la Praesumption" : "Pourquoy n'est-il loisible de mesme à un chacun de se peindre de la plume, comme il se peignoit d'un creon?" (Montaigne 653).

phenomenology.[49] In the "Apologie" chapter of the *Essais*, Montaigne describes nature as a veiled painting, or an enigmatic poem, that flickers between misleading appearances and imperfect conjecture[50]—for a painter to depict his environment, Montaigne suggests, he has to exercise his perception to unveil where the naked eye is in contact with the world, and has to paint that contact.[51] Titian's dismantling portrayal of Marsyas invites the viewer to perceive that contact.

In "Titian's Flaying of Marsyas: Thresholds of the Human and the Limits of Painting" Stephen Campbell compares Titian's depiction of Marsyas to a drawing by Giulio Romano [fig. 7.2] to show how Titian accomplishes a "creative un-making" in his later painting that redefines sixteenth-century naturalism.[52] He shows how both the "Flaying of Marsyas" and "Sacred and Profane Love," each in its own way, forge an immersive connection of viewer and painting.[53] Campbell argues that Titian's Marsyas is "the culmination of this preoccupation with bodies that might overcome their boundaries; the dissolution of bodies—not just that of Marsyas—and the radical equivalence between figure and ground, object and void."[54] This dissolution of body in Titian's painting is taken up by Daniela Bohde in "Skin and the Search for the Interior" in which she examines how skin simultaneously bears and conceals identity in both Titian's depiction of Marsyas and Michelangelo's St. Bartholomew. The exposure of the interior in both Titian's painting and in anatomical depictions of the human body, she argues, equivocate self with interiority. At the same time, in Titian's depiction of Marsyas, flesh and skin have been merged together.[55] The "radical equivalence between figure and ground" Campbell describes noticing is attributed by Jodi Cranston in *The Muddied Mirror* to Titian's oil paint medium, and the amorphousness of his

---

[49] All translations of Merleau-Ponty are mine unless otherwise indicated. (Merleau-Ponty 7).

[50] "ay-je pas veu en Platon ce divin mot, que nature n'est rien qu'une poësie oenigmatique? Comme peut estre qui diroit une peinture voilée et tenebreuse, entreluisant d'une infinite variété de faux jours à exercer nos conjectures" (II, 12, 536) ("It was in Plato (was it not?) that I came across the inspired adage, 'Nature is but enigmatic poetry,' as if to say that Nature is intended to exercise our ingenuity, like a painting veiled in mists and obscured by an infinite variety of wrong lights [566]).

[51] In *L'oeil et l'esprit*, Merleau-Ponty shows how the embodied artist, instead of recording a likeness, produces what he perceives on his canvas.

[52] Campbell, "The Flaying of Marsyas," 86.

[53] Ibid., 77.

[54] Ibid., 90.

[55] Bohde, 19.

brushwork. Examining Titian's Marsyas alongside Pietro Aretino's salacious sonnets, Cranston argues that the viewer *feels* the depicted body from the inside and shows how Titian opens the phenomenological dimension of painting. There is in Titian's later painting, she suggests, an interconnection between materiality and dematerialization. Campbell, Bohde, and Cranston each demonstrate how Titian's chosen subject and his method of depiction betray a preoccupation with material boundaries, and with how to render the fluid delineation of those boundaries.

Further, while Ovid's written depiction of Marsyas speaks—screams—in agony, Titian's Marsyas keeps his mouth firmly closed in a grimace and looks out directly at the viewer of the painting. Titian seems to reorient the moment of flaying away from the verbal and towards the visual, the silent gaze. None of the other figures in the painting look out at the viewer directly. Their eyes are downcast (the two figures on the right), directed upwards (the musician), or watching their own hands flay Marsyas (the apollonian blond and the satyr behind him). Yet Marsyas looks out towards the viewer. As though conscientious of creating a visual experience, Titian depicts Marsyas looking outwards, perhaps aware of being exposed to the viewer's gaze. The violence and agony of flayed skin is, like exposing the bare skin, closely entwined with an awareness of being looked at by an Other. Flaying, especially as it is rendered here, emphasizes the combination of the optic and the haptic in *feeling naked*.[56] The texture of the oil paint and of the brush strokes facilitates this combination and, at the same time, the specular and tactile dimensions of feeling naked—of nakedness—also facilitate the dismantling of body and the merging of form and ground.

The colors and forms of the tree branches and of Marsyas' legs blend together so that the inverted lower half of his body almost becomes part of the tree to which he is tied. This inversion, in addition to the echoing of color and form, integrates the humanlike figure of the satyr into his surroundings.[57] In this way, the painting accomplishes a simultaneous dismantling of body and dissolution of ontological categories. The figures themselves accomplish some of this dissolution: the dog lapping at the blood on the ground shows the ingestion of Marsyas' interior fluids by another organism and, as a result,

---

[56] In "Titian's Flaying of Marsyas: Thresholds of the Human and the Limits of Painting" Stephen Campbell suggests that in this and other late Titian paintings the dead or subjected body is subject of scrutiny and that, since the object has no capacity to look back, the specular becomes tactile (71).

[57] Campbell suggests Titan's Marsyas is a kind of inversion of the Vitruvian man ("Titian's Flaying of Marsyas," 67).

the continuity of matter between bodies. Titian's use of color also invites the viewer to perceive a kind of ontological homogenization: the blue of Marsyas' exposed veins is echoed in the apollonian figure's blue garment so that exterior vestments and interior blood vessels mirror one another. Similarly, the ruddy color of the blood colors the robes of the seated figure to the right so that the viewer of the painting sees the body's interior and exterior vestments blurred together in the composition of the painting. Ultimately, Titian's painting depicts the porosity between body and environment as much as the violence of flaying. In this painting, moreover, Titian embraces what Vasari argues painting should suppress: the surface materiality of the canvas and the indications of making should be concealed. For Vasari, "painting is a plane covered with patches" —Titian's painting of Marsyas also exposes the materiality of the painting itself like an anatomist exposing the materiality of human viscera under the skin.[58] Cranston describes Titian "operating on his painted subjects" yet he also seems to operate on the painting itself.[59]

Titian does more than titillate the viewer into imagining an immersive, haptic connection with the painting. In his "Flaying of Marsyas" he visually disintegrates the very boundary between interior and exterior that underlies this visual titillation. By encouraging the viewer to see skin and flesh as materially synonymous—sharing texture and color—Titian renders the impossibility of depicting nakedness and perception at once. Bare skin circumscribes the individual organism by demarcating bodily material from its surroundings. Stripping that integument then dismantles the body as a distinct entity and exposes its consubstantiality with its surroundings. Depicting flaying in painting exposes the continuity between interior and exterior matter. Whereas Ovid's Marsyas screaming "why are you stripping me from myself?" verbally articulates the violence of stripping away the naked skin, moreover, Titian's ambiguous blending of naked skin and exposed flesh in his painting manages to visually undo the distinction between integument and flesh, between interior and exterior.[60] In this way, Titian's very method of painting—his brushwork, his colors—is itself a kind of stripping. In *Le Moi-Peau*, Anzieu shows how the perception of this physical boundary between *my* body and the outside constitutes the functionality of the Skin Ego.[61]

---

[58] Cranston, 1.

[59] Ibid., 8.

[60] Campbell, 91.

[61] In Federn's work, Anzieu explains, to treat a psychotic is to help him to "se rendre compte de son corps comme partie du Moi, comme partie du monde extérieur et comme frontière entre le Moi et le monde" (Anzieu, 94) ("to notice his body as part of the Ego, as part of the exterior world and as border between the Ego and the world").

Marsyas, for Anzieu, codifies the psychic reality of the Skin Ego. Anzieu asks whether, "*si le Moi est une surface et la projection d'une surface est une structuration en Moi-Peau, comment peut-il (le Moi) passer à un autre système de fonctionnement, différencié du Moi corporel?*" ("if the Ego is a surface *and* the projection of a surface is a structuring as Skin-Ego, how can it (the Ego) transition to a system of functioning, differentiated from the corporal Ego?").[62] One of the ways of answering this, he explains, is to transform tactile experience into representations. Given the haptic quality of Titian's painting, then, Marsyas represents the disintegration of the skin barrier by means of the painter's—and viewer's—gaze, that sees flesh and skin echoed together in the texture and color of the environment.

Just as Titian's painting of Marsyas invites the viewer to perceive a kind of dissipation of skin and flesh into environment, Montaigne's naked self-portraiture exposes the consubstantiality of integument and surroundings. The introspection Montaigne strives for is counterintuitive because of the porous multi-functionality of naked skin. The open, tactile orientation of the human organism towards her environment conditions a way of looking that, as Titian's painting of Marsyas reveals, produces echoes between bodies and their surroundings. Being bounded by naked skin conditions a human way of looking that is constructed by outlined demarcations between form and ground. At the same time—on closer inspection—the porosity of bare integument facilitates a way of looking that disturbs those same demarcations and invites a painter to reveal visual continuity between one body and another. In Montaigne's written naked self-portraiture, introspection reveals internal variety that challenges cohesive representation. In turning inward, Montaigne discovers that the tactile relationship between self and world mirrors a human, inquisitive embrace of surroundings. In attempting to write a naked self, Montaigne ultimately disintegrates the skin's surface. Titian's depiction of Marsyas is similarly preoccupied with visual and tactile distinctions between skin and flesh. In attempting to portray the separation of integument from body, the painting exposes a way of looking that integrates the perception of one body into the perception of its surroundings, ultimately inviting the viewer to see glimpses of continuity between interior and exterior in her own perception. For both Montaigne and Titian, depiction—written or painted—invites an exploration of the liminal liveliness of naked skin that conditions a human way of looking.

---

[62] Anzieu, 136.

Figure 7.1: Titian's *Flaying of Marsyas* Oil on Canvas. Circa 1570-76.

Figure 7.2: Romano's *Flaying of Marsyas* Pen, Ink, and Wash over Chalk. Circa 1525-1535.

Chapter 8

'Et corps qu'est-ce?': Dismantling Body in Montaigne's *Essais* and Estienne's *La dissection des parties du corps humain en trois livres*

Elizabeth Anne Kirby

New York University

Abstract: "Et corps qu'est-ce?"— "and what is body?" Montaigne asks in the final chapter of the *Essais*. Attempting to depict himself naked (as he explains in the note to his reader) Montaigne discovers that divestment dismantles the body, and that nakedness emerges at the lively threshold of the breathing, moving, human integument. At its most visceral level, Montaigne suggests, body is unorganized matter, and motion is the essential fabric of the self. This chapter engages Montaigne's investigation of his bodily interior in conversation with Charles Estienne's 1546 illustrated anatomy. Drawing on Didier Anzieu's argument in *Le Moi-Peau* that each organism is constituted by a dialectical interaction between carapace and core, this chapter demonstrates that this dynamic between interior and exterior underlies both the human experience of nakedness and sixteenth-century anatomical study. Both anatomy and naked self-portraiture exercise a divesting, dismantling gaze by which Montaigne and Estienne each wrestle with how to look at and depict the naked body. Whereas Estienne examines the organization of a cadaver from without, Montaigne investigates his own visceral motion from within. Turning to Montaigne's description of his writing as a kind of dissection in "De l'exercitation" and reading his account of his own excrement and kidney stones in "De l'expérience," the chapter shows how, for Montaigne, the living body is always disintegrating — dismantling itself. Montaigne's introspection and Estienne's anatomizing each divest and dismantle the human body and each confronts the integumented structure of organism, body, and matter. Even as they discover that body is a question of interior and exterior, the exteriorizing depictions of sixteenth-century essayist and anatomist ultimately demonstrate the fragility and mobility of the interior-exterior binary.

Keywords: Montaigne, Estienne, skin, anatomy, nakedness, body, dissection

***

Introduction

In the final chapter of his attempts at a naked self portrait[1], Montaigne asks, *"et corps qu'est-ce?"*—and what is body? In essaying to expose himself fully to his reader, Montaigne delves past the surface of his naked skin in order to investigate—and attempt to represent—the inner workings of his body. By means of anatomical and material metaphors for his own writing, Montaigne discovers that his at the visceral level, he is made up of unorganized matter and that motion is the essential fabric of the self. For Montaigne, looking at and portraying nakedness is a process of divestment that ultimately dismantles the integrity of the body. The objectives of anatomy that underlie Montaigne's visceral imagery in the *Essais* facilitate a connection between nakedness—the *telos* of the *Essais*—and scientific investigation of anatomical organization. Both Montaigne's naked self-portraiture and sixteenth-century anatomical study demonstrate that the body as a phenomenon is a question of interior and exterior. This chapter examines Montaigne's written depiction of his visceral makeup alongside Charles Estienne's *La dissection des parties du corps humain en trois parties* (1546) in order to show that observation and depiction, shared by self-writing and natural science, necessitate exposure. Both Montaigne and Estienne show how looking and portraying involve a process of divestment that dismantles the body. At the same time, organismal unity facilitates the locomotion and perception that enable their written projects. Montaigne's depictions of visceral material and Estienne's anatomical methodology both demonstrate that the human body is a network of interconnected membranes, and that bodies are contiguous with their environment.

In "The Body's Moment" Jean Starobinski argues that, whereas Andreas Vesalius and Leonardo da Vinci transform the body into a spectacle, an Other at which we look, Montaigne's knowledge emerges from his bodily experience,

---

[1] "…je m'y fusse tres-volontiers peint *tout entier et tout nud*" ("I would most willingly have portrayed myself *whole, and wholly naked*" [1]). All citations refer to the Villey-Saulnier edition of the *Essais* (2004) and Michael Screech's English translation (2003).

from his sense perception.[2] By characterizing Montaigne's body-writing in relation to an anatomist and a painter, Starobinski invites other readers of Montaigne to consider the *Essais* in conversation with sixteenth-century anatomical study and painting. This chapter reexamines Starobinski's comparison by investigating Montaigne's depiction of his viscera alongside Estienne's anatomy, in order to demonstrate how the vantage point of anatomist converges with that of self-portraying essayist. In *The Body Emblazoned*, Jonathan Sawday shows how anatomical study fashions a new image of the human interior in the Early Modern period, and argues that this leads to a reconfiguration of self-hood.[3] The concept of body in the context of anatomizing, Sawday argues, is a question of interior and exterior,[4] and this preoccupation with configurations between interior and exterior provokes a distinction between *the* body and *my* body.[5] The preoccupation with exposure and this navigation of interior and exterior in Early Modern anatomical study, I will show in my reading of Montaigne and Estienne, intersects with the stakes of Montaigne's attempts at naked self-portraiture. Montaigne's anatomical self-depiction, moreover, results from his aim to depict a fully naked self in his writing. In "Montaigne Anatomiste" Jean Céard compares Montaigne's anatomical self-depiction in the *Essais* to a child in Pierre Boaistuau's *Histoires prodigieuses*, who is born with his stomach open and his intestines on view.[6] Montaigne's aim in writing the *Essais*, Céard argues, is to exhibit himself as if he were on a dissection table.[7] Reading the passage of "De l'exercitation" in which Montaigne uses the metaphor of a skeleton to describe his own writing, Céard draws attention to Montaigne's choice of the Greek *skeletos* over the French *squelette* and explains that for sixteenth-century French anatomist Ambroise Paré the Greek word specifically signifies the composition and structure of the skeleton. At the same time, he points out, Montaigne clearly wants to exhibit his veins, muscles, and tendons in addition to his bare bones.[8] Céard's reading of this passage in "De l'exercitation" demonstrates Montaigne's efforts to show the

---

[2] Jean Starobinski. 1983. "The Body's Moment." *Yale French Studies*, no. 64, 276.

[3] Jonathan Sawday, *The Body Emblazoned* (London: Routledge 1995), ix.

[4] Sawday, *The Body Emblazoned*, ix.

[5] Ibid., 7.

[6] Jean Céard, "Montaigne Anatomiste." *Cahiers de l'Association internationale des etudes françaises*, no. 55 (2003): 314-15.

[7] "Le dessein de Montaigne, c'est de s'étaler tout entier, de s'exposer tout entier, de se donner à voir tout entier, comme sur une table de dissection" (Céard, 313) ("Montaigne's design is to fully spread himself out, to fully expose himself, to fully show himself, as if on a dissection table").

[8] Céard, "Montaigne Anatomiste," 313.

inner workings of his body to his reader and not merely his external surface. Montaigne, writes Céard, "*oppose la 'montre' partielle, externe et incertaine du corps, au temps où il était vivant, et la montre complète, interne, et évidente de celui-ci que permet son anatomie*"[9] ("opposes partial 'exhibition,' external and unsure of the body, when he was alive, to the complete, internal, and obvious exhibition that his anatomy allows").[10] Like Sawday, Céard demonstrates a direct connection between anatomical investigation and self-knowledge: self-knowledge and both anatomical investigation and depiction are central to Montaigne's project[11] and the empirical connection between self-knowledge and anatomy continues into seventeenth-century anatomical studies. For example, seventeenth-century anatomist Nicolas Habicot's book title, *La semaine ou pratique anatomique, par laquelle il est enseigné par Leçons le moyen de disassembler les parties du corps humain les une d'avec les autre, sans les intéresser,* emphasizes how anatomy is essentially a taking apart, a fragmentation. The book's title page, moreover, announces that it is "*utile et nécessaire à ceux qui désirent parvenir à la parfaite connaissance d'eux-mêmes*"[12] ("useful and necessary to those who desire to achieve perfect understanding of themselves"). Montaigne's project of naked self-portraiture necessitates a similar investigation of the human interior yet, as I will show, the dismantling of body in the *Essais* is tempered by Montaigne's realization that anatomizing self-scrutiny ultimately muddies self-perception.

Reading Montaigne alongside Charles Estienne's illustrated anatomy text demonstrates that motion between clothing and nakedness, and the fraught distinction between clothes and skin, are as pervasive in sixteenth-century French anatomists' thinking about the human body as they are in the *Essais.* Both Montaigne and Estienne divest the body of its integument and dismantle its structure, and both are explicit about their project of portraiture. In his introduction, Estienne writes that he has included illustrations, "***portraits*** *des choses que pensions estre plus necessaires comme des os, ligaments, nerfs, veines et arteres*"[13] ("portraits of things that we thought were the most necessary, such as bones, ligaments, nerves, veins, and arteries") and tells his readers, "*vous plaira contenter vostre fantaisie des* ***portraits et figures*** *que trouverez en cette oeuvre jusqu'a...puissiez recouvrer quelque corps d'homme a*

---

[9] Céard, "Montaigne Anatomiste," 314.

[10] All translations are mine unless otherwise indicated.

[11] Céard, "Montaigne Anatomiste," 302.

[12] Céard, "Montaigne Anatomiste," 302.

[13] Charles Estienne, *La dissection des parties du corps humain, divisee en trois livres.* (Paris, 1546).

decoupper"[14] ("your imagination will enjoy these portraits and figures that you will find in this work until you are able to find a human body to take apart"). Whereas Montaigne compares his self-portraiture with a *plume* to an artist's with a *creon,*[15] Estienne compares his anatomical representations to painting: *"si les ecrits contentent l'esprit et la memoire aussi pouvons nous dire que la peinture contentera l'oeil et la vue de la chose absente"*[16] ("if writing satisfies the mind and the memory we can also say that painting satisfies the eye and vision with the absent thing"). Like Jean de Léry in his *Histoire d'un voyage*[17] and sixteenth-century herbalist Leonhart Fuchs,[18] Estienne instructs his readers to read text and image in conversation: *"les ecrits supplient la parole et les protraits (combien que muets) portent la forme et facon des choses devant les yeux en sorte qu'ils n'ont autre mestier de parole"*[19] ("the writing provides speech and the portraits (as mute as they are) have the form and fashion of things before the eyes so that they, too, speak"). The combination of text and image provides a complete representation in which the form, fashion, and description of the body merge into one explanation of human anatomy. Just as Montaigne aims to write a naked self-portrait, Estienne's anatomy writing aims to expose *and* to describe.[20] Estienne also understands description and depiction to be intimately entwined with knowledge.[21] In these ways, Montaigne's method of naked self-writing resembles the natural science and anatomy writing published twenty years before the first edition of the *Essais*[22].

---

[14] Ibid., 2, emphasis mine.

[15] Montaigne, Michel de. 2004. *Les Essais.* Edited by Pierre Villey. (Paris: Presses Universitaires de France), 653.

[16] Estienne, *La dissection des parties du corps humain*, 6, emphasis mine.

[17] "ce qu'outre la susdite description, je vous ay bien voulu encore representer par la figure suyvante, du danseur et du sonneur de *Maraca*" (Léry, 402) ("in addition to the description below, I also wanted to represent the dancer and Maraca player by means of the following figure").

[18] In the preface to his herbal, Fuchs explains, "En iceulx j'ay comprins en premier lieu, brefvement et en bon ordre la description d'une chascune plante. Puis apres jai mis *les protraitz* et figures d'icelles" (Fuchs, 11, emphasis mine).

[19] Estienne *La dissection des parties du corps humain*, 7.

[20] "exposer et descrire" (Estienne, 253) ("to expose and describe").

[21] Ibid., 217.

[22] Montaigne was acquainted with Swiss physician and natural historian Felix Platter, whose collages of preserved plants emphasized the role of representational images in medicine. See Florike Egmond's *Eye for Detail: images of plants and animals in art and science, 1500-1630*, 50.

Charles Estienne: Anatomy as Divesting

In addition to insisting on the integral role of perception and representation in scientific inquiry, Estienne's language explicitly describes dissection in terms of undressing throughout his book. For both Estienne and Montaigne, the body is a configuration of layered integuments. Estienne's anatomical methodology and Montaigne's introspective self-writing both work to strip away integuments like vestments and to depict what lies underneath, though from opposing vantage points. Whereas Montaigne's written undressing ultimately dismantles his own body, Estienne's anatomy unclothes several cadavers in order to represent anonymous archetypes of male and female bodies that he—and his reader—can use to visualize their own internal structures. Estienne's book is meant to re-present the anatomy of the cadaver he carefully opens before an audience so that the reader can recognize the skeletal and muscular strucutres, viscera and organs concealed beneath her own skin. There is nothing written, he explains, "*que nous n'ayons diligemment apperceu et connu a l'oeil...par la dissection de plusieurs corps*"[23] ("that we haven't diligently perceived and known with our eyes...by means of the dissecting of several bodies"). He explains that anatomy investigates parts of the body that we cannot immediately see.[24] Estienne, like Montaigne, describes his portraiture project as exercise.[25] For Estienne, scientific understanding of anatomy involves both *stripping* away coverings and *depicting* what the naked eye can capture. To dis-cover the workings of the body, he has to undress it. In the table of contents he maps out for his reader the design and function of the body, including its envelopes and membranes, clothing and covering. Estienne's division of the chapters of his book reveals that the integrity of the body is maintained by layers of vestments, from the "*cuir exterieur*" ("outer pelt")[26] to the inner membranes and envelopes

---

[23] Estienne *La dissection des parties du corps humain*, 2.

[24] "l'inquisition des parties du corps qui ne sont pas appercues par l'oeil" (Estienne, 4) ("the investigation of the parts of the body not perceived by the naked eye").

[25] "*L'exercitation* des professeurs en écrivant les matières anatomiques" (Estienne, 6, emphasis mine) ("the exercise of professors in writing anatomical materials"); "Les livres m'ont servi non tant d'instruction que *d'exercitation*" (III, 12, 1039, emphasis mine) ("Books have been useful to me less for instruction than as training" [1176]) .

[26] In Helkiah Crooke's *Mikrokosmographia* (1615), the skin is "an vnseamed garment couering the whole bodie" (Crooke 72, cit. Anderson 159). An earlier example of this vestment metaphor is in Erasmus's *De Civilitate Morum Puerilium*. Erasmus draws a parallel between clothing, "forme and fassion of the bodie" and "the habyte and apparyle of the inward mynde" (sig. B3r, cit. Anderson 159). Erasmus's vestment metaphor suggests the structural parallel between exterior and interior may have ramifications for thought.

wrapping muscle and organ tissue. The arrangement of these layers of clothing-integuments, moreover, structures the body's design and appearance—the "*façon ordinaire*" of a naked body that Montaigne aims to illustrate—rather than one exterior surface in Estienne's anatomy.[27] As Estienne reveals body to be structurally contingent on integumentation, his anatomizing also suggests that embodied subjectivity is inseparable from the relationship between an interior and an exterior. The orientation of interior to exterior of the living body is dismembered and inverted by dissecting a cadaver—as the anatomist investigates the cadaver's viscera as a substitute for his (and others') own insides. In this way, Estienne gestures towards the bodily subject's capacity for displacement towards dead matter. This substitution of the cadaver for understanding of the living body underlines the impossibility of visually perceiving one's own viscera or original fundament. In Jeffrey Masten's chapter on Leo Bersani's essay "Is the Rectum a Grave" and Early Modern English literature, he shows how the Early Modern English word "fundament" emphasizes a conception of the body attached to and articulated around the rectum and digestive tract.[28] Estienne's vestment-integument imagery for dissection similarly points to a bodily organization around a central integumentary structure—the digestive tract. Thinking of the digestive tract as foundational origin (both structurally and gestationally) is substantiated by modern science: the invagination of the digestive tract is the *beginning* of cellular bodily growth. Whereas Masten argues that the fundamental position of the large intestine up-ends traditional bodily-social hierarchies, I suggest here that the visceral and superficial membrane structures in Estienne's anatomy are in-verted by dissection. Rather than conceptualizing the body in terms of head and tail, moreover, Estienne's fascination with internal membrane structures illustrates embodiment in terms of inside and outside—in the anatomy, turned inside-out.

Estienne notices in his dissections how this network of integuments functions at once as protective covering, structural adhesive, and porous conductor. His dissections reveal that body is really constituted by this membranous network.[29] Integumentation emanates from the skeleton to the

---

[27] In *Le Moi-Peau,* Anzieu similarly describes the skin as "un ensemble d'organes differents" (Anzieu, 13) ("a collection of different organs").

[28] See Chapter Seven of *The Body in Parts* (1997), edited by David Hillman and Carla Mazzio.

[29] "faut dire ny avoir un corps qu'une membrane continue par tout: laquelle procede des os et fait son discours a toutes les autres parties jusqu'au dedans de la peau" (Estienne, 88) ("a body only needs one continuous membrane throughout: which proceeds from the bones and makes its way to all the other parts into the skin").

outer surface: the integument is, for Estienne, what makes a body a body.[30] He describes the double function of the outer layer of the pulmonary artery as both its "*vetement et couverture*" ("vestment and covering") and seam holding blood vessel and lung tissue together.[31] In his chapter on the pericardium, Estienne explains that its name means "*un vêtement et couverture entourant le coeur*"[32] ("a vestment and covering surrounding the heart"). Each bone is "*vestu de sa propre membrane*" ("clothed with its own membrane") so tightly that "*a grand peine les peut-on separer des os*"[33] ("it is very difficult to separate them from the bones"). This structure facilitates the function of the bones' membranes to join the skeleton together.[34] In this way, Estienne discovers in the cadaver that the living body's motion is facilitated by a network of integuments that protect, connect, and breathe. His vestment metaphor for the membranes throughout human anatomy helps Estienne to illustrate the slippage between skin and organ, membrane and bone, and how often the anatomist struggles to draw a substantial distinction between an individual part and its integument. The clothing-like "tunique" designates a clothing, protective function of an inner part[35]: "*quand on l'appelle **membrane** c'est à cause de sa substance et quand on le nomme **tunique** c'est à raison de son usage et office*"[36] ("one calls it membrane for its substance and one calls it tunic for its function and purpose"). These protective membranes are bodily *tissue* in both senses—the brain's membrane, for example, looks like the threads of spiders' webs: "*tellement estrainte et embrassée la cervelle qu'il semble qu'elle luy soit unye et naturelle...elle ne se remonstre que comme quelque bien tenue et delyée toile d'araigne*"[37] (the brain is so constrained and embraced by it that [the membrane] seems naturally united with it...it is only visible as a well-kept, unraveled spider's web"). By comparing the brain's

---

[30] Anzieu shows how this definition of body by its integument structures different kinds of psyches in *Le Moi-Peau* when he argues, "tous systèmes psychiques obéissent à une interaction dialectique entre écorce et noyau" (Anzieu, 37) ("all psychic systems obey one dialectical interaction between carapace and core").

[31] "cette membrane qui retient et arrete toutes les pieces des poumons ensemble" (Estienne, 87) ("this membrane that retains and holds all the pieces of the lungs together").

[32] Estienne, *La dissection des parties du corps humain*, 227.

[33] Ibid, 88.

[34] "car le membrane qui couvre quelque os autour de la jointe est aussi par le moyen d'icelle jointe commune a l'autre" (Estienne 1546, 88) ("for the membrane that covers a bone around the joint also joins the bones together").

[35] For example, "les tuniques des intestins" (Estienne, 182) ("the tunics of the intestines").

[36] Estienne, *La dissection des parties du corps humain*, 243, emphasis mine.

[37] Ibid. 259.

membrane to threads of spider's web, Estienne emphasizes the likeness between bodily membrane and woven, vestment-like textile,[38] further blurring the distinction between clothing, skin, and inner anatomy.

Estienne suggests that the design and function of the intact body is facilitated by its network of integuments and at the same time shows how the membranes of, for example, individual bones are practically inseparable from their inner matter. As he navigates the relationship between corpus and integument, he also makes an effort to distinguish between flesh and body—the muscles (each encased by their own membrane) are pieces of flesh[39] and their function, Estienne argues, is like that of clothing. These pieces of flesh cover and ornament the as yet unformed mass that is the human body[40]: musculature protects against blows and extreme temperatures and, at the same time, functions as a kind of ornament.[41] Flesh covers and ornaments the body and by doing so gives it its natural form[42]—what might this mean, incidentally, for Montaigne's aim to depict his "*façon naturelle*"? Covering and ornamentation are distinct ways of relating to human nakedness[43]—Estienne's description of human musculature collapses these together by demonstrating how musculature gives form to the body while protecting and clothing the skeleton. Like muscle, human breasts serve to cover and adorn the heart[44] and "*rechauffent comme les vetemens de laine*"[45] ("they warm like woolen clothing"). Estienne captions a couple of his printed illustrations of musculature "*le devant du corps **revestu** de ses muscles*"[46] ("the front of the

---

[38] In Crooke's *Mikrokosmographia* (1615), this vestment metaphor for nervous tissue intertwines structure with function: nerves are "membranes wherein the Braine itself is inuested" (Crooke 824, cit. Anderson 103).

[39] "pieces de chair" (Estienne, 90) ("pieces of flesh").

[40] "couvrent et ornent cette rude masse n'ayant encore sa forme naturelle" (Estienne, 90) ("cover and ornament this raw mass that doesn't yet have its natural form").

[41] "contre les coups donne couvertrure...il nous eschauffe contre le froid...et contre le chaud il donne ombre...très bonne couverture contre les dangers exterieurs...quelque defense sert encore de singulier ornement à ce corps" (Estienne 1546, 90) ("gives protection against blows...it keeps us warm against the cold...and against heat gives shade...very good protection against external dangers...some protection serves as a singular ornament to this body").

[42] See Sawday on dissection and thinking about "design, fashioning, and fabric" of the human body in the sixteenth century (Sawaday, The Body Emblazoned, 6).

[43] Ornamentation and clothing, different relations to nakedness, are contrasted in both Montaigne's "Des cannibales" and Léry's *Historie d'un voyage.*

[44] "couvrir et garner le coeur" (Estienne, 217) (to cover and to decorate the heart").

[45] Estienne, *La dissection des parties du corps humain*, 217.

[46] Ibid., 96, emphasis mine.

body reclothed with its muscles"), and "*deux figures desquelles la premiere est du tout **desnuée** de sa chair*"[47] ("two figures of which the first is completely stripped of its flesh"), suggesting that the anatomist is divesting and reclothing cadavers [fig. 1]. Estienne's language asks his readers to consider: can a corpse be naked? This question diverges from Montaigne's introspective attempts at naked self-portraiture in that for Montaigne, as this chapter will demonstrate, the essential fabric of the self is *motion* and nakedness exists at the lively threshold of the human integument. For Montaigne, a cadaver might be able to show the anatomist the structural organization of internal and external membranes, but nakedness—contingent on the organismal integrity of the human body—vanishes. Montaigne and Estienne converge methodologically: whereas Montaigne's attempts at naked self-portraiture ultimately dismantle the body, Estienne's dissection of the body—and his subsequent depictions of the dismantled body—conceptualize the dissected cadaver in terms of clothing and nakedness.

In the third section of his anatomy book, in which Estienne explains how to dissect, he writes that the anatomist should cover "*la face et la partie honteuse dudict corps a ce que le regard d'icelles parties ne puisse retirer et distraire la fantaisie des spectateurs*"[48] ("the face and the shameful part of this body so that the gaze of these parts cannot distract the imagination of the spectators"). If the face and the genitalia of the cadaver have to be covered, and if these parts have a gaze ("regard") that can distract the public—and perhaps even the anatomist—then the cadaver seems to retain its capacity to be naked, if only in relation to its dissectors and spectators. Nakedness is, for Estienne, a visual phenomenon and the naked body—even after dying—has a certain capacity to confront the anatomist's gaze. The capacity to feel naked depends on a capacity to look and to feel looked at—in Estienne's anatomy, this visual dynamic is sustained, but warped, between anatomist and cadaver. The anatomist strips the corpse apart in place of his own body, in order to see, to describe and, eventually, to depict an approximate likeness of his own inner organization—what Montaigne calls "*la presse domestique que j'ay dans mes entrailles et dans mes veines*" in "De mesnager sa volonté"[49] ("I have enough to do to order and arrange those pressing affairs of my won which lie within my veins and vitals").[50] The cadaver is of course devoid of life, motion, and the capacity to feel naked—but the surface of the cadaver troubles the anatomist enough to be

---

[47] Ibid., 92, emphasis mine.
[48] Estienne, *La dissection des parties du corps humain*, 374.
[49] Montaigne, *Les Essais*, 1004.
[50] Montaigne, *The Complete Essays*, 1135.

endowed with a kind of initial nakedness. The anatomist's main objective—*to look* inside the body—facilitates the metaphorical connection between stripping and dissecting. Estienne captions another print: "*le corps mort **desnué et despouillé** de sa gresse: avec la separation et distinction d'iceux*"[51] ("the dead body stripped of its fat"). In order to anatomize the parts of the body, Estienne has to strip them away, so that the anatomy book portrays the human cadaver in varying states of undress: "*desgarny de son cuir...revestu de sa gresse*"[52] ("unadorned of its pelt...reclothed with its fat"). Once the genitalia are divested of their integument, the cadaver might appear less disarming, and make the anatomist feel less as though he is looking at a naked body. Nakedness is an essential facet of human anatomical observation, and consequently of the anatomy texts, like Estienne's, published in the sixteenth century.[53] The only way to investigate a living body instead of a cadaver is to observe *from the vantage point* of that body—that is, what Montaigne essays to depict. The only way anatomy can be viewed as a spectacle, on the other hand, is as a cadaver. Estienne and Montaigne are, in this sense, each attempting self-depiction from different vantage points, each wrestling with how to look at and depict nakedness.

Montaigne's Dismantled Body

Whereas in "Au lecteur" Montaigne uses un-anatomized matter to connect his body to his writing,[54] in "De l'exercitation" Montaigne uses an anatomically organized metaphor for his *Essais*, which he breaks down in order to reveal that the motions and emotions of the uncovered body constitute his essential fabric. Diverging from Richard Regosin's reading of exposure in the *Essais*, which focuses on the incarnation—the becoming body—of Montaigne's thoughts, I consider here how Montaigne strips his own flesh and bone of their protective integument in his writing and examine the ways Montaigne's exposure of his interior organs problematizes what and where body is. Regosin suggests that Montaigne's writing stages a kind of ontogenesis from a

---

[51] Estienne *La dissection des parties du corps humain*, 99, emphasis mine.

[52] Ibid., 151.

[53] In *Dissection on Display*, Christine Quigley shows how the history of dissection reveals the ways in which it was a public spectacle—often, dissection was "a dramatic violation of family honor through publicly exposing the naked body" (Quigley, 78). The voyeuristic dimension of anatomical study is, as Jonathan Sawday argues in *The Body Emblazoned*, a consequence of the impossibility of gazing within our own bodies—making the interior of other bodies so compelling (Sawday 1995, 5, cit. Quigley, 3).

[54] "Ainsi, lecteur, je suis moy-mesmes la matiere de mon livre" (Au lecteur, 3) ("And therefore, Reader, I myself am the subject of my book" [1]).

mass of unformed pieces of flesh.[55] Montaigne's writing as a mode of undressing, however, strips his self-depiction so far as to dismantle the body into flesh and bone, kidney stones and excrement. His writing captures a "subject informe" and, in essaying his "façon naturelle et ordinaire", Montaigne fragments the apparent integrity of embodied existence instead of fashioning an *entire* portrait ("tout *entier* et tout nud").[56]

In "De l'institution des enfans" Montaigne shows how unexciting prose is stripped of flesh—and consequently of meaning.[57] The incisive writing Montaigne attempts himself, on the other hand, skins the body to reveal his flesh. In "De l'exercitation" for example, the flesh initially appears organized into distinct structures: "Je m'estalle entier: c'est un skeletos où, d'une vue, les veines, les muscles, les tendons paroissent, chaque piece en son siege"[58] ("I am *all* on display, like a mummy on which at a glance you can see the veins, the muscles and the tendons, each piece in its place".[59] But this uncovered body is jostled by the motions and emotions in the following sentence: "L'effect de la toux en produisoit une parti; l'effet de la palleur ou battement de coeur, un'autre, et doubteusement"[60] ("Part of me is revealed—but only ambiguously—by the act of coughing; another by my turning pale or by my palpitations").[61] These motions, Montaigne insists, are not accidental to the self, but its essential fabric: "Ce ne sont mes gestes que j'escris, c'est moy, c'est mon essence"[62] ("It is not what I do that I write of, but of me, of what I *am*").[63] The verb "étaler" already suggests a kind of dissipation of Montaigne's bodily matter—that it is spread out into displayed fragments—yet Montaigne's syntax moves in opposition to that of a scalpel, from his skeleton into his veins, muscles and tendons. The reader is invited to look *from* the skeleton ("*où, d'une vue…*") *onto* surrounding structures that move Montaigne's body.

---

[55] Regosin Richard. 1977. *The Matter of my Book: Montaigne's Essais as the book of the self.* (Berkeley: University of California Press), 248.

[56] In Cynthia Marshall's *The Shattering of the Self: Violence, Subjectivity, and Early Modern Texts,* she opposes self-shattering and self-fashioning in Early Modern literature.

[57] "J'avois trainé languissant apres des parolles Françoises, si exsangues, si descharnées et si vuides de matiere et de sens…" (I, 26, 147). See Regosin, Richard. 1977. *The Matter of my Book: Montaigne's Essais as the book of the self.* Berkeley: University of California Press.

[58] Montaigne, *Les Essais,* 379.

[59] Montaigne, *The Complete Essays,* 426.

[60] Montaigne, *Les Essais,* 379.

[61] Montaigne, *The Complete Essays,* 426.

[62] Montaigne, *Les Essais,* 379.

[63] Montaigne, *The Complete Essays,* 426.

Montaigne's project of naked self-portraiture, in dismantling his body, enables him to examine the insufficiency of language to pin down any kind of universals. Contemplating the insubstantial, verbal contestations of the Reformation in "De l'expérience", Montaigne considers his mineral insides and asks bluntly, what is body? *"Une pierre c'est un corps. Mais qui presseroit: et corps, qu'est-ce?—Substance,—et substance quoi? ainsi de suite, acculeroit en fin le respondant au bout de son calepin...la test de Hydra"* (III, 13, 1069) ("A stone is a body.—But if you argue more closely: 'And what is a body?'—'Substance'— 'And what is substance?' And so on' you will eventually corner your opponent on the last page of his lexicon...it is a Hydra's head"[64]).[65] Here Montaigne dismantles the concept of body as he strips body down to substance. If a stone is a body, does it follow that Montaigne's *gravelle* are also tiny bodies, or are they merely fragments of mineral matter? Spreading his own matter, Montaigne is lead to an impasse: what is body? Material substance is as far as Montaigne seems willing to strip body down, since he neglects to pursue the hydralike multiplicity of his lexicon. At the same time, however, Montaigne implies that stripping anatomical organization down to material tissues will lead to a multifarious body instead of an intact, singular body.

It is language, moreover, that Montaigne wrestles with—and seems to find insufficient—as he questions what body is. This moment in "De l'expérience" disputes the compatibility of Montaigne's chosen written medium for self-portraiture with his own embodiment. As Regosin rightly argues, "to speak of entity and of language as an incarnating medium extends the implications of the book as interiority externalized, as the invisible made visible, and echoes another incarnation, one also expressed in the juxtaposition of word and substance."[66] Montaigne's exposure of his inner material organization in his skeletal metaphor for his own writing is precisely the kind of externalization and making visible Regosin describes. Yet the image of Montaigne spread on a dissection table, together with his excremental metaphors in "De la vanité," do even more to dismantle the concept of body than to incarnate.

Like Estienne's anatomical investigation, Montaigne's bodily—and psychological—introspection strips away his integument, so that his naked self-

---

[64] Ibid., 1213.

[65] See Antoine Compagnon's *Nous, Michel de Montaigne*. Compagnon shows how in this instance Montaigne's line of questioning demonstrates his hesitant attitude towards universals. Ann Hartle also suggests in *Michel de Montaigne: Accidental Philosopher* that there is a "nominalist slant to the Essays" so that for Montaigne, only particulars truly are (58).

[66] Regosin, *The Matter of My Book*, 199-200.

portraiture dismantles his body and exposes the fragile porosity of the intact, naked body. The self-depiction in this chapter of the *Essais* emphasizes the material motion of Montaigne's viscera[67] and consequently shows how Montaigne's body is consubstantial with his environment, taking in and excreting surrounding matter through pores and orifices. In "De l'exercitation" Montaigne's depiction of mental introspection mirrors both the activity and structure of the digestive tract. Montaigne's adjective *espineuse* gives a tactile, sensuous quality to mental agitation: "*C'est une espineuse entreprinse, et plus qu'il ne semble, de suyvre une alleure si vagabonde que celle de nostre esprit*"[68] ("It is a thorny undertaking—more than it looks—to follow so roaming a course as that of our mind's").[69] To essay the interior of one's own vagabond mind—to expose it in a written portrait—is a prickly, uncomfortable enterprise. In the second half of the sentence, essaying resembles vivisection: "*de penetrer les profondeurs opaques de ses replies internes; de choisir et arrester tant de menus airs de ses agitations*"[70] ("to penetrate its dark depths and inner recesses, to pick out and pin down the innumerable characteristics of its emotions").[71] The mind is made up of moving folds that resemble the folds of the small intestine and that need to be dissected—or vivisected—in order to pinpoint individual movements. Essaying a depiction of one's own psychological and visceral depths requires a self-othering in which Montaigne writes as both anatomist and as the body on the table. Whereas Estienne substitutes a cadaver for his own body and for the bodies of his readers and spectators, Montaigne essays a written vivisection of his own insides and, in the process, engages directly with the motion of visceral matter.

The opening of "De la vanité," in which Montaigne depicts writing as mental excrement, suggests that writing is the medium best suited to the moving, living nakedness he is essaying. Montaigne's excremental metaphors for his writing allow him to depict not just excrement but also excretion: they demand that the reader examine Montaigne's bodily processes as much as— perhaps more than—his bodily material. Montaigne's description of a man who communicates literally by means of his bowel movements accentuates the exhibitionism that is central to his naked self-portraiture: "*Si ay-je veue un*

---

[67] See Drew Leder's *The Absent Body*. He argues that the viscera "disappear" from our immediate experience of our environment because we do not use them for perception. Montaigne, on the other hand, depicts how his viscera *appear* and makes them visible to his reader.

[68] Montaigne, *Les Essais*, 378.

[69] Montaigne, *The Complete Essays* 424.

[70] Montaigne, *Les Essais* 378.

[71] Montaigne, *The Complete Essays*, 424.

*Gentilhomme qui ne communiquoit sa vie que par les operations de son ventre: vous **voyez** chez luy, **en montre,** un ordre de bassins de sept ou huict jours"*[72] ("Thus did a nobleman I once knew reveal his life only by the workings of his bowels: at home he paraded before you a series of seven or eight days' chamber pots").[73] Moreover, it literalizes and materializes what the Oracle at Delphi says at the end of the same chapter[74]. By describing this man, Montaigne is able to literalize his own metaphor of excrement for reading and thinking: "*c'estoit son estude, ses discours; tout autre propos luy puoit*"[75] ("He thought about them, talked about them: for him any other topic stank").[76] Though Montaigne exposes his mental excrement in a slightly more civilized way by writing it, he maintains a metaphorical connection between mind and digestive tract, and explains the fluctuating quality of the *Essais* by pointing to the shared mortality of mind and viscera: "*Ce sont icy, un peu plus civilement, des excremens d'un vieil esprit, dur tantot, tantot lache et toujours indigestes*"[77] ("Here (a little more decorously) you have the droppings of an old mind, sometimes hard, sometimes squittery, but always ill-digested").[78]

The form of Montaigne's written medium—the *essai*—mirrors Montaigne's undigested excrement. He slides deftly from his metaphor ("*ce sont icy des excremens*") to reminding his reader that his writing *represents* moving and mutating thoughts: "*Et quand seray-je a bout de **representer** une continuelle agitation et mutation de mes pensees, en quelque matiere qu'elles tombent, pusique Diomedes remplit six mille livres du seul subject de la grammaire?*"[79] ("And when shall I ever have done describing some commotion and revolution of my thoughts, no matter which subject they happen upon, when Diomedes wrote six thousand books on the sole subject of philology?").[80] Montaigne's excremental metaphor for his writing enables him to depict his thinking as constant motion between interior and exterior. His initial question about writing his thoughts incorporates Lucretian motion, change, and matter: his thoughts are as yet unformed matter that is in continuous

---

[72] Montaigne, *Les Essais,* 946.
[73] Montaigne, *The Complete Essays,* 1070.
[74] "Regardez dans vous, reconnoissez vous, tenez vous à vous" (III, 9, 1001) ("Look back into yourself; get to know yourself; hold onto yourself" [1132]).
[75] Montaigne, *Les Essais,* 946.
[76] Montaigne, *The Complete Essays,* 1070.
[77] Montaigne, *Les Essais,* 946.
[78] Ibid., 946.
[78] Montaigne, *The Complete Essays,* 1070.
[79] Montaigne, *Les Essais,* 946, emphasis mine.
[80] Montaigne, *The Complete Essays,* 1070.

agitation and mutation. In this way Montaigne's medium of representation imitates the embodied, mutating motion and thinking of its subject.

Montaigne's explicit comparison of writing to excrement in "De la vanité" emerges from his aim to write a naked self-portrait. Montaigne's writing about excrement also exposes the consubstantiality of body and environment and the porosity between them. The *Essais* are not so much swollen with extra material as they spread out and expose textual matter.[81] Both Montaigne's excrement and his *gravelle* are kinds of bodily excretion—material that is part of Montaigne until it is exteriorized. Excretion and stripping both exteriorize—and consequently make visible—bodily tissue, but in distinctive ways. Montaigne's depictions of his inner anatomy show his reader what is beneath his skin, whereas purging rids the body of waste matter. Montaigne's *gravelle* and his mental and physical excrement are exterior, material traces of inner bodily movements that subsequently acquire their own, independent vitality. Montaigne's attempts to portray his nakedness, on the other hand, constitute a purging of exterior, superfluous outer layers. Like stripping, purging from the inside eliminates the superfluous. Each mode of exteriorizing—undressing and excreting—are motions contingent on the integrity of bodily interior and exterior, yet exteriorizing also underscores the fragility and mobility of this interior-exterior binary.

Montaigne uses writing to depict his undressed anatomy and at the same time uses his own anatomy to depict his writing. Exposing what lies beneath the surface of his skin ultimately reveals Montaigne's mortality: age complicates and interrupts the material composition and movement of his organs. *"L'age affoiblit la chaleur de mon estomac; sa digestion en estant moins parfaicte, il renvoye cette matiere crue à mes reins. Pourquoy ne pourra...nature s'acheminer à prendre quelque autre voye de purgation?...Pourquoy non ces excremens, qui fournissent de matiere à la grave"*[82] ("Old age reduces the heat of my stomach, which therefore digests things less perfectly and dispatches waste matter to my kidneys: so why [shouldn't]...Nature find some other means of purging it?...why

---

[81] Referencing Montaigne's admission "j'ajoute mais je ne corrige pas" (III, 9, 963), Gisèle Mathieu-Castellani suggests in "Des excréments d'un vieil esprit: Montaigne Coprographe" that for Montaigne excrement is a supplement that resembles the many additions "qui gonflent le corps de l'essai" (Mathieu-Castellani, 16). See also "Excremens d'un vieil esprit: le register corporel dans les Essais" in which Maria Proshina examines Montaigne's parallel between ingestion/digestion and education/imitation in order to show how his excrement metaphor for written material diverges from the image of clothing for borrowed textual material in Erasmus.

[82] Montaigne, *Les Essais*, 1093.

not then those excretions which furnish the raw material for my gravel?").[83] His verbs *affaiblir, renvoyer,* and *fournir* (to weaken, to send, to provide) portray Montagine's visceral movements, of which the kidney stones (and excrement) are traces. The kidney stones facilitate at once a more intimate self-portrait than a merely unclothed Montaigne—they emerge from his most intimate insides— and a complete dismantling of the body upon which his nakedness depends.

Depicting his kidney stones and excrement problematizes for Montaigne where body begins and ends. In divesting his body of both clothing and skin, he discovers that at his most intimate depths his body consists of constantly moving matter.[84] In "De l'expérience" Montaigne depicts his *gravelle* almost as an independently acting entity, a living organism coexisting with his own bodily matter. He establishes that living itself is a kind of disintegrating motion, that alters and scatters bodily material: "*Mais tu ne meurs pas de ce que tu es malade; tu meurs de ce que tu es vivant...la cholique est souvent non moins vivace que vous*"[85] ("You are not dying because you are ill: you are dying because you are alive...your colic is often no less tenacious of life than you are").[86] Whether sick or healthy, the living body is always disintegrating. *La cholique* is similarly alive: it consists of the production and motion of tiny pieces of gravel (kidney stones) and eventually ceases—or dies—once the human body is no longer hospitable: "*il se voit des hommes ausquels elle a continué depuis leur enfance jusques à leur extreme vieillesse...vous la tuez plus souvent qu'elle ne vous tue*"[87] ("we know of men in whom it has lasted from childhood to extreme old age...Men kill the stone more than it kills men."[88] The apparent dysfunction of the human digestive tract is for Montaigne merely another accident of embodied existence.

Instead of depicting his kidney stones as foreign matter, Montaigne shows his reader that inside he is made of rocks, and that these rocks' motion is part of his life, rather than part of an invasive illness. He writes that they purge him from superfluities, working to rid his body of waste matter:

---

[83] Montaigne, *The Complete Essays,* 1241.

[84] See Cynthia Marshall's *The Shattering of the Self: Violence, Subjectivity, and Early Modern Texts* in which she places Early Modern conceptualizations of a *dispersive* self (Marshall, 10) and of a "fluid, volatile and vulnerable self" (Marshall, 9) in dialogue with modern psychoanalysis. The dispersiveness she sees in Early Modern subjectivity more generally is, I argue, apparent in explicitly bodily terms in Montaigne's writing.

[85] Montaigne, *Les Essais,* 1091-92.

[86] Montaigne, *The Complete Essays,* 1239.

[87] Montaigne, *Les Essais,* 1092.

[88] Montaigne, *The Complete Essays,* 1239-40.

Depuis ma cholique je me trouve deschargé d'autres accidens, plus ce me semble que je n'estois auparavant, et n'ay point eu de fievre depuis. J'argumente que les vomissemens extremes et frequens que je souffre me purgent... et nature vuide en ces pierres ce qu'elle a de superflu et nuysible.[89]

The kidney stones have eliminated other accidents and materials from Montaigne's body, but these excretions are difficult to endure. The motion of kidney stones is still an acute suffering, even if they are a way to naturally rid the body of other accidents and useless matter. By accentuating the painful effects of kidney stones and by designating them as superfluous material, Montaigne emphasizes the disease's otherness: the kidney stones may be materially generated inside his body, but their motion acts on his body independently. They begin as his most intimate matter but are at the same time an othered, superfluous material his body automatically eliminates.

Whereas other diseases disrupt the functionality of the whole body, Montaigne explains that kidney stones do not impede all of our faculties. Montaigne keeps the actions of other diseases in the third person, maintaining their otherness by describing their actions *on* the human organism:[90] "*Les autres maladies ont des obligations plus universelles,* **geinent** *bien autrement nos actions,* **troublent** *tout nostre ordre et* **engagent** *à leur consideration tout l'estat de la vie*"[91] ("The constraints of other illnesses are more all-embracing: they are far more restricting on our activities, upsetting our normal ways of doing anything and requiring us to take account of them throughout the entire state of our lives").[92] The first verbs, *gener, troubler,* and *engager* describe all illnesses except kidney stones acting on the whole body. They disrupt the organization and movements of the body ("nostre ordre, nos actions") and as a result maintain embodied attention at all times. Montaigne's use of the inclusive "nous" for general bodily organization resembles the

---

[89] Montaigne, *Les Essais,* 1094. "Since my stone I find that I have been freed from the load of other ailments and that I seem to feel better than I ever did before. I have not had a temperature since! I reason that the frequent and extreme vomiting which I suffer purges me...Nature voiding with those stones all her noxious superfluities" [1242].

[90] See Jean-Luc Nancy's essay "The Intruder" in *Corpus*. Nancy describes his own heart transplant and questions the degree of otherness of this new organ grafted into his body. Montaigne's kidney stones are not transplanted, but they are similarly othered in his description.

[91] Montaigne, *Les Essais,* 1094, emphasis mine.

[92] Montaigne, *The Complete Essays,* 1242.

archetypal illustration of human anatomy by his contemporaries—bodily organization is shared between Montaigne's embodiment and his reader's.

Kidney stones, on the other hand, do not convulse the body as a whole, but only pinch the skin so that understanding, will, and language remain untouched: "*Cette-cy ne faict **que pinser** la peau; elle vous **laisse** l'entendement et la volonté en vostre disposition, et la langue, et les pieds, et les mains; elle vous **esveille** plutost qu'elle ne **vous assopit**"*[93] ("Mine does no more than pinch the epidermis: it leaves you free to dispose of your wit and your will as well as of your tongue, your hands and your feet. Rather than battering you numb, it stimulates you").[94] *La cholique* shifts physical suffering from the universal to the particular and as a result heightens physical awareness of a particular pain. In leaving Montaigne his faculties of understanding, desire, and language, kidney stones awaken his bodily awareness instead of weakening and deadening physical sensation ("*elle vous esveille plustot qu'elle ne vous assopit*"). In addition to shifting from the third person plural in the first sentence to the third person singular in the second, Montaigne switches from a universal *nous* ("*nostre ordre*") to a demonstrative *vous*: "*elle **vous** laisse l'entendement et la volonté en **vostre** disposition…elle **vous** esveille plutost qu'elle ne **vous** assopit.*" The direct object pronoun nestled between the subject (*la cholique*) and the verbs emphasizes the otherness of the disease, acting on the body as a foreign entity.

In distinguishing kidney stones from other diseases, Montaigne explains that, unlike other afflictions, *la cholique* does not debilitate the psyche. The sequence of passive verbs in the following sentence establish the active position of disease with respect to the passive psyche: "*L'ame est frapée de l'ardeur d'une fievre, et **atterrée** d'epilepsie, et **disloquée** par une aspre micraine, et en fin **estonnée** par toutes les maladies qui **blessent** la masse et les plus nobles parties*"[95] ("It is your soul which is attacked by a burning fever, cast to the ground by epilepsy, dislodged by an intense migraine and, in short, struck senseless by those illnesses which attack all the humours and the nobler organs").[96] The psyche is struck by fever, distressed by epilepsy, fragmented by intense migraines, and overwhelmed by the illnesses that wound the whole. The only active verb, *blesser*, is done by illnesses to the living organism. Kidney stones, Montaigne tells his reader, are nothing like this because they do not attack the psyche: "*Icy, on ne l'ataque point*"[97] ("Such

---

[93] Montaigne, *Les Essais,*1094, emphasis mine.

[94] Montaigne, *The Complete Essays,*1242.

[95] Montaigne, *Les Essais,* 1094, emphasis mine.

[96] Montaigne, *The Complete Essays,* 1242.

[97] Montaigne, *Les Essais,* 1094.

are not attacked in my case").[98] In this case, the mind is in charge of its own wellbeing, and of steering itself. "*S'il luy va mal, à sa coulpe; elle se trahit elle mesme, s'abandonne et se desmonte*"[99] ("If things go ill for my soul, too bad for her! She is betraying, surrendering, and disarming herself").[100] It is the mind's fault if it suffers, Montaigne explains, because it splinters from itself. The reflexive verbs Montaigne chooses in this sentence, *se trahir, s'abandonner,* and *se desmonter* all capture a kind of fragmentation, but *se desmonter* specifies a kind of stripping apart—a dismantling of the psyche from itself. Dismantling, Montaigne suggests, can become an autoimmune, destructive disintegration. The only thing to do, Montaigne argues, is to allow the material of the kidney stones to hold together and to behave as a cohesive body within his own body's viscera. Only irrational people (whose minds have been partially dismantled) are persuaded that the hard mass produced inside our kidneys can be disintegrated by intervention: "*Il n'y a que les fols qui se laissent persuader que ce corps dur et massif qui se cuyt en nos roignons se puisse dissoudre par breuvages*"[101] ("Only fools let themselves be persuaded that a solid, massy substance concocted within our kidneys can be dissolved by draughts of medicine".[102] The kidney stone will be excreted no matter what medications we ingest: "*parquoy, depuis qu'il est esbranlé, il n'est que de luy donner passage; aussi bien le prendra il*"[103] "So, once it starts to move, all you can do is to grant it right of passage: it will take it anyway".[104]

Just as kidney stones are resistant to pulverization, Montaigne notices how mercury resists being molded by the children's hands. Towards the beginning of "De l'expérience," Montaigne's ruminations on the representation of nature in painting and language lead to an image of children playing with mercury. This image follows a line from Seneca, arguing that excessive division ends with a disintegration of order: "*Confusum est quidquid usque in pulverem sectum est*"[105] ("Cut anything into tiny pieces and it all becomes a mass of confusion."[106,107] This confusion is then embodied in the mercury that the children *essay* to mold together into one solid mass: "*Qui a veu des enfants*

---

[98] Montaigne, *The Complete Essays,* 1242.
[99] Montaigne, *Les Essais,* 1094.
[100] Montaigne, *The Complete Essays* 1242.
[101] Montaigne, *Les Essais,* 1094.
[102] Montaigne, The Complete Essays 1242.
[103] Montaigne, *Les Essais,* 1094.
[104] Montaigne, *The Complete Essays* 1242.
[105] Montaigne, *Les Essais,* 1067.
[106] Ibid., 1094.
[107] Montaigne, *The Complete Essays* 1209.

essayans de renger à certain nombre une masse d'argent vif?"[108] ("Have you ever seen children making assays at arranging a pile of quicksilver into a set number of segments?".[109] By using the verb *essayer* here Montaigne aligns his self-writing with the children's attempts to organize and grasp slippery mercury. The textual material of the *Essais*—which Montaigne compares to excrement, kidney stones, and other bodily material in the same chapter—has the same tendency as quicksilver to divide and move in spite of Montaigne's *essais* to represent it all together. The following sentence suggests that writing mental excrement and shaping it into a naked self-portrait resembles poking and prodding at quicksilver, ultimately agitating it so much that it escapes artifice: "*Plus ils le pressent et pestrissent et s'estudient à le contraindre à leur loy, plus ils irritent la liberté de ce genereux metal: il fuit à leur art et se va menuisant et esparpillant au delà de tout compte*"[110] ("The more they press it and knead it and try to make it do what they want the more they exasperate the taste for liberty in that noble metal: it resists their art and proceeds to scatter and break down into innumerable tiny parts").[111] Like the dissipation of the human individual Montaigne describes at the end of "De la vanité,"[112] the image of mercury in "De l'expérience" captures matter's resistance to any kind of containment—and consequently to any kind of stable perception, or representation.

Conclusion

The objectives of sixteenth-century anatomy—to perceive and to represent the internal mechanisms of the human body—establish a connection between anatomy and nakedness. The body is, in both cases, a question of the relationship between interior and exterior. In Estienne's anatomical study, and in Montaigne's written self-portraiture in particular, depicting the body often demands a representation of *exteriorizing* the internal. Both self-writing and scientific investigation are contingent on the empirical connection between observation and depiction: to know something, including one's own body, involves representing perceived phenomena. Estienne's anatomical study and

---

[108] Montaigne, *Les Essais*, 1067, emphasis mine.

[109] Montaigne, *The Complete Essays* 1209.

[110] Montaigne, *Les Essais*, 1067.

[111] Montaigne, *The Complete Essays,* 1209-10.

[112] "vostre esprit et vostre volonté, qui se consomme ailleurs, ramenez la en soy; vous vous escoulez, vous vous respandez…on vous trahit, on vous dissipe, on vous desrobe à vous" (III, 9, 1001) ("Bring yourself back to your self your mind and your will which are being squandered elsewhere; you are draining and frittering yourself away. Consolidate yourself; rein your self back. They are cheating you, distracting you, robbing you of your self" [1132]).

Montaigne's written self-portraiture, however, approach the body from opposing vantage points. Whereas the anatomist investigates the cadaver from without in order to see an approximation of his own internal organization, Montaigne depicts the motion of his viscera from within, including the effects of these movements on his whole organism. Estienne's methodology and language establish that the human body is ultimately a network of integuments and that the anatomist's process of investigation, in divesting the body, dismantles the integumentary structure. Montaigne's project of naked self-portraiture aims to divest the body of superfluities, consequently discovering the visceral layers of the body to be a constant exteriorizing of unformed matter. The complex, unstable configurations between bodily interior and exterior dismantle apparent boundaries between body and surroundings, and expose the continuity between living body and environment.

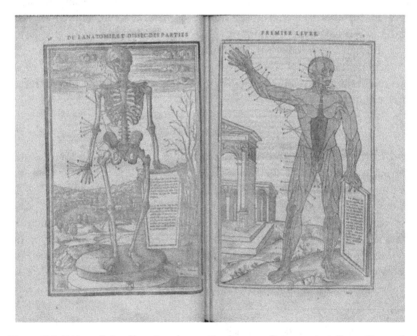

Figure 8.1: Estienne's *La dissection des parties du corps divisee en trois livres.* Simon de Colines, Paris 1546.

Chapter 9

Gardens in the Anatomy Theater: Recreating the Garden of Eden in Leiden's Anatomy Theater

Kaleigh Hunter

Bergische Universität Wuppertal

Abstract: This chapter explores anatomy theaters and their relationship to botanical spaces and concepts through depictions of Leiden University's anatomy theater and the ways in which this space used the garden of Eden to display ideas of morality and death. The anatomy theater and botanical garden were aspects to the grander "theater of knowledge," each working independently and complimenting each other in the pursuit of understanding natural history. Knowledge between these two spaces would be shared throughout the year: winter dissections to explain the physical causes of illness and summer observations of plants to be used in their treatment. Observations of both the body and of plants worked together to create a more complete view of the study of medicine. This relationship can be seen on the engraved title pages of garden catalogs from Leiden, which often display the theater in the distance. Each space was complimented with collections. Just as botanical gardens are "living collections" for the study of botany, so do the dissections performed in the theater add a more vivid and temporary addition to the other objects of wonder displayed in the room. This chapter identifies the anatomy theater as not solely a space for dissection, but as a complimentary factor to the botanical garden in understanding the natural world and a place where the garden of Eden is used to contemplate morality.

Keywords: Botany, Anatomy, Leiden, Mortality, Eden

***

Introduction

In the early seventeenth century, Jan Jaszn Orlers published a description of the city of Leiden, under the appropriate title *Beschrijvinge der stad Leyden*. The still-young university of the city was described in detail, especially the many new academic facilities offered there. After describing the botanical garden, Orlers moves on to the anatomy theater where he writes on the uses and layout of the room. The skeleton of a man and woman under a tree is mentioned as a reference of the death of mankind.[1] After noting this detail, he goes on to list the many other animals whose bones also accompany the humans before describing other items from this collection, such as dried human intestine, a piece of a human skin, and medical tools used for dissection. He goes on to discuss the dissections that would take place in the coldest months and the people who would attend them — not only students of medicine, but anyone who wanted an education on the "self" — before moving on to describe the university's library.[2] This description, although brief, touches upon the many different aspects of the anatomy theater: a space of curiosity and religious morality not solely for anatomical dissections.

With each description of different facilities at the university came illustrations in a similar style to the engraving series of Leiden University done by Willem van Swanenburgh, after Jan Cornelis Woudanus, in 1610. The university was well equipped with the most current types of facilities of its time such as the aforementioned permanent anatomical theater, library, botanical garden, and collections of curiosity that made it a popular destination. The account by Jan Jaszn Orlers was only one of many travel accounts of both Leiden and its university and was also not the only one to make use of illustrations. The four copperplate engravings of Leiden University published in 1610 display many of the ways in which studies of the natural world were approached in The Netherlands during the sixteenth century, especially the ones of the botanical garden and anatomy theater. Another engraving of the anatomy theater in 1609 by Bartholomeus Dolendo also displays it in a similar fashion, including the Adam and Eve recreation, which have now been moved aside to frame the dissected body.

The anatomy theater specifically holds many details that reflect ideas regarding natural history of the sixteenth and seventeenth centuries, especially in the small detail of Eden which both Orlers describes, and engravings of this room display. The use of this reference as a tale on morality

---

[1] Orlers 1614, 149.
[2] Ibid., 149.

is clear, however, it also gives further insight into the intertwined relationship between the different spaces of knowledge at the university and the ways in which the natural world was studied and understood. The anatomy theater and botanical garden in Leiden were both established in fairly close succession and this closeness is clear in their early history. The anatomy theater was more than a space for dissections; these depictions of it reflect the many other roles that both the theater and the study of anatomy played in seventeenth century thought. The collections housed within this room created a microcosm of nature and accentuated the complicated task of understanding both the human body and nature as a whole. Not only do the objects housed within this space transform it beyond the scope of anatomy, but the ways in which they are displayed highlight the emblematic and moralistic thinking that came with natural history. Tim Huisman discusses the history of Leiden's anatomy theater in detail in *The Finger of God* and describes the multifaceted role of this space and its 1610 depiction: "The role of the prints as well as the role of the skeletons is in keeping with the humanist ideal of moral education and emblematic imagery..."[3]

This chapter looks at how the Leiden anatomy theater reflected certain mindsets regarding the study of natural history; how it was one part of the larger whole of studying nature, alongside the botanical garden and collections; and how the theater, garden, and their collections were used in similar ways to pursue knowledge. There are many ways in which this theater encompasses these concepts, however, the detail of Eden, as can be seen in seventeenth-century references, is an especially potent aspect of this space that highlights many of the ideas which will be discussed here. Leiden's anatomy theater makes for an interesting study of these ideas, as its explicit visual display of Eden is somewhat unique. The goal of this chapter is to explore one of the ways that the natural world was studied in the sixteenth and seventeenth centuries and how the Leiden anatomy theater reflected these pursuits.

Establishing the Garden and Theater at the University

Both the botanical garden and anatomy theater were established at Leiden University in the latter half of the sixteenth century. Having direct access to nature as an object of study to accompany texts was gaining in popularity, especially within the realms of natural history. Nature itself, in some areas of thought in the sixteenth and seventeenth centuries, was regarded as a book written by God full of as much knowledge as Scripture: "the book of nature."[4]

---

[3] Huisman, 37-38.
[4] Jorink, 71; Smith, 160-161.

These new spaces of knowledge allowed for hands-on contact to nature, creating access to the "book of nature" to accompany the literal books of the library.[5] As Eric Jorink describes it in *Reading the Book of Nature in the Dutch Golden Age*: "Nature was a book of God's wonders that lay waiting to be read, understood and pondered."[6] The idea of nature as a book next to scripture was a prominent method of study in the Dutch Republic during this time.[7] Nature was something created by God that possessed certain kinds of knowledge that could be learned through direct "reading" of this book. The motto for the emblem of Aadriaan van der Venne reflects these ideas where "God is visible in the miniature" is accompanied by an illustration of men in a garden examining the plants.[8] The idea that an invisible God can be seen in the visible world of His creation is something echoed in texts on natural history and anatomy.[9]

In 1588, a Lutheran pastor, Conrad Rosbach, complied an illustrated book of plants titled *Paradise Garden* for the purpose of readers to take into fields to read about the plants they encountered.[10] This book presents an example not only of a growing interest in studying the physical plants alongside texts, but also expands upon how the study of nature was also a spiritual pursuit, as each plant was accompanied with descriptions of their medical uses and spiritual meanings.[11] While this book does encourage the reader to use it in nature, the author compiled the text through consulting both herbals and scripture. These sources of studying nature were intertwined and physical spaces such as botanical gardens would become a part of this network. These are the types of mindsets that brought on the need for facilities like a botanical garden and anatomical theater. Paula Findlen discusses these spaces (anatomy theater, botanical garden, and natural history collections), describing them as: "...a direct result of the medical fascination with experience in the early sixteenth century."[12] Direct, "living" counterparts to texts were important for studies of the natural world. These needs would be filled at the Leiden University in the latter half of the sixteenth century.

---

[5] Crowther, 224; Jorink, 71-72.
[6] Jorink, 11.
[7] Huisman, 58.
[8] Jorink, 71.
[9] Crowther, 203; Jorink, 232.
[10] Crowther, 213.
[11] Ibid., 213.
[12] Findlen, 273-274.

The *hortus botanicus* was established in 1594 as one of the earliest institutionalized botanical gardens of this kind after their introduction in Pauda in 1545.[13] An early professor of medicine at Leiden, Pieter Pauw, played a large role in the establishment of both the botanical garden and the anatomy theater; however, he will be discussed in more detail when discussing the latter space. Another figure who had a strong impact on the early history of the botanical garden was Carolus Clusius, the director of the garden from 1592 who would remain in Leiden until his death in 1609.[14] Clusius had a strong network throughout Europe and was able to procure a large variety of plants for the garden. The hortus began to gain a renowned esteem under the direction of Clusius and his established reputation. He had an interest in plants beyond their medical uses with a specific affinity for plants known for their beauty and rarity.[15] Unlike Pauw, as we will see later, Clusius' responsibilities and focuses did not land on teaching or directly working in the garden. Instead, his resources for acquiring a variety of rare plants and his ability to identify them were valuable and during his time at the garden, some of his prized exotics (specifically, the tulip) were on display near the garden entrance.[16] The garden itself, while primarily a medical garden, did go beyond only medical uses. At one point, one section delt specifically with poisonous plants.[17] The usefulness or interests in plants, even in the context of a botanical garden for medical study, had far-reaching goals more than simply displaying plants of medical value. Beyond the content of the garden itself, this larger intention can be seen in the inclusion of the *naturalia* collection that followed the establishment of the garden. In 1599, the *ambulacram* was constructed along the western wall of the garden to shelter visitors in bad weather and plants in the winter.[18] For students, the garden would be a living counterpart to their texts where they could identify what they read.[19] Access to plants was a primary use of this garden, but this space was also used to study nature on a larger scale.[20] This collection of *naturalia* would accompany this space, creating a more complete view of the natural world. Other objects such as maps and prints would also be included in this

---

[13] Grämiger, 236.
[14] Swan, 178.
[15] Grämiger, 249.
[16] Ibid., 240, 249.
[17] Ibid., 246.
[18] Ibid., 180.
[19] Jorink, 71.
[20] Ibid., 175.

collection.[21] This collection housed many exotic animals, and ethnographic objects that would complement the exotic plants growing in the garden were large components to this collection. The 1610 Swanenburgh print displays these exotic objects on the lower boarder, showing the many types of objects other than living plants that could be seen when visiting the garden and its *ambulacram.* Both the practical and wonderous aspects of the garden are on view with, in this case, more focus on the wonderous.[22]

Not long after the establishment of the botanical garden, discussions began for a permanent space for anatomical dissections. As mentioned, Pauw had much influence over this construction of Leiden's anatomy theater and the early state of its collection. Pauw studied not only in Leiden, but also Rostock and Paris before eventually travelling to Padua, an influential site for anatomical research and the main institution where Andreas Vesalius prepared his *De Humani Corporis Fabrica.*[23] Upon his return to Leiden in 1589, he would perform a public human dissection in the *Faliede Bagijnkerk* that same year. The *Faliede Bagijnkerk* was a secularized church whose different facets would be used by the university for lectures, but plans for more permanent uses in this building would begin around 1590. The university library would be moved into this repurposed church and plans for a more permanent dissection space in this same building also began. Construction of the theater began in 1591 and was completed in 1594.[24]

Pauw had many contacts with many people outside of the field of medicine, such as artists and others within Dutch humanist circles, one of whom was the beforementioned Orlers.[25] These relationships reflect the flexibility of interest in subjects like anatomy, which was not bound specifically to medical students or practitioners.[26] The theater was not limited to a purely academic audience: it was a public space and dissections were open to anyone who wanted to know more about man and by extent God. The theater was open for anyone who wanted to learn about the human body, themselves, wonderous aspects of nature, or God through both observation and contemplation of dissections and the collection of curiosity. Pauw would also start this collection of curiosities, which would evolve with new professors of anatomy

---

[21] Swan, 180.

[22] Ibid., 182.

[23] Huisman, 21.

[24] Huisman, 74.

[25] Huisman, 37.

[26] Ibid., 37.

over time; he had also initiated the *ambulacram* at the botanical garden.[27] Pauw put a strong emphasis on this emblematic view of studying nature, which is clearly reflected in this early display of the theater. The study of anatomy in this century went beyond just the human body, but it worked as an effort to understand oneself, the role of humans on earth, and morality.[28] Findlen writes that "the Dutch theaters engaged more actively with the religious connotations of dissection as an art that inquired into the secrets of life through the observation of death."[29] She notes how the objects Pauw put in this space, specifically the skeletons of humans and animals along with the Latin phrases, were used for "moralizing the deaths of many of the criminals whose bodies ended up on the dissecting table."[30] The aspiration to study one's "self" can be seen in the description by Orlers referenced earlier and within the anatomy theater itself with the phrase "know thyself" on display. To study the human body intently was to study one of God's greatest creations and dissections were public affairs to provoke wonder in this workmanship.[31]

This relation of knowing oneself in both an anatomical and spiritual sense is reflected in anatomical texts from this time as well. In *Microkosmographia: A Description of the Body of Man* from 1615, a section dedicated to "How profitable and helpfull Anatomy is to the knowledge of God" describes the use of anatomy and dissections as a method to gain knowledge of oneself that can lead to the more "useful profit" of gaining knowledge of God.[32] The human body was an elaborate piece of creation that could be directly observed for spiritual gain. To further quote *Microkosmographia*, "infinite goodnesse and bounty of God shineth in this excellent workemanship."[33] God is referenced as either a workman or author in relation to the body and the "frame of body" itself is mentioned as "The Book of God."[34] Walter Ryff's 1541 anatomical text also reflects many of these same ideas as he states that investigations of the construction of one's body can bring man nearer to knowledge of God.[35] Pauw emphasized the study of anatomy as a study of both "body and soul" to contemplate the world and humankind's place within it; as Tim Huisman puts

---

[27] Swan, 180.

[28] Huisman, 37.

[29] Findlen, 278.

[30] Ibid., 278.

[31] Crowther, 56, 61-62; Waddington, 101.

[32] Crooke, 14-15.

[33] Ibid., 14-15.

[34] Ibid., 14-15.

[35] Crowther 2010, 205.

it, the Leiden anatomical theater was a "place of edification".[36] Johnathan Sawday in *The Body Emblazoned* describes the 1610 print of the Leiden anatomy theater as reflecting its status as a place for more than simple dissections, and also, "the theater was an architectural lesson in human mortality – a cabinet of death."[37] He also notes how the positioning of the skeletons also displays not just the story of Eden, but specifically the exact moment of the Fall, as Eve is extending the fruit to Adam.[38] Adam's spade and the skeletal appearance of the figures both give reference to the results of this offering of fruit while simultaneously displaying the moment before it happens.

This relationship to theology and anatomy was not limited to spaces like anatomy theaters or anatomical treatises. Medical metaphors or examples would sometimes be used in sermons or religious texts, specifically in Reformed Pietistic literature where detailed medical procedures or anatomical descriptions could be used as moralistic metaphors to accompany religious discussions.[39] The human body alone was not the only way the anatomy theater offered reflection. The theater was fitted a collection of animal skeletons that held their own associations. Animals could hold specific religious or moral implications and were included in these collections; for example, storks, which embody lessons on practicality and loyalty as opposed to the swan that warns against laziness or bad temperament.[40] The *naturalia* itself among these collections, along with their medical values, encouraged religious reflection as nature was, within itself, an object of knowledge created by God.[41] These two spaces were not only connected through being two "halves" of the same pursuit, but also by their identical methods of that pursuit.

The anatomy theater and the garden were closely linked as being two parts in the larger role of studying medicine and understanding nature. Cluadia Swan, in *Art, Science, and Witchcraft*, describes these two intuitions as "twin provinces of medical study."[42] These two places were indeed two parts of the same goal of studying medicine. The garden would be used in the warmer seasons and the anatomy theater in the winter, allowing for observations of both physical ailments on the body and their remedies throughout the year. This closeness among the garden, theater, and collections of curiosities can be

---

[36] Huisman, 10-11, 37.
[37] Sawday, *The Body Emblazoned*, 73.
[38] Ibid., 73.
[39] Lieburg, 137.
[40] Crowther, 208-209.
[41] Jorink, 71; Smith, 160.
[42] Swan, 54.

seen in many visual representations of these spaces. This is clear in the earlier mentioned engravings of the university from 1609 and 1610, where the anatomy theater especially is displayed both in use for dissection and as a space to display its collection.

The four copperplate engravings of Leiden University published in 1610 show that the botanical garden has pieces from its own collection on display on the boarder, giving a similar effect to the print of the anatomy theater where the space would be somewhat incomplete with some view of their collection of curiosities. The many different uses of each space are on display simultaneously, especially in the example of the theater. Like the depiction of the garden, the theater is shown in multiple roles. It is currently in use for a dissection while the collection of curiosities is in full display. People are roaming the space, discussing what is on display with one group in the bottom right corner handling flayed skin. The theater is not being depicted in a specifically realistic way, but in a way that reveals all its seasonal uses: as a space for dissection and to display its collection. Like the garden, the collection that accompanies this space is important to display, even if it is not an accurate portrayal. All of these facilities — the garden, theater, and collections — worked together and relied on one another to create a complete view of nature. For instance, Gregory Grämiger gives an example of kidney stones to show the connections between the garden, anatomy theater, and collections. Specifically, the bladder of Issac Casaubon and kidney stones (an affliction Clusius also suffered from) that were a part of the anatomy theater's collection.[43] In this example, a specific ailment could be viewed in the theater and its remedy in the garden when other objects relating to this affliction (bladders or kidney stones) could be viewed in the collection of curiosities.

The relationship between the anatomy theater and botanical garden can also be seen in other prints from this time. In the 1615 engraving by Stock, after Jacques de Gheyn II, which displays Pauw giving a public dissection, lavender can be seen scattered on the dissection table and floor of the theater to mask the scent of the dissection, showing the usefulness of plants in this endeavor.[44] This detail of including plants also matches the dedicatory poem that describes Pauw as a "Botanist and Anatomist" and was framed with some copies of this print.[45] This type of visual relationship is not confined to Leiden, as can be seen on the title page to *Pancreas Pancrene* (1668), where a dissection is taking place in the foreground while the botanical garden can be seen in the distance.

---

[43] Grämiger, 246-247.
[44] Swan, 60.
[45] Ibid., 60.

Botanical references in general can also be seen with anatomical illustrations. The 1613 collection of anatomical flap engravings by Lucas Kilian uses an oversized flower as one of the flaps covering Adam. The use of plants or references to botany as part of the study of medicine can be seen in similar examples. Not only botanical references, but moralizing imagery was also common for anatomy beyond the anatomy theater of Leiden.

Botany and anatomy held a close relationship during this period, and Pieter Pauw emphasizes this when he mentions his dual province of "anatomy and botany" in his 1615 *Primitiae anatomicae*, as these two fields were the responsibility of professors of medicine.[46] The botanical garden, anatomical theater, and their collections were all aspects of natural history, both independently and also as a larger whole.[47] While each held their own unique roles that can be individually observed, their relationships to each other transform these spaces into more than just a garden or room for dissection. The collection in the anatomy theater achieves similar goals to that of the garden, but the use of this room as a place to display these objects and the way in which they are displayed greatly illustrated the emblematic and moralizing thinking towards natural studies. Like the garden, the collected objects on display within the theater complimented this space in multiple ways and their portrayals on the copperplate engravings of Leiden University encompass the roles of the anatomy theater in natural history and humanistic thought.

Eden, Gardens, and Anatomy

With this broader understanding of the use of collections to study and understand nature, the example of the Adam and Eve in the anatomy theater can be used to further explore these ideas. The story of Eden was a potent biblical reference for many aspects of natural history; however, for the scope of this chapter, its use in anatomy and botany will be the focus. This section focuses on the reference to the story of Eden, how it was used in discourse for both botany and anatomy, and how its use in the anatomy theater in Leiden encompasses and accentuates all the ideas presented in this chapter.

References to Eden and the fall of mankind highlight the network of associations within natural history during the Renaissance. Eden specifically had strong associations with both botany and anatomy. Adam and Eve were sometimes used in anatomical illustrations. The 1613 collection of anatomical engravings by Lucas Kilian uses Adam and Eve along with other moralizing

---

[46] Swan, 56.
[47] Jorink, 278.

images such as the snake from Eden and a skull. In editions of Adam Lonitzer's medical text, *Kreuterbuch*, Adam and Eve are sometimes used multiple times at the beginning of sections, such as the 1593 edition that displays Adam, Eve, and the Tree at the beginning of the section on plants and again at the section on animals. This scene of Eden also appears on the title page to the second edition of Helkiah Crooke's anatomical text, *Microkosmographia: A Description of the Body of Man* (1651). A direct reference to Eden displayed in an anatomy theater was not only found in Leiden; a description of an anatomy theater for Barber-Surgeons in London also includes a detail of a skeletal Adam and Eve recreation added in 1645.[48] While the lessons on the fragility of life are clear when it comes to the story of Eden, there were many more associations.

The figure of Adam represented a primordial knowledge that he possessed, wisdom directly from God, an Adamic knowledge that was lost after the fall of mankind; he used his wisdom to give all plants and animals their name. The garden of Eden and its lost knowledge held an influence over the scholarly interests in collecting *naturalia* and the study of etymology as a pursuit of an encyclopedic and comprehensive knowledge of God's creation.[49] This reference is not only a symbol to reflect on how sin affected mankind, but also to reflect on how mankind's sin affected the earth.[50] After the fall, not only was knowledge lost, but nature itself became more hostile and laborious and the body became prone to sickness. In *The Anatomy of Melancholy*, "the impulsive cause of man's misery and infirmaries" or "destruction of God's image" was caused by the sin of Adam in eating the fruit due to his "disobedience, pride, ambition, intemperance, incredulity, curiosity."[51] The fall is not only a reminder to be humble or too be cautious, but it is also a reminder of the knowledge that was lost while also being displayed in a space that is attempting to gain back this knowledge — to quote again Tim Huisman, "to restore mankind to the state of Adam in Paradise."[52] The story of Eden is often used in anatomical contexts with clear lessons on the fragility of life, however, this biblical reference was also common within the field of botany. The use of Eden between anatomy and botany held many of the same associations and implications, but the ways in which they were used differ.

---

[48] Sawday, 76-77.
[49] Jorink, 261, 289.
[50] Ibid., 75, 218-219.
[51] Burton, 2-3.
[52] Huisman, 64-65.

Adam was an often-used figure on title pages of herbals during this period and he was also a symbol of this "natural" knowledge. Adam named all the plants and animals and possessed this potent form of knowledge. As John Parkinson writes in his address "To the Reader" from *Paradisi in sole paradisus terrestris* (1629), when God created Adam, he "inspired him [Adam] with the knowledge of all naturall things."[53] When Adam is used in these botanical contexts, it is usually within the context of the garden before the fall of mankind. As is continued in *Paradasi*, "as he [Adam] was able to giue names to all the liuing Creatures, according to their seuerall natures; so no doubt but hee had also the knowledge."[54] This garden was planted by God so that Adam could "exercise his knowledge." This section from *Paradasi* also tells of the warnings of this biblical reference, urging readers to not be like Eve and "set their affections so strongly on the pleasure in them, as to deserue the losse of them in this Paradise."[55] While this title "Paradisi in Sole Paradisus Terrestris" also works as a pun, the use of Eden on the title page and references to biblical Paradise in the text make the biblical implications clear. On the title page to the 1633 edition of *The Herball*, revised by Thomas Johnson, the top of the page refers to the Bible verse of Genesis 1:29, which describes God providing Eden with every seed-bearing plant and fruits for food; under the verse is a natural scene with many varieties of trees and flowers, like Eden. The original garden and its inhabitants give both an aspirational image of knowledge and how gardening can be used to achieve it as well as a moralizing reminder to not seek only pleasure or use this knowledge improperly. While Eden in botanical contexts often referenced the ideal Paradise, the moral implications were not lost here.

As mentioned, Adam is a fairly common figure on title pages to herbals or other botanically themed books in the sixteenth and seventeenth centuries, however, how he is portrayed varies. The title page to *Rariorum plantarum historia* (1601) displays Adam with the biblical king Solomon in a pre-fall fashion, still in the nude before their removal from the garden, similar to the title page of *Paradisi*. However, Adam can also be displayed in post-fall imagery, as we see on another work by John Parkinson, *Theatrum Botanicum* (1640), where Adam is now clothed and holds a shovel — similar to the Adam in Leiden's anatomy theater — to express that after the fall, he must work the land.[56] This text also references humankind as fallen after Adam - "FROM a

---

[53] Parkinson, *Paradasi*, A2r.
[54] Ibid.
[55] Ibid.
[56] Huisman, 41.

Paradise of pleasant Flowers, I am fallen (Adam like)."[57] These effects of the fall of humankind are also referenced in other botanical books, not just on their title pages. In Adam Lonitzer's *Kreuterbuch*, the consequences of that sin in the garden promote much consideration and lamentation.[58] In this text, Lonitzer describes the idealized state of Eden where knowledge of nature (specifically, of plants) was complete and perfect and so was human's control over it before human's sin created a separation.[59] He then goes on to describe the difficulty and alienation between man and nature as a result of this act, while the rest of the herbal goes on to attempt to recapture some of what was lost. As Juliette Ferdinand puts it, when speaking of the history of gardens and of Eden, "nature possessed of a potent knowledge that, used improperly, is the cause of the degradation of mankind and his environment."[60]

On a 1592 edition of Walther Hermann Ryff's *New Albertus Magnus*, a book about the "secrets of nature," Adam and Eve are displayed on the title page with the Tree of Knowledge, which is shown as a skeleton with outstretched arms.[61] This display of the tree as a skeleton is seen in earlier engravings by Barthel Beham from 1520-1543 and would also be used by Jakob Lucius later in the sixteenth century. The dangers of excessive curiosity or of botanical study were not only implied through the various connections to biblical references, but also through the plants themselves. Most of the plants displayed in Leiden's botanical garden were of medical importance, however, there were also plants on display for the sake of their exotic status or beauty.[62] This also included the space composed exclusively of poisonous plants.[63] In *Paradise Garden*, these moralizing lessons combined with the use of "Paradise" in the title illustrate the ways in which the story of Eden influence some aspects of botany. One of the herbs in this book, "devils bite," does cover a moral lesson relating to the fall, urging the reader to consider the damage done to us by the devil when looking at the damaged appearance of this herb's roots.

Each space emphasizes two different ways of reflecting on Eden: the "living" collection of natural knowledge and the "death" of humankind and the resulting loss of said knowledge. The two sides of this reference overlap between each space, as the uses and conceptualizations between the garden and theater also

---

[57] Parkinson, 1.
[58] Crowther, 218-219.
[59] Ibid., 219-220.
[60] Ferdinand, 9.
[61] Crowther, 145, 222.
[62] Ferdinand, 9.
[63] Grämiger, 246.

overlapped. These two spaces are not just physical areas for the study of plants or anatomy, but for a condensed experience through the idealized Eden and moralizing fall of man when moving from the garden to the theater. This display of Adam, Eve, and the Tree of Knowledge would be potent for not only the anatomy theater, but also for the garden. While these two spaces were not physically close, their closeness in use and displays of natural objects connected them. Especially in the 1610 series of prints, the garden and theater can be viewed in succession, allowing their traits to further blend. The fall is not only a lesson in humility and the dangers of knowledge, but also a sign of the lost knowledge of Adam and of Eden. In this reference in the theater, Adam and Eve represent a warning against "excessive curiosity" inside a space that attempts to recapture what was lost; a reference to a time when Adam named every creature and a humbling reminder of the consequence of sin.[64]

While all of the contents of the anatomy theater's collection embody the mindsets around the study of nature, the added detail of Adam, Eve, and the Tree of Knowledge further highlight these concepts and give the already close relationship between the theater and botanical garden a furthered closeness. Each space attempts to create a complete view of nature for the purpose of providing areas of observation to be studied alongside texts, a space where the "book of nature" can be used to recapture a form of knowledge that has been lost — a purist more directly referenced in the theater — with the added warning to be cautious.[65] The consequence of sin not only separated humankind from its knowledge, but also from its health, bodily perfection, and escape from death.[66] The potency of Eden in fields such as anatomy displays how inseparable concepts of nature, religion, and morality were in the many pursuits of knowledge. Adam and Eve in the theater cover the type of knowledge that this space is trying to restore, a warning on excessive curiosity, and contemplation on the effects of sin.

Conclusion

These engravings of Leiden University, especially of the anatomical theater, highlight the emblematic view of natural history and the many different associations that come with objects found in collections. The anatomy theater embodied the many different aspects of natural history not only for academic audiences, but also for anyone who was curious and wanted to become closer to God through observing nature. The anatomy theater held a close relationship

---

[64] Cook, 166; Jorink, 283.
[65] Jorink, 288-289.
[66] Cook, 166; Crowther, 75, 88.

to the botanical garden as two parts of understanding nature for simultaneous academic and religious means. The garden and theater were two parts of a larger whole, sharing seasonal uses and year-round collections. The closeness between these two spaces is reflected in visual representations of the university and on title pages from other publications. The early life of the Leiden anatomy theater and its collection embody much of the ways in which the "book of nature" was understood. A longer look at this theater (especially its collection) and how it changes over the years would likely see a similar evolution into modernized methods of studying anatomy and natural sciences.[67] For the purpose of this chapter, the early establishment of the theater gives an introduction to how this space was used to emphasize the emblematic and religious connections to natural objects and to the study of nature itself. Objects from nature – plants, animals, the human body – all held lessons in not only academic-based knowledge, but also in religion and morality. The depictions of the Leiden anatomy theater show how this space went beyond the simple study of anatomy and how it compasses the natural world and its splendor, curiosity, and lessons. All of these associations to religion, morality, and knowledge are further reflected and condensed by the recreation of Adam, Eve, and the Tree of Knowledge looming near the place of dissection in the center of the theater. The biblical garden of Eden is brought inside the anatomy theater for the visitors of that space to consider what was lost after the fall and reflect on how the different spaces at the university – the garden and theater – were used as vessels to regain some of the knowledge that was lost.

---

[67] For a broader view on the anatomical collections in Leiden over a longer span of time, see Hendriksen, Marieke. *Elegant Anatomy: The Eighteenth-Century Leiden Anatomical Collections.* (Leiden: Brill, 2015), and Knoeff, Rina, and Robert Zwijnenberg, eds. *The Fate of Anatomical Collections.* (London: Routledge, 2016).

Conclusion: Expanding the Spaces of Renaissance Anatomy Theater

Leslie R. Malland

University of Texas Permian Basin

The point is that no matter what you choose to do with your body when you die, it won't, ultimately, be very appealing. If you are inclined to donate yourself to science, you should not let images of dissection or dismemberment put you off. They are no more or less gruesome, in my opinion, than ordinary decay or the sewing shut of your jaws via your nostrils for a funeral viewing.

– Mary Roach

The space of Renaissance anatomy theaters continues to reach us today as each of us contemplate what to do with our bodies. Though the cadavers studied in this collection often did not choose (nor did they have a choice) to donate their bodies to anatomy, most modern humans are fortunate to have the choice of the space of anatomy theater for their body's final performance. Medical students, anthropologists, and even military researchers continue to utilize spaces that intersect with anatomy theaters in their classrooms, Body Farm, or field tests.[1] As this collection demonstrates, we cannot consider the anatomy theater as a place isolated from its culture. Instead, we should consider how the space of anatomy theaters intersects with and resonates within their culture. From the nationalist concerns of anatomical publication authorship to the sexualization of female corpses, the anatomy theater commentates its culture, its participants, and the world outside its doors.

This interdisciplinary collection situates itself within the space of the Renaissance anatomy theater and demonstrates how researchers and scholars can (and should) combine their common interests to locate cultural intersections between anatomy and the world outside the anatomy theater.

---

[1] "Forensic Anthropology Center." University of Tennessee. https://fac.utk.edu/.

We have collaborated through a global pandemic, across continents, and around the world to develop our unique insight into Renaissance culture. Sharing the common interest of anatomy, we worked tirelessly to overcome many hurdles, including nationwide lockdowns and limited access to resources, to develop a new conversation about anatomy theaters. Going forward, we would like the conversation to continue developing the *spaces* of anatomy. The study of human bodies continues to benefit human culture; thus, the culture must continue to recognize how anatomy influences its education, art, and understandings of the world beyond the literal space of the anatomy theater.

Bibliography

Agrimi, Jole, and Chiara Crisciani. *Edocere Medicos: Medicina Scolastica nei Secoli XIII-XV.* Napoli: Guerini e Associati, 1988.

Anonymous. *Memorials of the Duttons of Dutton in Cheshire: With Notes Respecting the Sherborne Branch of the Family.* London: Henry Sotheran & Co., 1901.

Anzieu, Didier. *Le Moi-Peau.* Paris: Bordas, 1985.

Archivo Historico de la Universidad de Salamanca, AUSA, Libros de Visitas de Cátedras, Años 1560-1838, 947, fl. 77v. Original transcribed by Luiz E. Rodriguez-San-Pedro Bezares, "Universidad de la Monarquía Católica, 1555-1700," in *Historia de la Universidad de Salamanca,* vol. I-Trayectoria y Vinculaciones. Salamanca: Ediciones Universidad de Salamanca, 2002.

Aristotle. *The Politics of Aristotle.* Translated by B. Jowett. London: Oxford University Press, 1885.

Armin, Robert. *Quips upon Questions, or, a Clownes Conceite on Occasion Offered Bewraying a Morrallised Metamorphoses of Changes Upon Interrogatories.* London: W. Ferbrand, 1600.

Aspin, Richard K., "John Evelyn's Tables of Veins and Arteries: A Rediscovered Letter." *Medical History,* no. 39 (1995): 493-499.

Bachelard, Gaston. *The Poetics of Space.* Translated by Maria Jolas. Boston: Beacon Press, 1994.

Bakhtin, Mikhail. *Rabelais and His World.* Translated by Hélène Iswolsky. Bloomington: Indiana University Press, 1984.

Baldasar Heseler, Andreas Vesalius' first Public Anatomy at Bologna, 1540, An Eyewitness Report... together with His Notes on Matthaeus Curtius' Lectures on Anatomia Mundini. Edited by Ruben Eriksson. Uppsala and Stockholm: Almqvist & Wiksells boktryckeri, 1959.

Banister, John. *The Historie of Man.* London, 1578. Da Capo Press, 1969.

Baudry, Hervé. "La réception d'Ambroise Paré au Portugal aux XVIe et XVIIe siècles." In *Ambroise Paré (1510-1590): Pratique et écriture de la science à la Renaissance,* 355–77. Paris: Classiques Garnier, 2003.

Becedas González, Margarita. "Introducción a la Exposición." In *A Defunctis Interdum Viventes Erudiuntur: Los Estudios de Anatomía en la Universidad de Salamanca. Exposición Bibliográfica,* 11-15. Salamanca: Universidad de Salamanca Servicio de Archivos y Bibliotecas, 2001.

Bednarz, James P. *Shakespeare and the Truth of Love: The Mystery of "The Phoenix and Turtle."* New York: Palgrave Macmillan, 2012.

Bejan, Teresa M. *Mere Civility: Disagreement and the Limits of Toleration.* Cambridge: Harvard University Press, 2017.

Billing, Christian. "Modelling the Anatomy Theater and Indoor Hall Theater: Dissection on the Stages of Early Modern London." *Early Modern Literary Studies,* Special Issue 13, no.3 (2004): 1-17.

Bliss, Lee. "What Hath a Quarter-Century of Coriolanus Criticism Wrought." *The Shakespearean International Yearbook 2: Where are We Now in Shakespearean Studies*. Edited by W. R. Elton and John M. Mucciolo. New York: Routledge Press, 2018.

Bohde, Daniela. "Skin and the Search for the Interior." In *Bodily Extremities: Preoccupations with the Human Body in Early Modern European Culture*. Edited by Florike Egmond, 10-47. Florence: Taylor and Francis, 2003.

Borsetti, Ferrante. *Historia Almi Ferrariae Gymnasii*. Vol. I, Ferrara: Bernardino Pomatelli, 1735.

Brandão, Mário. *Actas dos Conselhos da Universidade de 1537 a 1557*. Vol. II, 3.ª parte. Coimbra: A. U. C., 1969.

Brito, A. da Rocha. "As Primeiras Dissecações Humanas na Universidade de Coimbra. O Primeiro Teatro Anatomico." *Folia Anatomica. Universitatis Conimbrigensis* XVII, no. 4 (1942): 1–16.

Brockbank, Philip. "Introduction." In William Shakespeare's *Coriolanus*, 1-89. London: Bloomsbury, The Arden Shakespeare, 2007.

Brockbank, William. "Old Anatomical Theaters and what Took Place Therein." *Medical History* 12, n. 4 (1968): 371–84.

Brockliss, Laurence. "Curricula." In *A History of the University in Europe: Universities in Early Modern Europe (1500-1800)*, 2:565–620. Cambridge: Cambridge University Press, 2003.

Burton, Robert. *The Anatomy of Melancholy vvhat it is. VVith all the Kindes, Causes, Symptomes, Prognostickes, and Seuerall Cures of it*. Oxford: Printed by Iohn Lichfield and Iames Short, for Henry Cripps, Anno Dom. 1621.

Bylebyl, Jerome J. "The School of Padua: Humanistic Medicine in the Sixteenth Century." In *Health, Medicine and Mortality in the Sixteenth Century*. Edited by Charles Webster, 335-70. Cambridge: Cambridge University Press, 1979.

Bylebyl, Jerome. "Medicine, Philosophy, and Humanism in Renaissance Italy." In *Science and the Arts in the Renaissance*. Edited by John W. Shirley and F. David Hoeniger, 27-49. Washington: Folger Library, 1985.

Campbell, Ruth. "Sentence of Death by Burning for Women." *The Journal of Legal History* 5, no. 1 (1984): 44-59.

Campbell, Stephen. "Titian's Flaying of Marsyas: Thresholds of the Human and the Limits of Painting." In *Renaissance Posthumanism*, edited by Joseph Campana and Scott Maisano, 64-98. New York: Fordham University Press, 2016.

Campion, Thomas. "Cherry-Ripe." In *The New Oxford Book of English Verse, 1250-1950*, edited by Helen Gardner, 162. New York: Oxford University Press, 1972.

Carlino, Andrea. *Books of the Body: Anatomical Ritual and Renaissance Learning*. Translated by John Tedeschi and Anne C. Tedeschi. Chicago & London: The University of Chicago Press, 1999.

Carlino, Andrea *La Fabbrica del Corpo: Libri e Dissezione nel Rinascimento*. Torino: Einaudi, 1994.

Carpenter, John. *The Plaine Man's Spirituall Plough Containing the Godly and Spirituall Husbandrie*. London: Thomas Creede, 1607.

Carreras Panchón, Antonio. "La Medicina, Siglos XVI-XIX." In *Historia de la Universidad de Salamanca*, III.1, Saberes y confluencias, 303–44. Salamanca: Ediciones Universidad de Salamanca, 2006.

Carruthers, Jo. "'Neither Maide, Wife or Widow': Ester Sowernam and the Book of Esther." *Prose Studies: History, Theory, Criticism* 26, no. 3 (2003): 321-343.

Carvalho, Joaquim Martins Teixeira de, and Santos Costa. *A Universidade de Coimbra no séc. XVI: Guevara: Notas e Documentos*. Coimbra: Imprensa da Universidade de Coimbra, 1922.

Caswell, Marisha. "Flames and Ashes: The Significance of Death by Burning in Europe, 1400-1800." *International Journal of Arts and Sciences* 9, no. 3 (2016): 197-204.

Cavell, Stanley. "'Who Does the Wolf Love?' Reading *Coriolanus*." *Representations*, No. 3, (1983): 1-20.

Caviness, Madeline H. *Visualizing Women in the Middle Ages: Sight, Spectacle, and Scopic Economy*. Philadelphia: University of Pennsylvania Press, 2001.

Céard, Jean. "Montaigne Anatomiste." In *Cahiers de l'Association Internationale des études Francaises*, no. 55, (2003): 299-315.

Cefalu, Paul. *Revisionist Shakespeare: Transitional Ideologies in Texts and Contexts*. New York and Hampshire: Palgrave Macmillan, 2004.

Colombo, Realdo. *De re Anatomica Libri XV*. Venice: Niccolo Bevilacqua, 1559.

Cook, Harold J. *Matters of Exchange: Commerce, Medicine, and Science in the Dutch Golden Age*. New Haven: Yale University Press, 2007.

Cooke, James. *Mellificium chirurgiæ: or, the marrow of chirurgery. With the anatomy of humane bodies, according to the most modern anatomists; Illustrated with many Anatomical Observations. Institutions of Physick, with Hippocrates's Aphorisms largely Commented upon. The marrow of physick, Shewing the Causes, Signs, and Cures of most Diseases incident to Humane Bodies. Choice Experience'd Receipts for the Cure of Several Distempers. The sixth edition, enlarg'd with many additions. Illustrated in its several parts with 12 copper cutts. By the Late Eminent Dr James Cooke, of Warwick, Practitioner in Physick and Chirurgery Revis'd, Corrected, and Purg'd from many Faults that escap'd in the former Editions, by Tho. Gibson, M. D. and Fellow of the College of Physicians in London. Licens'd by the said College of Physicians and fitted for the Use of all Sea-Surgeons*. London, MDCCXVII, 1717. *Eighteenth Century Collections Online*. Gale. University of Kentucky Libraries.

Correia, Maximino. "Esbôço da História da Anatomia em Coimbra." *Jornal da Sociedade das Sciências Médicas de Lisboa* LXXXVIII (1925): 3–39.

Corsini, Andrea. "Andrea Vesalio nello studio di Pisa." In *Volume Pubblicato nel XXX anno di Direzione Sanitaria del Prof. D. Barduzzi delle RR. Terme di S. Giuliano 1915*. Siena: S. Bernardino, 1915.

Cranston, Jodi. *The Muddied Mirror: Materiality and Figuration in Titian's Later Paintings*. University Park: Pennsylvania University Press, 2010.

Crooke, Helkiah. *Mikrokosmographia a Description of the Body of Man*. London: Printed by William Iaggard, 1615.

Crowther, Kathleen M. *Adam and Eve in the Protestant Reformation*. Cambridge: Cambridge University Press, 2013.

Cunningham, Andrew. *The Anatomist Anatomis'd: An Experimental Discipline in Enlightenment Europe*. Farnham: Ashgate, 2010.

Cunningham, Andrew. *The Anatomical Renaissance: The Resurrection of the Anatomical Projects of the Ancients*. England: Aldershot, 1997.

Dauber, Noah. *State and Commonwealth: The Theory of the State in Early Modern England 1549-1640*. New Jersey: Princeton University Press, 2016.

Dawson, Lesel. *Lovesickness and Gender in Early Modern English Literature*. Oxford University Press, 2018.

De Angelis, Simone. "From Text to the Body. Commentaries on *De Anima*, Anatomical Practice and Authority around 1600." In *Scholarly Knowledge. Textbooks in Early Modern Europe*, 205–27. Genève: Librairie Droz S.A., 2008.

Deleuze, Gilles. *Francis Bacon: Logique de la Sensation*. Paris, Éditions de la Différence, 1981.

Demerson, Paulette. "La chaire et le Théâtre d´Anatomie de L´Université de Salamanque (1771-1792)." *Mélanges à la mémoire de Jean Sarrailh*. Centre de Recherches de L´Institut D´Etudes Hispaniques edição, 1966.

Diana, Esther. "Anatomy between Public and Private in 14th-16th Century Europe: Social Contexts, Scenarios and Personages." In *Anatomy and Surgery. From Antiquity to the Renaissance*, 329-74. Amesterdam: Adolf M. Hakkert Publishing, 2016.

Dittmann, Joo Young. "'Tear him to Pieces:' De-Suturing Masculinity in Coriolanus." *English Studies* 90, no. 6 (2009): 653-72.

Doelman, James "The Religious Epigram in Early Stuart England." *Christianity and Literature* 54, no. 4 (2005): 497-520.

Dolan, Frances E. *Dangerous Familiars: Representations of Domestic Crime in England, 1550-1700*. Ithaca, New York: Cornell University Press, 1994.

Dolan, Frances E. "Tracking the Petty Traitor Across Genres." In *Ballads and Broadsides in Britain, 1500-1800*. Edited by Patricia Fumerton, Anita Guerrini, and Kris McAbee, 149-171. Burlington, Vermont: Ashgate, 2010.

Dugan, Holly. *The Ephemeral History of Perfume: Scent and Sense in Early Modern England*. Baltimore: The Johns Hopkins University Press, 2011.

Dulieu, Louis. *La médecine à Montpellier*. Vol. I. Avignon: Presses Universelles, 1975.

Duplessis, Robert S. *Transitions to Capitalism in Early Modern Europe*. Cambridge: Cambridge University Press, 1997.

Eastman, Nate. "The Rumbling Belly Politic: Metaphorical Location and Metaphorical Government in *Coriolanus*." *Early Modern Literary Studies* 13, no. 1 (2007): 2.1-39.

Easton, Martha "Saint Agatha and the Sanctification of Sexual Violence." *Studies in Iconography* 16 (1994): 83-118.

Edgar, Thomas. *The Lawes Resolutions of Womens Rights: or, The lawes provision for woemen A methodicall collection of such statutes and customes* [...]. London: John More, 1632.

Egmond, Florike. *Eye for Detail: Images of Plants and Animals in Art and Science 1500-1630*. London: Reaktion Books Ltd, 2017.

Egmond, Florike. "Execution, Dissection, Pain and Infamy- A Morphological Investigation." In *Bodily Extremities: Preoccupations with the Human Body in Early Modern European Culture*, edited by Florike Egmond and Robert Zwijnenberg, 92-127.Vermont: Ashgate, 2003.

Eriksson, Ruben. *Andreas Vesalius First Public Anatomy at Bologna: An Eyewitness Report by Baldassar Heseler.* Uppsala and Stockholm: Alqvist and Wiksells, 1959.

Estienne, Charles. *La Dissection des Parties du Corps Humain, Divisee en Trois Parties.* Paris: Estienne, 1546.

Evelyn, John. *The Diary of John Evelyn*, edited by Richard Garnett. Project Gutenberg, 2012.

Evelyn, John, and William Cowper. "An Account of Divers Schemes of Arteries and Veins, Dissected from Adult Human Bodies, and Given to Repository of the Royal Society by John Evelyn, Esq; E.R.S. To Which are Subjoyn'd a Description of the Extremities of Those Vessels, and the Manner the Blood is Seen, by the Microscope, to Pass from the Arteries to the Veins in Quadrupeds When Living: With Some Chirurgical Observations, and Figures After Life, by William Cowper, F.R.S." *Philosophical Transactions* 23 (1702): 1177-1201.

Fabroni, Angelo. *Historiae Academiae Pisanae.* Vol. II, Pisa: Gaetano Mugnainio, 1792.

Facciolati, Jacobo. *Fasti Gymnasii Patavini.* Vol. II, Padua: Giovanni Manfrè, 1757.

Favaro, Giuseppe. *Gabriele Falloppia Modenese (MDXXIII - MDLXII).* Modena: Tipografia Editrice Immacolata Concezione, 1928.

Ferdinand, Juliette. "In the 'Hoiius Universalis:' Science, Technique, and Delight in Gardens." In *From Art to Science: Experiencing Nature in the European Garden*, edited by Juliette Ferdinand, 8–17. Treviso: ZeL Edizioni, 2016.

Fernández Luzón, Antonio. *La Universidad de Barcelona en el siglo XVI.* Barcelona: Publicacions i Edicions de la Universitat, 2005.

Ferrari, Giovanna. "Anatomy Lessons and the Carnival: The Anatomy Theater of Bologna." *Past & Present* 117 (1987): 50-106.

Findlen, Paula. "Anatomy Theaters, Botanical Gardens, and Natural History Collections." In *The Cambridge History of Science*, edited by Lorraine Daston and Katharine Park, 272–89. Cambridge: Cambridge University Press, 2006.

Fiolhais, Carlos. "Livros Médicos do Renascimento: Tesouros do Conhecimento." *Medicina Interna. Revista da Sociedade Portuguesa de Medicina Interna* 26, no. 4 (2019): 274–82.

Fissell, Mary E. *Vernacular Bodies: The Politics of Reproduction in Early Modern England.* Oxford: Oxford University Press, 2004.

Fletcher, Phineas, *The Purple Island, or The Isle of Man. Together with Piscatorie Eclogs and Other Poeticall Miscellanea.* Cambridge: Printed by the Printers to the Universitie of Cambridge, 1633.

Fonseca, Fernando Taveira da. "A Medicina." In *História da Universidade em Portugal*, I tomo II (1537-1771):835–75. Coimbra, Lisboa: Universidade de Coimbra, Fundação Calouste Gulbenkian, 1997.

Fontana, Velarde Perez. *Andreas Vesalius Bruxellensis y su epoca.* Montevideo, Imprenta Nacional, 1963.

"Forensic Anthropology Center." University of Tennessee. https://fac.utk.edu/

Forset, Edward. *A Comparative Discourse of the Bodies Natural and Polituque Wherein out the principles of Nature, is fet forth the true forme of a Commonweale, with dutie of Subiects, and the right of the Soueraigne.* London: Printed by John Bill, 1606.

Foucault, Michel. "From the Power of Sovereignty to Power over Life," March 17, 1976. In *Society Must be Defended: Lectures at the Collège De France, 1975-76,* edited by Mauro Bertanie and Alessandro Fontana, translated by David Macey, 239-263. New York: Picador, 2003.

Foucault, Michel. *Discipline and Punish: The Birth of the Prison.* 2nd Vintage Books ed., Vintage Books, 1995.

Foucault, Michel. *History of Sexuality.* Vols. 1-3, translated by Robert Hurley. New York: Random House, 1986.

Foucault, Michel. *Security, Territory, Population: Lectures at the College de France, 1977-1978,* edited by Michel Senellart, translated by Graham Burchell. New York: Palgrave Macmillan, 2007.

Fountain, Kenny T. *Rhetoric in the Flesh: Trained Vision, Technical Expertise, and the Gross Anatomy Lab.* New York: Routledge, 2014.

Foxe, John. *The Unabridged Acts and Monuments Online or TAMO.* HRI Online Publications, Sheffield, 2011. http//www.johnfoxe.org.

Fuchs, Leonhardt. *Commentaires Tres Excellens de l'hystoire des Plantes.* Paris: Jacques Gazot, 1547-48.

Gamba, A. "Il primo teatro anatomico stabile di Padova non fu quello di Fabrici d"Acquapendente." In *Atti e memorie dell'Accademia patavina di scienze, lettere ed arti* 99, no. 3 (1986): 157–61.

García Ballester, Luis. "Medical Science and Medical Teaching at the University of Salamanca in the 15th Century." In *Universities and Science in the Early Modern Period,* 37–64. New York: Springer, 2006.

Gay, Edwin F. *The Midland Revolt and the Inquisitions of Depopulation of 1607.* Royal Historical Society, 1904.

Goodall, Charles. *The Royal College of Physicians of London.* London: Walter Kettilby, 1684.

Goodcole, Henry. *The Adultresses Funerall Day in Flaming, Scorching, and Consuming Fire; or, The Burning Downe to Ashes of Alice Clarke.* London: N. and I. Okes, 1635.

Grämiger, Gregory. "Reconstructing Order: The Spatial Arrangements of Plants in the Hortus Botanicus of Leiden University in Its First Years." In *Gardens, Knowledge and the Sciences in the Early Modern Period,* edited by Volker Remmert, Hubertus Fischer, and Joachim Wolschke-Bulmahn, 235–51. Basel: Birkhäuser, 2016.

Grande, Nuno. "Os estudos anatómicos em Portugal até ao fim do século XIX." In *Academia de Ciências de Lisboa. História e desenvolvimento da ciência em Portugal,* 479–95. Lisboa: Publicações do II Centenário da Academia de Ciências de Lisboa, 1986.

Greenblatt, Stephen. *Renaissance Self-fashioning: from More to Shakespeare.* Chicago: University of Chicago Press, 1980.

Grossman, Joel. "Remembering and Dismembering Henry Howard: Blazon and Beheading in Sir John Cheke's Elegy on the Earl of Surrey." *Review of English Studies, New Studies* (2020): 1-20.

Guild, Elizabeth. *Unsettling Montaigne: Poetics, Ethics and Affect in the Essais and Other Writings.* Cambridge: Cambridge University Press, 2014.

Hale, David George. *The Body Politic: A Political Metaphor in Renaissance English Literature.* The Netherlands: Mouton & CO. N.V., Publishers, 1971.

Harris, Jonathan Gill. *Foreign Bodies and the Body Politic: Discourses of Social Pathology in Early Modern England.* Cambridge: Cambridge University Press, 1998.

Hartle, Ann. *Michel de Montaigne: Accidental Philosopher.* Cambridge: Cambridge University Press, 2007.

Harvey, William. *Lectures on the Whole of Anatomy.* Translated by Charles D. O'Malley, F.N.L. Poynter, and K.F. Berkley: University of California Press, 1961.

Henderson, Katherine Usher, and Barbara F. McManus. *Half Humankind: Contexts and Texts of the Controversy about Women in England, 1540-1640.* Chicago: University of Illinois Press, 1985.

Hickerson, Megan. *Making Women Martyrs in Tudor England.* London: Palgrave Macmillan, 2005.

Hildebrandt, Sabine. "Capital Punishment and Anatomy: History and Ethics of an Ongoing Association." *Clinical Anatomy* 21, no. 1 (2008): 5-14.

Hill, John Spencer. "The Phoenix." *Religion & Literature* 16, no. 2 (1984): 61-66.

Hobbes, Thomas. *Leviathan or, The Matter Frome, and Power of a Commonwealth Ecclesiasticall and Civil.* London: Printed for Andrew Crooke, 1651.

Hopkins, D. J. *City/Stage/Globe: Performance and Space in Shakespeare's London.* New York: Routledge, 2008.

Hudson, Hoyt H. "Edward May's Borrowings from Timothe Kendall and Others." *The Huntington Library Bulletin*, no. 11 (1937): 23-58.

Huisman, Tim. *The Finger of God: Anatomical Practice in 17th-Century Leiden.* Leiden: Primavera Press, 2009.

Huisman, Tim. "Resilient Collections: The Long Life of Leiden's Earliest Collections." In *The Fate of Anatomical Collections*, edited by Robert Zwijnenberg and Rina Knoeff, 73–92. London: Routledge, 2015.

Isidore of Seville. *The Etymologies of Isidore of Seville.* Translated by Stephen A. Barney, W. J. Lewis, Isnardi, Lorenzo, and Emanuele Celesia. *Storia della Università di Genova.* Genova: Coi tipi del R.I. de'sordo-muti, 1867.

Jagendorf, Zvi. "*Coriolanus*: Body Politic and Private Parts." *Shakespeare Quarterly* 41. no. 4 (1990): 455-469.

Jones, Ann Rosalind and Peter Stallybrass. "The Politics of *Astrophel and Stella.*" *Studies in English Literature* 24 (1984): 73-87.

Jorink, Eric. *Reading the Book of Nature in the Dutch Golden Age, 1575-1715.* Translated by Peter Mason. Leiden: Brill, 2010.

Kantorowicz, Ernst H., *The King's Two Bodies: A Study in Medieval Political Theology.* Princeton: Princeton University Press, 1957.

Kay, Sarah. 2006. "Original Skin: Flaying, Reading, and Thinking in the Legend of Saint Bartholomew and Other Works." *Journal of Medieval and Early Modern Studies* 36, issue 1 (2006): 35-74.

Keltridge, John. *Two Godlie and Learned Sermons Appointed and Preached, Before the Jesuites, Seminaries, and Other Adversaries to the Gospell of Christ in the Tower of London.* London: J. Charlewood and Richard Ihones, 1581.

King, John. *Foxe's Book of Martyrs and Early Modern Print Culture.* Cambridge: Cambridge University Press, 2006.

Klestinec, Cynthia J. *Theaters of Anatomy: Students, Teachers, and Traditions of Dissection in Renaissance Venice.* Baltimore: The Johns Hopkins University Press, 2011.

Klestinec, Cynthia. "A History of Anatomy Theaters in Sixteenth-Century Padua." *Journal of the History of Medicine and Allied Sciences* 59, n. 3 (2004): 375–412.

Klestinec, Cynthia J. "A History of Anatomy Theaters in Sixteenth Century Padua." *Journal of the History of Medicine and Allied Sciences* 59, no. 4 (2004): 375-412.

Klestinec, Cynthia. "Civility, Comportment, and the Anatomy Theater: Girolamo Fabrici and His Medical Students in Renaissance Padua." *Renaissance Quarterly* 60 (2007): 434–63.

Knott, John R. "John Foxe and the Joy of Suffering." *The Sixteenth Century Journal* 27, no. 3 (Autumn 1996): 721-734.

Knott, John R. *Discourses of Martyrdom in English Literature, 1563-1694.* Cambridge: Cambridge University Press, 1993.

Langis, Unhae. "Coriolanus: Inordinate Passions and Powers in Personal and Political Governance." *Comparative Drama* 40, No. 1 (2010): 1-27.

Laqueur, Thomas W. *The Work of the Dead: A Cultural History of Mortal Remains.* New Jersey: Princeton University Press, 2015.

Laurenza, Domenico. *Art and Anatomy in Renaissance Italy. Images from a Scientific Revolution.* New York: Metropolitan Museum of Art, 2012.

Lefebvre, Henri. *The Production of Space.* Translated by Donald Nicholson-Smith. Oxford: Basil Blackwell, 1991.

Leite, Serafim. *Estatutos da Universidade de Coimbra* (1559). Coimbra: Por ordem da Universidade, 1963.

Lemos, Maximiano. *História da Medicina em Portugal. Doutrinas e Instituições.* Vol. I. Lisboa: Publicações D. Quixote/Ordem dos Médicos, 1991.

Léry, Jean de. *Histoire d'un Voyage Faict en la Terre du Brésil.* Edited by Frank Lestringant. Paris: Librairie Générale Française, 1994.

Lieburg, Mart van. "Religion and Medical Practice in the Netherlands in the Seventeenth Century: An Introduction." In *The Task of Healing: Medicine, Religion and Gender in England and the Netherlands 1450-1800,* edited by Hilary Marland and Margaret Pelling, 135–44. Rotterdam: Erasmus, 1996.

Lind, Levi Robert. *Studies in Pre-Vesalian Anatomy: Biography, Translations, Documents.* Philadelphia: American Philosophical Society, 1975.

Livy. *The History of Rome, Books 1-5*. Translated by Valerie M. Warrior. Indianapolis & Cambridge: Hackett Publishing Company, 2006.

Lockwood, Matthew. "From Treason to Homicide: Changing Conceptions of the Law of Petty Treason in Early Modern England." *The Journal of Legal History* 34, no. 1 (2013): 31-49).

López Piñero, José M. "The Faculty of Medicine of Valencia: Its Position in Renaissance Europe." In *Universities and Science in the Early Modern Period*, 65-82. Dordrecht: Springer, 2006.

López Piñero, José M. "The Vesalian Movement in Sixteenth-century Spain." *Journal of the History of Biology*, no. 12 (1979): 45–81.

Lucretius. *De rerum natura*. Translated by W.H.D. Rouse. Cambridge: Loeb Classical Library, 1975.

Macalister, Alexander. "An Address on the History of Anatomy in Cambridge." *British Medical Journal* 1, no. 1574 (1891): 449–52.

Maclean, Ian. *The Renaissance Notion of Woman: A Study in the Fortunes of Scholasticism and Medical Science in European Intellectual Life*. Cambridge: Cambridge University Press, 1980.

Malabou, Catherine. *L'avenir de Hegel: plasticité, temporalité, dialectique*. Paris: J.Vrin, 1996.

Mandressi, Rafael. "Of the Eye and the Hand: Performance in Early Modern Anatomy." Translated by Elizabeth Claire. *The Drama Review* 59, no. 3 (2015): 60-76.

Mandressi, Rafael. *Le regard de l'anatomiste: Dissection et invention du corps en Occident*. Paris: Seuil, 2003.

Marchesi, Patricia. "'Limbs Mangled and Torn Asunder:' Dismemberment, Theatricality, and the Blazon in Christopher Marlowe's *Doctor Faustus*," in *Staging the Blazon in Early Modern English Theater*. Studies in Performance and Early Modern Drama (London: Routledge, 2016), 93.

Margócsy, Dániel, Mark Somos, and Stephen N. Joffe. *The 'Fabrica' of Andreas Vesalius: A Worldwide Descriptive Census, Ownership, and Annotations of the 1543 and 1555 Editions*. Leiden: Brill, 2018.

Marshall, Cynthia. *The Shattering of the Self: Violence, Subjectivity, and Early Modern Texts*. Johns Hopkins University Press, 2002.

Martínez-Vidal, Àlvar and José Pardo-Tomás. "Anatomical Theaters in Early Modern Spain." *Medical History* 49, n. 3 (2005): 251–80.

Martinotti, Giovanni. *L'insegnamento dell'anatomia in Bologna prima del secolo XIX*. Bologna: Azzoguidi, 1911.

Marvell, Andrew. "To His Coy Mistress." In *Andrew Marvell: The Complete Poems*. Edited by Elizabeth Story Donno, 50-51. New York: Penguin Books, 1996.

Masten, Jeffrey. "Is the Fundament a Grave?". In *The Body in Parts*, Edited by David Hillman and Carla Mazzio. London: Routledge, 1997.

Mathieu-Castellani, Gisèle. "Des excréments d'un vieil esprit: Montaigne Coprographe." In *Littérature*, no. 62 (1986): 14-24.

May, Edward. *Epigrams Divine and Morall*. London: John Beale for John Grove, 1633.

May, Edward. "On a woman burned in Smithfield the 20 of April 1632. who dyed a Wife, a Widdow, and a true maide, by her owne free confession." In *Epigrams Divine and Morall*, C2. London: John Beale for John Grove, 1633.

Merleau-Ponty, Maurice. 1945. *Phénoménologie de la perception*. Paris: Éditions Gallimard.

Mitchell, Perry, *The Purple Island and Anatomy in Early Seventeenth-Century Literature, Philosophy, and Theology*. Teaneck: Fairleigh Dickinson University Press, 2007.

Montaigne, Michel de. *Les Essais*. Edited by Pierre Villey. Paris: Presses Universitaires de France, 2004.

Montaigne, Michel de. *The Complete Essays*. Translated by M.A. Screech. London: Penguin Books, 2003.

Munro, Ian. *The Figure of the Crowd in Early Modern London: The City and its Double*. New York and Hampshire: Palgrave Macmillan, 2005.

Muratori, Giulio. *Su alcuni documenti inediti relativi ad un insigne anatomico ferrarese: G. B. Canani*. Ferrara: Emiliana, 1943.

Nancy, Jean-Luc. *Corpus*. Translated by Richard Rand. New York: Fordham University Press, 2008.

Nardi, Michele Giuseppe. "Statuti e documenti riflettenti la dissezione anatomica umana e la nomina di alcuni lettori di medicina nell'antico Studium generale fiorentino." *Rivista di storia delle scienze mediche e naturali* 47 (1956): 237–49.

Neiberg, Linda K. "Exquisite Corpses: Fantasies of Necrophilia in Early Modern English Drama." Ph.D. Dissertation, Graduate Center, City University of New York, 2014. CUNY Academic Works, https://academicworks.cuny.edu/gc_et ds/1420/.

Nunn, Hillary. "On Vegetating Virgins: Greensickness and the Plant Realm in Early Modern Literature." In *The Indistinct Human in Renaissance Literature*, edited by Jean E. Feerick and Vin Nardizzi, 159-77. New York: Palgrave Macmillan, 2012.

Nunn, Hillary. *Staging Anatomies: Dissection and Spectacle in Early Stuart Tragedy*. Aldershot: Ashgate, 2005.

O'Brien, John. 2009. "Fashion." In *Montaigne after Theory/Theory after Montaigne*, edited by Zahi Zalloua, 55-74. Seattle: University of Washington Press, 2009.

Ongaro, Giuseppe. "La medicina nello Studio di Padova e nel Veneto." In *Storia della cultura veneta. Dal primo Quattrocento al Concilio di Trento*, 75–134. Vicenza: Neri Pozza, 1980.

O'Malley, Charles D. "Pedro Jimeno: Valencian Anatomist of the Mid-sixteenth Century." In *Science, Medicine and Society in the Renaissance*, vol. 1, 69–72. London: Heinemann, 1972.

O'Malley, Charles D. *Andreas Vesalius of Brussels, 1514-1564*. Berkeley: University of California Press, 1964.

Orlers, Jan Janszn. *Beschrijvinge Der Stad Leyden: Inhoudende 't Begin, Den Voortgang, Ende Den Wasdom Der Selver: De Stichtinghe van de Kercken, Cloosteren, Gasthuysen*. In *Commercial Visions: Science, Trade, and Visual*

Culture in the Dutch Golden Age, edited by Dániel Margócsy. Chicago: The University of Chicago Press, 2014.

Pardo Tomás, José. *Un lugar para la ciencia. Escenarios de práctica científica en la sociedad hispana del siglo XVI.* Tenerife: Fundación Canaria Orotava de Historia de la Ciencia, 2006.

Park, Katharine. *Secrets of Women: Gender, Generation, and the Origins of Human Dissection.* New York: Zone Books, 2006.

Park, Katharine. "The Rediscovery of the Clitoris: French Medicine and the Tribade, 1570-1620." In *The Body in Parts: Fantasies of Corporeality in Early Modern Europe,* edited by David Hillman and Carla Mazzio, 171-193. New York: Routledge, 1997.

Park, Katharine. "The Criminal and the Saintly Body: Autopsy and Dissection in Renaissance Italy." *Renaissance Quarterly* 47, no. 1 (1994): 1-33.

Parker, Patricia. *Literary Fat Ladies: Rhetoric, Gender, Property.* New York: Methuen, 1987.

Parkinson, John. *Paradisi in Sole Paradisus Terrestris, or, A Garden of All Sorts of Pleasant Flowers Which Our English Ayre Will Permitt to Be Noursed vp: With a Kitchen Garden of All Manner of Herbes, Rootes, and Fruites, for Meate or Sause Vsed with vs, and an Orchard of All Sorte of Fruit Bearing Trees and Shrubbes Fit for Our Land Together with the Right Orderinge Planting & Preseruing of Them and Their Vses & Vertues.* London: Printed by Humfrey Lownes And Robert Young, 1629.

Parkinson, John. *Theatrum botanicum.* London: Printed by Tho. Cotes, 1640.

Paster, Gail Kern. *The Body Embarrassed: Drama and the Disciplines of Shame in Early Modern England.* Ithaca: Cornell University Press, 1993.

Paster, Gail Kern. "'In the Spirit of Men There Is No Blood:' Blood as Trope of Gender in *Julius Caesar.*" *Shakespeare Quarterly* 40, no. 3 (1989): 284–298.

Peachey, George Charles. *A Memoir of William and John Hunter.* Plymouth: William Brendon and Son, 1924.

Pedersen, Olaf. "Tradition and Innovation." *A History of the University in Europe: Universities in Early Modern Europe (1500-1800),* 2: 452–88. Cambridge: Cambridge University Press, 2003.

Piccinni, Gabriella. "Tra scienza ed arte: lo Studio di Siena e l'insegnamento della medicina (sec. XIII-XVI)." In *L'Università di Siena: 750 anni di storia.* Milan: Silvana Editoriale, 1991.

Pita, João Rui. "Medicina, Cirurgia e Arte Farmacêutica na Reforma Pombalina da Universidade De Coimbra." In *O Marquês de Pombal e a Universidade,* 2ª., 141–78. Coimbra: Imprensa da Universidade de Coimbra, 2014.

Poe, Edgar Allan. "The Philosophy of Composition." In *The Complete Works of Edgar Allan Poe, Vol. XIV: Essays and Miscellanies,* edited by J. A. Harrison, 193-208. New York: Society of English and French Literature, 1902.

Poulantzas, Nicos. *State, Power, Socialism.* Translated by Patrick Camiller. London and New York: Verso Press, 2014.

Prieto Carrasco, Casto. "La enseñanza de la Anatomía en la Universidad de Salamanca." In *X Congreso Internacional de Historia de la Medicina, Madrid, 23-29 septiembre 1935. Libro de Actas. Tomo primero,* 187–88. Madrid: Bolaños y Aguilar, 1935.

Quigley, Christine. *Dissection on Display: Cadavers, Anatomists, and Public Spectacle*. Jefferson, N. C.: McFarland & Co., 2012.

Raccolta de nomi, e cognomi, et anni, ne' quali pubblicamente furono fatti morire per delitti, dal principio della repubblica fino a' nostri giorni in questa città di Venezia, de' quali si ha potuto ritrovare più certa memoria, principiando dall'anno 728 in giù, or *Registro dei giustiziati in Venezia: dal principio della repubblica veneta fino ai giorni nostri, per la prima volta stampato* [Venice, Santini, c.1850].

Raynalde, Thomas, and Eucharius Rösslin. *The Birth of Mankynde Otherwyse Named the Womans Booke. Newely Set Foorth, Corrected, and Augmented. Whose Contentes Ye May Reade in the Table of the Booke, and Most Playnely in the Prologue*. By Thomas Raynalde Phisition. By Richard Jugge, 1565.

Read, Alexander, *A Treatise of All the Muscules of the Whole Bodie*. London: Printed by R.T. for F. Constable, 1637.

Regosin, Richard. *The Matter of My Book: Montaigne's Essais as the Book of the Self*. Berkeley: University of California Press, 1977.

Roach, Mary. *Stiff*. New York: W.W. Norton & Company, 2003.

Rodrigues, Isilda Teixeira, and Carlos Fiolhais. "O ensino da medicina na Universidade de Coimbra no século XVI." *História, Ciências, Saúde - Manguinhos* 20, no. 2 (2013): 435–56.

Rodrigues, Manuel Augusto. *Memoria professorum Universitatis Conimbrigensis*. Vol. 1: 1290-1772. Coimbra: Arquivo da Universidade, 2003.

Rodrigues, Manuel Augusto. *Os primeiros Estatutos da Universidade de Coimbra*. Coimbra: Arquivo da Universidade de Coimbra, 1991.

Rodríguez-San Pedro Bezares, Luis Enrique. "Universidad de la Monarquía Católica, 1555-1700," Em *Historia de la Universidad de Salamanca*, I-Trayectoria y vinculaciones: 97–147. Salamanca: Ediciones Universidad de Salamanca, 2002.

Rodríguez-San Pedro Bezares, Luis Enrique. *La Universdiad Salamantina del Barroco. Período 1598-1625*. Vol. 2. Salamanca: Ediciones Universidad de Salamanca, 1986.

The Royal College of Physicians. "The Anatomical Tables" https://www.rcplondon.ac.uk/news/anatomical-tables. Accessed on 14 January 2021.

The Royal College of Physicians. *The Story Behind "Curious Anatomys."* YouTube. https://www.youtube.com/watch?v=StDwfY-kiyY.

Sammern, Romana. "Red, White and Black: Colors of Beauty, Tints of Health and Cosmetic Materials in Early Modern English Art Writing." *Early Science and Medicine* 20 (2015): 397-427.

Santamaría Hernández, María Teresa. "Collado, Luis." In *Diccionario biográfico y bibliográfico del humanismo español (siglos XV-XVII)*, 224-28. Madrid: Ediciones Clásicas.

Santander, Teresa. "La iglesia de San Nicolás y el antiguo teatro anatómico de la Universidad de Salamanca." *Revista Española de Teología*, no. 43 (1983): 253–74.

Saunders, John Bertrand Decusance and Charles D. O'Malley. *The Illustrations from the Works of Andreas Vesalius of Brussels*. New York: Dover Publications, 1973.

Sawday, Jonathan. *The Body Emblazoned: dissection and the human body in Renaissance culture.* London: Routledge, 1995.

Sawday, Jonathan. "Bodies by Art Fashioned: Anatomy, Anatomists and English Poetry 1570-1680." PhD Diss, University of London, 1988.

Sawday, Jonathan. "The Fate of Marsyas: Dissecting the Renaissance Body." In *Renaissance Bodies: The Human Figure in English Culture c. 1540-1660.* Edited by Lucy Gent and Nigel Llewellyn, 111-35. London: Reaktion Books, 1990.

Schoenfeldt, Michael. "Fables of the Belly in Early Modern England." In *The Body in Parts: Fantasies of Corporeality in Early Modern Europe,* edited by David Hillman and Carla Mazzio, 243-62. New York and London: Routledge, 1997.

Scholz, Susan. *Body Narratives: Writing the Nation and Fashioning the Subject in Early Modern England.* New York: Macmillan, 2000.

Schwarz, Kathryn. "Missing the Breast: Desire, Disease, and the Singular Effect of Amazons." In *The Body in Parts: Fantasies of Corporeality in Early Modern Europe,* edited by David Hillman and Carla Mazzio, 147-69. New York: Routledge, 1997.

Schwarz, Kathryn. "Death and Theory: Or, the Problem of Counterfactual Sex." In *Sex Before Sex: Figuring the Act in Early Modern England,* edited by James M. Bromley and Will Stockton, 53-88. Minneapolis: University of Minnesota Press, 2013.

Schmitt, Charles. "Science in the Sixteenth and Early Seventeenth Centuries." In *The Aristotelian Tradition and Renaissance Universities,* 35-56. London: Variorum Reprints, 1984.

Schmitt, Charles. "The Problem of Continuity." In *The Aristotelian Tradition and Renaissance Universities,* 104-23. London: Variorum Reprints, 1984.

Semenzato, Camillo, Vittorio Dal Piaz, and Maurizio Rippa Bonati. *Il teatro anatomico. Storia e restauri.* Padua: Università degli Studi di Padova, 1994.

Seventh Report of the Royal Commission on Historical Manuscripts, Part 1, Appendix, "The Manuscripts of Geo. Alan Lowndes, Esq., of Barrington Hall, Co. Essex," edited by Alfred J. Horwood. London, 1879.

Shakespeare, William. *Coriolanus.* Edited by P. Holland. London: Bloomsbury Arden Shakespeare, 2013.

Shakespeare, William. *Hamlet. The Arden Shakespeare.* Edited by Ann Thompson and Neil Taylor. London: Bloomsbury, 2006.

Shakespeare, William. *The Taming of the Shrew.* Edited by Robert B. Heilman. New York: Signet, 1966.

Shapiro, James. *The Year of Lear: Shakespeare in 1606.* New York: Simon & Schuster, 2015.

Shuger, Debora. "'Society Supernatural:' The Imagined Community of Hooker's Laws." *Religion and Culture in Renaissance England,* edited by Claire McEachern and Debora Shuger, 116-41. Cambridge: Cambridge University Press, 1997.

Sidney, Philip. *The Poems of Sir Philip Sidney.* Edited by William A. Ringler, Jr. Oxford: Clarendon Press, 1962.

Silverman, Lisa. *Tortured Subjects: Pain, Truth, and the Body in Early Modern France.* Chicago, The University of Chicago Press, 2001.

Siraisi, Nancy. G. *Medieval & Early Renaissance Medicine: An Introduction to Knowledge and Practice.* Chicago and London: The University of Chicago Press, 1990.

Siraisi, Nancy G. *The Clock and the Mirror. Giordano, Cardano and Renaissance Medicine.* New Jersey: Princeton University Press, 1997.

Siraisi, Nancy G. "The Faculty of Medicine." In *A History of the University in Europe,* I. Universities in the Middle Ages, 360–87. Cambridge: Cambridge University Press, 2007.

Siraisi, Nancy G. "Vesalius and Human Diversity in *De humani corporis fabrica.*" *Journal of the Warburg and Courtauld Institutes* 57 (1994): 60–88.

Siraisi, Nancy G. "Vesalius and the Reading of Galen's Teleology." *Renaissance Quarterly* 50, no. 1 (1997): 1–37.

Slack, Paul. "The Response to Plague in Early Modern England: Public Policies and their Consequences." In *Famine, Disease and the Social Order in Early Modern Society,* edited by John Walter and Roger Schofield, 167-188. Cambridge: Cambridge University Press, 1989.

Smith, Pamela H. *The Body of the Artisan: Art and Experience in the Scientific Revolution.* Chicago: University of Chicago Press, 2004.

Smyth, Richard. *The Obituary of Richard Smyth.* Edited by Henry Ellis. London: Camden Society, 1849.

Soja, Edward W. *Postmodern Geographies: The Reassertion of Space in Critical Social Theory.* London and New York: Verso Press, 1989.

Solmi, Edmondo. "Per gli studi anatomici di Leonardo da Vinci." In *Miscellanea di studi critici pubblicati in onore di Guido Mazzoni,* I, 343–60. Firenze: Tipografia Galileiana, 1907.

Spenser, Edmund. *The Faerie Queene.* London: Routledge, 2013.

Spicci, Mauro. *Corpo e ibridazioni discorsive nell'Inghilterra elisabettiana.* Catania: Editpress, 2009.

Starkey, Thomas. *A Dialogue between Reginald Pole and Thomas Lupset.* Edited by Kathleen M. Burton. London: Chatto & Windus, Oxford University Press, 1948.

Starobinski, Jean. "The Body's Moment." In *Yale French Studies* no. 64 (1983): 273-305.

Statuta Almae Universitatis Doctorum Philosophium et Medicorum, cognomendo Artistarum, Patavini Gymnasii, denuo correcta et emendata et nonnullis Apostillis aucta. Padua, 1607.

Statutos d'el Rei Dom Manoel para a Universidade de Lisboa. 1937. Em Noticias Chronologicas da Universidade de Coimbra, 2a. Vol. 1. Coimbra, 1937.

Stolberg, Michael. "Learning Anatomy in Late Sixteenth-century Padua." *History of Science* 56, no. 4 (2018): 381–402.

Stow, John. *A Survey of London by John Stow: Reprinted from the text of 1603. Volume 1.* Edited by Charles Lethbridge Kingsford. Oxford: Clarendon Press, 1908.

Swan, Claudia. *Art, Science, and Witchcraft in Early Modern Holland: Jacques de Gheyn II (1565-1629).* New York: Cambridge University Press, 2005.

Swan, Claudia. 2008. "Making Sense of Medical Collections in Early Modern Holland: The Uses of Wonder." In *Making Knowledge in Early Modern Europe:*

Practices, Objects, and Texts, 1400-1800, edited by Benjamin Schmidt and Pamela H Smith, 199–213. Chicago: University of Chicago Press.

Swan, Claudia. 2010. "Of Gardens and Other Natural History Collections in Early Modern Holland: Modes of Display and Patterns of Observation." In *Museum, Bibliothek, Stadtraum: Räumliche Wissensordnungen 1600- 1900*, edited by Robert Felfe Felfe and Kirsten Wagner, 173–90. Berlin: LIT Verlag.

Tassini, Giuseppe. *Alcune delle più clamorose condanne capitali eseguite in Venezia sotto la Repubblica*. Venice: Cecchini, 1866.

Tawney, R. H. *The Agrarian Problem in the Sixteenth Century*. New-York: Burt Franklin Research & Source Work Series # 13, 1967.

Tennenhouse, Leonard. "Family Rites: City Comedy and the Strategies of Patriarchalism." *New Historicism & Renaissance Drama*, edited by Richard Wilson and Richard Dutton. London: Logman Publishing, 1992.

The Declaration of the Diggers of Warwickshire. British Library, Harley MS 787, f. 9v, Papers found in William Dell's study, Laud's secretary. 1607.

Trigge, Francis. *To the Kings most excellent Maiestie. The humble petition of two sisters the Church and Common-wealth*. Londini: Georgi Bishop, 1604.

Uman, Deborah, and Sara Morrison. *Staging the Blazon in Early Modern English Theater*. Studies in Performance and Early Modern Drama. London: Routledge, 2016.

Underwood, Edgar Ashworth. "The Early Teaching of Anatomy at Padua. With Special Reference to a Model of the Padua Anatomical Theater." *Annals of Science* 19 (1963): 1-26.

Vesalius, Andreas, and Thomas Raynalde. *A Compendious Declaration of the Excellent Uertues of a Certain Lateli Inuentid Oile, Callid for the Uuorthines Thereof Oile Imperial VVith the Maner Hou the Same Is to Be Usid, to the Benefite of Mankind, against Innumerable Diseasis. Vuriten by Thomas Rainold Doc. of Phisick. Ioan. Gryphius Excudebat*, 1551.

Vesalius Andreas. *Anatomicarum Gabrielis Falloppii Observationum Examen*, Venice, Francesco de' Franceschi, 1564.

Vesalius, Andreas. *Andreae Vesalii Bruxellensis, Scholæ medicorum Patauinae professoris de Humani corporis fabrica Libri septem*. Basle, Johann Oporinus, 1543.

Vesalius, Andreas. *Epistola, rationem modumque propinandi radicis Chynae decocti… & praeter alia quaedam, epitola cuiusdam ad Iacobum Sylvium sententiam recensens, veritatis ac potissimum humanae fabricae studiosis perutilem: quum in illa nimium Galeno creditum sit, facile commonstret*. Basle, Johann Oporinus, 1546.

Vesalius, Andreas. *The Bloodletting Letter of 1539: An Annotated Translation and Study of the Evolution of Vesalius's Scientific Development*. H. Schuman, 1947.

Vicary, Thomas. *The Anatomie of The Bodie of Man, 1548*. Edited by Fredk J. Furnivall, M.A., Hon. Dr. Phil, and Percy Furnivall. Oxford: Oxford University Press, 1888.

Vicary, Thomas. *The Englishemans Treasure*. Imprinted by George Robinson for John Perin, 1587.

Vickers, Nancy J. "Diana Described: Scattered Women and Scattered Rhyme." *Critical Inquiry* 8 (1981): 265-279.

Vickers, Nancy J. "Members Only: Marot's Anatomical Blazons." In *The Body in Parts: Fantasies of Corporeality in Early Modern Europe.* Edited by David Hillman and Carla Mazzio, 3-21. New York: Routledge, 1997.

Waddington, Keir. *An Introduction to the Social History of Medicine: Europe since 1500.* New York: Palgrave Macmillan, 2011.

Wiesner-Hank, Merry E. *Women and Gender in Early Modern Europe*, Third Edition. Cambridge: Cambridge University Press, 2008.

Woodbridge, Linda. *Women and the English Renaissance: Literature and the Nature of Womankind, 1540-1620.* Urbana and Chicago: The University of Illinois Press, 1984.

Yeo, Colin. "'The Grave Where Buried Love Doth Live:' Hearts-Imagery and Bakhtinian Grotesque in Early Modern English Poetry." In *The Feeling Heart in Medieval and Early Modern Europe: Meaning, Embodiment, and Making,* edited by Katie Barclay and Bronwyn Reddan, 129-142. Boston: Degruyter, 2019.

Zaccagnini, Guido. *La vita dei maestri e degli scolari nello Studio di Bologna nei secoli XIII e XIV.* Genève: L.S. Olschki, 1926.

Zampieri, Laura. "Il ruolo dell'anatomia nello Studio pisano e i suoi *Lectores* (1543-1860)." In *Alla ricerca dell'arte di guarire: Storia della sanità a Pisa dal Medioevo al 1861,* edited by Alberto Zampieri and Laura Zampieri, 195-224. Pisa: ETS, 2006.

Works Consulted

Alejo Montes, and Francisco Javier. "La Universidad de Salamanca en el siglo XVI: la reforma educativa en D. Juan de Zúñiga (1594)." *Studia historica. Historia moderna*, no. 8 (1990): 151–62.

Alston, Mary Niven. "The Attitude of the Church towards Dissection before 1500." *Bulletin of the History of Medicine* 16, no. 3 (1944): 221–38.

Andrioli, Giancarlo, and Giuseppe Trincia. "Padua: The Renaissance of Human Anatomy and Medicine." *Neurosurgery* 55, no. 4 (2004): 746–55.

Arnaut, Salvador Dias. 1997. "A Medicina." In *História da Universidade em Portugal*, I-Tomo I (1290-1536): 285–302. Coimbra-Lisboa: Universidade de Coimbra-Fundação Calouste Gulbenkian.

Baker, Moira P. "'The Uncanny Stranger on Display:' The Female body in Sixteenth- and Seventeenth-Century Love Poetry." *South Atlantic Review* 56, no. 2 (1991): 7-25.

Banerjee, Pompa. *Burning Women: Widows, Witches, and Early Modern European Travelers in India*. Basingstoke: Palgrave Macmillan, 2003.

Barcia Goyanes, Juan José. *El mito de Vesalio*. Valencia: Real Academia de Medicina– Universitat de Valencia, 1994.

Bennett, Jane. *Vibrant Matter: A Political Ecology of Things*. Durham: Duke University Press, 2010.

Braga, Teófilo. *Historia da Universidade de Coimbra. Nas suas relações com a Instrucção Publica Portugueza*. Vol. II 1555 a 1700. Lisboa: Por ordem e na Typographia da Academia Real das Sciencias, 1895.

Browne, Edward Granville. *Islamic Medicine*. Goodword Books, 2001.

Carlino, Andrea. "L'anatomia a teatro tra didattica, celebrazione e edificazione." In *L'anatomia tra arte e medicina. Lo studio del corpo nel tardo Rinascimento*, 13–23. Milano: Silvana, 2010.

Castro, Zília Osório de. "A reforma de D. Francisco de Bragança." In *Universidade(s), História, Memória, Prespectivas*, 1:111–21. Coimbra: Comissão Organizadora do Congresso "História da Universidade," 1991.

Castro-Correia, José. "Sobre o estudo e o ensino da Anatomia." *O Médico*, no. 770 (1966): 1–19.

Ciranni, Rosalba. "Andrea Vesalio nello Studio Pisano di Cosimo I de'Medici." *Athenet online* 29 (2009): 1–8.

Cisney, Vernon W. and Nicolae Morar. "Why Biopower? Why Now?" *Biopower: Foucault and Beyond*, edited by Vernon W. Cisney and Nicolae Morar, 1-25. Chicago: The University of Chicago Press, 2016.

Compagnon, Antoine. *Nous, Michel de Montaigne*. Paris: Seuil, 1980.

Coole, Diana and Samantha Frost. "Introducing the New Materialisms." In *New Materialisms: Ontology, Agency, and Politics*, edited by Diana Coole and Samantha Frost, 1-43. Durham: Duke University Press, 2010.

Corradi, Alfonso. *Dello Studio e dell'insegnamento dell'anatomia in Italia nel Medioevo e in Parte del Cinquecento*. Milano: [s.n.], 1873.

Costa, Jaime Celestino. "O estudo da medicina até ao fim do século XIX." In *Academia de Ciências de Lisboa. História e desenvolvimento da ciência em Portugal*, 1:498–508. Lisboa: Publicações do II Centenário da Academia de Ciências de Lisboa, 1986.

Cunningham, Andrew. "The Kinds of Anatomy." *Medical history* 19, no. 1 (1975): 1–19.

Dall'Osso, Eugenio. *L'organizzazione medico legale a Bologna e Venezia nei secoli XII-XIV.* Cesena: Università di Bologna, 1956.

Descriptive Catalogue of the Physiological Series in the Hunterian Museum of The Royal College of Surgeons of England, Part II. Livingstone: Edinburgh and London, 1971.

Diana, Esther. "Società, corpo morto, anatomia: i luoghi e i personaggi." In *Anatomia e storia dell'anatomia a Firenze. Dal gabinetto Fisiologico al Museo Anatomico*, 9-41. Firenze: Edizioni Medicea, 1996.

Diehl, Huston. *Staging Reform, Reforming the Stage: Protestantism and Popular Theater in Early Modern England.* Ithaca: Cornell University Press, 1997.

Esperabé Artega, Enrique. *Historia pragmática e interna de la Universidad de Salamanca.* Vol. 1. Salamanca: F. Nuñez Izquierdo, 1917a.

Esperabé Artega, Enrique. *Historia pragmática e interna de la Universidad de Salamanca.* Vol. 2. Salamanca: F. Nuñez Izquierdo, 1917b.

Fletcher, Joseph. *The Historie of the Perfect-Cursed-Blessed Man.* London: M. Flesher, 1628.

Gavigan, Sheely A. M. "Petit Treason in Eighteenth Century England: Women's Inequality Before the Law." *Canadian Journal of Women and the Law* 3, no. 2 (1989-1990): 335-374.

Gelfand, Toby. "The 'Paris manner' of Dissection: Student Anatomical Dissection in Early Eighteenth-century Paris." *Bulletin of the History of Medicine* 46, no. 2 (1972): 99–130.

Ginn, Sheryl R., and Lorenzo Lorusso. "Brain, Mind, and Body: Interactions with Art in Renaissance Italy." *Journal of the History of the Neurosciences* 17, no. 3 (2008): 295–313.

Green, Mary Anne Everett (Ed). *Calendar of State Papers, Domestic Affairs, Elizabeth, 1595-97.* London: Longmans, Green, Reader, and Dyer, 1869.

Hendriksen, Marieke. *Elegant Anatomy: The Eighteenth-Century Leiden Anatomical Collections.* Leiden: Brill, 2015.

Kiene, M. "Piccole e grandi università a confronto. Insediamenti universitari in Europa dal XVI al XVIII secolo." In *Le università minori in Europa (sec. XV-XIX). Convegno Internazionale di Studi (Alghero 1996)*, 189–300. Sassari, 1998.

Kusukawa, Sachiko. *Picturing the Book of Nature: Image, Text, and Argument in Sixteenth-Century Human Anatomy and Medical Botany.* Chicago: University of Chicago Press, 2012.

Landucci, Luca, and Antonio Lanza. *Diario fiorentino dal 1450 al 1516: continuato da un anonimo fino al 1542.* Florence: Sansoni Editore, 1985.

Leder, Drew. *The Absent Body.* Chicago: University of Chicago Press, 1990.

Lo, Melissa. "Cut, Copy, and English Anatomy: Thomas Geminus and the Recording of Vesalius's Canonical Body." In *Andreas Vesalius and the 'Fabrica' in the Age of Printing: Art, Anatomy, and Printing in the Italian Renaissance.*

Edited by Rinaldo Fernando Canalis and Massimo Ciavolella, 225-56. Belgium: Brepols, 2018.

López Piñero, José M. "La disección y el saber anatómico en la España de la primera mitad del siglo XVI." *Cuadernos de historia de la medicina Espanola* 13 (1974): 51–110.

Matsen, Herbert. "Alessandro Achillini (1463-1513) as Professor of Philosophy in the 'Studio' of Padua (1506-1508)." *Quaderni per la storia dell'Universita di padova* 1 (1968): 91–109.

McLean, Antonia. *Humanism and the Rise of Science in Tudor England.* New York: Neale Watson Academic Publications, Inc., 1972.

Monta, Susannah Brietz. *Martyrdom and Literature in Early Modern England.* Cambridge: Cambridge University Press, 2005.

Mortazavi, M. M., N. Adeeb, K. Watanabe, A. Deep, B. Latif, C. J. Griessenauer, R. S. Tubbs, and T. Fukushima. "Gabriele Fallopio (1523–1562) and His Contributions to the Development of Medicine and Anatomy." *Child's Nervous System* 29 (2013): 877–80.

Nancy, Jean-Luc. *Corpus.* Translated by Richard Rand. New York: Fordham University Press, 2008.

O'Malley, Charles D. "Los saberes morfológicos en el Renacimiento: la anatomía." In *Historia Universal de la Medicina,* 4 (1973): 43–77.

Powell, Alison. "Self-Dissecting Devotional Bodies, Torture, and the State." *Shakespeare en devenir,* no. 5 (2011), consulted on 04/07/21.

Proshina, Maria. "Excremens d'un vieil esprit: le registre corporel dans les Essais." In *Bulletin de la Société international des amis de Montaigne,* no 58 (2013): 95-110.

Rasteiro, Alfredo. *O Ensino Médico em Coimbra, 1131-200.* Coimbra: Quarteto, 1999.

Rasteiro, Alfredo. "A Universidade e a Medicina Portuguesa no Século XVI." In *Universidade(s), História, Memória, Prespectivas,* 1:101–10. Coimbra: Comissão Organizadora do Congresso "História da Universidade," 1991.

Renaissance Clothing and the Materials of Memory. Edited by Ann Rosalind Jones and Peter Stallybrass. Cambridge: Cambridge University Press, 2000.

Romano, Andrea. *Università in Europa: le istituzioni universitarie dal Medio Evo ai nostri giorni: strutture, organizzazione, funzionamento.* Soveria Mannelli: Rubbettino, 1995.

Romero y Huesca, Andrés, Julio Ramírez-Bollas, Francisco Javier Ponce-Landín, Juan Carlos Moreno-Rojas, and Miguel Ángel Soto-Miranda. "La cátedra de Cirugía y Anatomía en el Renacimiento." *Cirugía y Cirujanos* 73, no. 2 (2005): 151–58.

Sánchez López, Juan Antonio. "Corpus insolitus: libros de anatomía, imágenes heterodoxas y manierismo surrealista en la cultura visual europea." *Revista de Historia das Ideias* 33 (2012): 183–216.

San Vicente, Angel. *Monumentos diplomáticos sobre los edificios fundacionales de la Universidad de Zaragoza y sus constructores.* Zaragoza: Diputación Provincial, Institución "Fernando el Católico," 1981.

Spitz, Lewis. "The Importance of the Reformation for the Universities: Culture and Confessions in the Critical Years." In *Rebirth, Reform and Resilience, Universities in Transition 1300-1700*, 42-67. Columbus: The Ohio State University Press, 1984.

Suki, Christine. "'Stella is Not Here:' Sidney's Acts of Writing as Acts of Erasing." *Etudes Epistémè: revue de littérature et de civilisation* 21 (2012). http://journals.openedition.org/episteme/411; DOI: https://doi.org/10.4000/episteme.411.

The Fate of Anatomical Collections. Edited by Rina Knoeff and Robert Zwijnenberg. London: Routledge, 2016.

Tourneur, Cyril, and Lawrence J. Ross. *The Revenger's Tragedy*. Regents Renaissance Drama Series. Lincoln: University of Nebraska Press, 1966.

Truman, James C. W. "John Foxe and the Desires of Reformation Martyrology." *ELH* 70, no. 1 (2003): 35-66.

Ward, Joseph P. *Metropolitan Communities: Trade Guilds, Identity, and Change in Early Modern London*. Stanford: Stanford University Press, 1997.

Williams, Grant. "Early Modern Blazons and the Rhetoric of Wonder: Turning Towards an Ethics of Sexual Difference." In *Luce Irigaray and Premodern Culture: Thresholds of History*, edited by Elizabeth D. Harvey and Theresa Krier, 126-137. New York: Routledge, 2004.

Consulted Collections

Archivio Antico dell'Università di Padova (AAUP): Raccolta Minato, seria 20, Teatro anatomico, filza 665; Atti dell'Università Artista, filza 675, busta 12 (1554-1557).

Archivio di Stato di Firenze (ASF): Archivio Mediceo del Principato; Archivio Guidi.

Archivio di Stato di Padova (ASP): Studio Patavino; Ufficio di Sanità; Libri dei morti; San Giovanni della Morte.

Archivio di Stato di Venezia (ASV): Lettere dalli Riformatori dello Studio scritte ai diversi Rettori (1555-1559), filza 63.

Biblioteca Classense di Ferrara: ms. 426.

Biblioteca Marciana di Venezia: Classe VII, cod. DII.

Biblioteca Nazionale Centrale di Firenze (BNCF): Fondo Palatino, Autografi Palatini.

University of Salamanca:
Historical Archive of the University of Salamanca
(Archivo Historico de la Universidad de Salamanca-AUSA)

Libros de Visitas de Cátedras, Años 1560-1838, 947.

Caja 2870.

Libros de Claustros, 18.

Libros de Claustros, 19.

Libros de Claustros, 20.

Libros de Claustros, 21.

Libros de Claustros, 35.

Historical Library of Salamanca
(Biblioteca General Histórica-BGU)

Andrés de León, *Tratados de medicina, cirugia y anatomia*. En Valladolid: por Luis Sanchez, 1603. BGU. 36.278.

Andrés Laguna, *Anatomica methodus, seu de sectione humani corporis contemplatio...* Parisiis: apud Ludovicum Cynaeum, 1535. BGU. 36.413.

Andreas Vesalius, *De humani corporis fabrica libri septem*. Basileae: ex officina Ioannis Oporini, 1543. BGU. 12.545.

Avicena, *Codex... totius scientiae medicine principis ...* [Venetiis: Lucae Antonii de Giunta], 1523. BGU 12.237.

Bartolomé Hidalgo, *Thesoro de la verdadera cirugia y via particular contra la comun*. En Barcelona: por Sebastián de Cormellas, 1624. BGU. 35.684.

Claudio Galeno, *Galeni Opera ex septima Iuntarum editione ...* Venetiis: apud Iuntas, 1597. BGU. 12.605-12.609.

Gabriele Fallopio: *Opera omnia.* Francofurti: apud haeredes Andreae Wecheli, 1600. BGU. 12.308.

Juan Valverde de Amusco: *Historia de la composicion del cuerpo humano.* En Roma: impressa por Antonio Salamanca y Antonio Lafrerii, 1556. BGU. 35.573.

Luis de Mercado, *Institutiones chirurgicae iussu regio factae pro chirurgis in praxi examinandis ... in duos libros dissectae et a caeterus Protomedicis approbate.* Madriti: excudebat Ludovicus Sánchez, 1594. BGU. 35.888 (Compañía de Jesús).

University of Coimbra:
Coimbra University Archive
(Arquivo da Universidade de Coimbra-AUC)

Arquivo da Universidade de Coimbra, AUC, *Atas dos Conselhos*, 1545-1551, IV-1.ªD-1-2-50.

Arquivo da Universidade de Coimbra, AUC, *Atas dos Conselhos*, 1553-1557, IV-1.ªD-1-2-51.

Arquivo da Universidade de Coimbra, AUC, *Atas dos Conselhos*, 1557-1560, IV-1.ªD-1-2-52.

Arquivo da Universidade de Coimbra, AUC, *Atas dos Conselhos*, 1560-1563, IV-1.ªD-1-2-53.

Arquivo da Universidade de Coimbra, AUC, *Atas dos Conselhos*, 1563-1566, IV-1.ªD-1-2-54.

Arquivo da Universidade de Coimbra, AUC, *Atas dos Conselhos*, 1566-1570, IV-1.ªD-1-2-55.

General Library of the University of Coimbra
(Biblioteca Geral da Universidade de Coimbra-BGUC)

Biblioteca Geral da Universidade de Coimbra, BGUC, *Opus mixtum ex fabrica corporis humani et singularum partium morbis*, ms. 2870.

Biblioteca Geral da Universidade de Coimbra, BGUC, *Opus mixtum ex fabrica corporis humani et singularum partium morbis*, ms. 2879.

Biblioteca Geral da Universidade de Coimbra, BGUC, *Tractatus anatomicus de universa corporis humani fabrica*, ms. 2856.

Biblioteca Joanina, BJ, *Andreae Vesalii Bruxellensis, Scholae Medicorum Patavinae Professoris, De humani corporis fabrica libri septem*, Basileia: ex officina Ioannis Oporini, 1543. 4 A-21-14-1.

Biblioteca Joanina, BJ, Ambroise Paré, *Opera.* Paris: apud Iacobum Du-Puys, 1582. 4 A-21-2-16.

Annexes

Annex 1

Archivio Antico dell'Università di Padova, filza 665, Raccolta Minato, seria 20, Teatro anatomico, De Anatomia singulis annis facienda XXVIII (Statuti Artistarum, lib. 2, p. 98), f. 263r:

Adhaerentes non solum antiquis statutis nostris, sed universitati, omniumque italicarum laudatissimae consuetudinis non modo ad nostrorum scholarium utilitatem, sed etiam totius humani generis salutem, statuimus quod post principium studii, et ante finem Febr[uarii] quilibet Rector sub paena periurii, et lib. 50 et quilibet Consiliarius sub paena lib. 20 efficaciter procurare teneatur, ut habeatur aliquod cadaver cuiuspiam delinquentis, de quo ab ipsis Praetoribus supplicium sumptum est. videlicet unius maris, et unius foeminae, vel saltem unius ipsorum. Ut autem communi utilitati consulatur confirmari petimus, specialiter, et de gratia speciali, quod vigore praesentis statuti teneantur ipsi Praetores, nisi tales delinquentes fuerint de Territorio Patavino, aut civis Venetus sub paena lib. 1000 tale cadaver. D. Rectori et scolaribus ad eorum requisitionem assignari facere. et si infra praedictum tempus aliquis delinquens non occurrat: si citadellae, aut alio quovis loco territorii accidat de aliquo supplicium capitis esse sumendum, teneantur Praetores dictorum locorum, non obstante decreto aliquo aut consuetudine, vel aliis quibuscumque ordinibus sub paena praedicta tale cadaver pro praedicta causa, ut supra rectoribus, et scolaribus assignare.

Annex 2

Angelo Fabroni, *Historiae Academiae Pisanae volumen II*, Pisa, 1792, Statuta L, pp. 73-4:

Perutilis et necessaria inspectio est earum, quae in humano corpore clauduntur his, qui perfectam medendi artem adipisci volunt. Quis enim languoribus, & morbis hominum interioribus, a visuque humano penitus semotis, aptum, aut perfectum scierit adhibere remedium? Totius igitur humani generis saluti prospicientes, statuimus quod Rector, singulis annis, tempore hyemali, cum illi commodius videbitur, teneatur providere quam accuratissime poterit, ut habeantur duo cadavera, de quibus Anatomia fieri possit, unum maris, alterum feminae, si commode haberi potuerint, sin minus saltem unum. Ut autem hoc facilius fieri possit, ordinamus, quod D. Commissarius Pisarum teneatur assignare Rectori dicta cadavera aliquorum Delinquentium, de quibus supplicium sumendum sit, ad omnem ejus requisitionem. Si vero sub tempus Anatomiae Pisis nullus occurret talis Deliquens, tunc Rector scribat Florentiam ad Dominos Octo Custodiae, & Baliae ad hoc, ut commode dicta cadavera habeantur. Declarantes quod Anatomia fieri non possit de corpore alicujus Civis Florentini, vel Pisani, aut alicujus Doctoris vel Scholaris, nisi proximiores eorum ad id consenserint.

Annex 3

Biblioteca Classense di Ravenna, ms. 426, Statutum LX, De Anathomia quolibet anno fienda, f. 35v:

Quoniam ad industriam, & utilitatem Scholarium spectat, & pertinet facere Anathomiam, statuerunt, quod Potestas Civitatis Ferrariae teneatur ad requisitionem D. Rectoris dare, & assignare Anathomistis singulo anno unum corpus humanum. Et quià plerumque consueverunt rixae, & rumores, in reperiendis, seu quaerendis corporibus, ex quibus, seu de quibus Anathomia fieri debeat, statuerunt, & ordinaverunt, quod aliquis Doctor, aut Scholarius, aut quivis alius non audeat, nec praesumat, sibi acquirere aliquod corpus mortuum pro dicta Anathomia fienda, nisi primo licentia praehabita à D. Rectore, qui pro tempore fuerit, qui quidem Rector teneatur, & debeat, in dando licentiam inter Doctores, & Scholares qualitatem, & ordinem observare, cum dicta licentia petita fuerit.

Annex 4

Archivio Antico dell'Università di Padova, filza 665, Raccolta Minato, seria 20, Teatro anatomico, Cap. 17 super 28 de Anatomia facienda singulis annis, f. 264r:

Quod maxime necessarium est, maxime cura appetendum est, quapropter cum statutum fuisset per statutum 28 huius secundi voluminis, quod singulis annis fieret anatomia, quodque pro ea perficienda Rectores urbis, et territorii tenerentur cadaver uniuscunque delinquentis, de quo capitis supplicium sumeretur, dare anatomiae deputatis, nisi cadaver esset alicuius civis veneti aut patavini, quum iam annis multis dicta anatomia raro facta fuerit cadaverum defectu. Ideo utilitati non modo scholarium, sed etiam universo mortalium generi consulentes, non in aliquorum vilipendium, statuitur quod urbis praesides, ac omnium locorum Patavini districtus Praetores teneantur dictis nostris anatomistis dare quodcumque cadaver uniuscunque delinquentis capitis supplicio puniti, nisi sit Venetus aut Paduanus civis, vel ex comitate ex aliqua familia alicuius aestimationis, et nisi consanguinei eius et eadem familia contradicant, vel advena nobilis, vel alicuius existimationis, sub paena in dicto statuto contenta, ad quam videndam omnes scholares nostri matriculati possint intrare.

Annex 5

Archivio Antico dell'Università di Padova, filza 665, Raccolta Minato, seria 20, Teatro anatomico, f. 271:

Essendo in vero cosa impia, et inhumana, et da tutte le leggi divine, et humane improbata, il cavava delli corpi morti delle loro sepolture, come pare, si facciano levito di fare alcuni temerarii, et scelerati nella Città Vostra di Padoa, per fare Anotomie particolari, et per far grassi, et vendere li ossi. Questa Magnifica Communità, mossa da tale impietà, ha prega parte nel suo General Consiglio sotto 14: del mese di Febraro 1547 : –, che sia supplicato alla Signoria Nostra, che non essendo eseguite le pene datte dalle leggi communi a tali violatori de sepolcri, si debba da novo statuire tenere pene contra di loro. Il che non si dovendo mancare di far cosi per la qualità della cosa, come per satisfatione di essa Magnifica Citta. L'anderà parte, che sia imposto al Podestà di Padova, et successori, che sel si troverà in ogni tempo alcuno cosi terrieno, come forestiero di qualunque grado, et conditione esser si voglia, che andrà per modo alcuno, o via che escogitare si possa, cavar alcun corpo delle sepolture, e cimiterii, per far Anatomia, est ut sapra, quello debbano punire severamente, come in vero richiede la qualità di tal delitto.

Annex 6

Jacopo Facciolati, *Fasti Gymnasii Patavini*, Padua, 1757, vol. 2, 208-9:

MDL. nonis sextil. Gellius a Valle Vicetimus, Prorector. Ex litter. Ducal. Anatomicum studium in dies magis cum vigeret, non publicæ modo, sed privatæ quoque exercitationes passim habebantur; quibus si forte cadavera non suppeterent, ne sepultis quidem juventus parcebat. Quapropter Senatus consultum VI. id. febr. factum est gravissimarum poenarum sanctione adversus illos, qui per hujusmodi caussas sepulchra violarent. Modus etiam aliquis privatis exercitationibus quinquennio post positus est, ne fierent, nisi cessantibus publicis.

Annex 7

Archivio di Stato di Firenze, Archivio Mediceo del Principato, filza 1171, fasc. VI, c. 286: letter by Marzio de Marzii, bishop in Marsico, to Pier Francesco Riccio, secretary to Duke Cosimo de' Medici (Pisa, January 22nd, 1544):

Molto R.^{do} S.^{r} mio. È arrivato qua il Vessalio per fare la notomia et la venuta sua assai ha dato piacere a S. Ecc.^{tia} et vassia ordinando tutta volta, per farla con tutte quelle cerimonie et modi possibili. La cagione perchè si spaccia questa staffetta è solo per havere a questo effecto di costà duoi corpi d'huomini morti et m'ha comandato S. Ecc.^{tia} lo scriva alla S. V. R. che subito subito si dia alla busca nello spedale di S.^{a} Maria nuova per haverne duoi non vecchi, ma quanto più siano giovini non importerà dice il Campana, quando ve ne fussi uno di donna non importerà, et trovati questi corpi lei gli farà chiudere in due casse et gl'invierà giù per lo arno in un barchetto, o navicello et con quella più celerità possibile gli farà condurre qua. Questo negotio V. S. R. lo farà fare secretamente si di levar gli corpi come di fargli addurre, et gli farà consegnare qua nel convento di San Franc.^{o} de frati conventuali dove sarà l'ordine. La S. V. R. è tutta diligentia, pero in questo non li diro altro se non la sollecitudine. L'astrologia di m.^{ro} Don Basilio è accetta nel modo che si gira il capo, non è creduta, hora la puo rispondere a lui come le parrà. S. Ecc.^{tia} fece honore al Guicc.^{no}, et ando alla sua letione et sodisfece. Saranno con questa alchune resposte et le mie racc.^{ni} alla S. V. R. che Dio la contenti. Di Pisa li 22 di Genn.^{o} 1543 hore 3 ½. Ser.re Martio Vesc. di Marsico.

Annex 8

Archivio di Stato di Firenze, Archivio Guidi, Guidi 571, n. c.: letter by Gabriele Falloppio to Giacopo Guidi, ducal secretary in Livorno (Pisa, November 27th, 1550):

Signor moi sempre oss:ᵐᵒ. Questi giorni scrissi al Sʳ. Lelio ricordandoli che s'avicina la Pasqua di Natale nella quale facciamo l'Anatomia, non sapiamo anchora se vi sono soggietti o no. Mi rispose che cio toceava a V. S. alla quale scriverebbe. et che io dovessi negotiar' seco poichè era presente. Ho aspettato il ritorno di V. S. et poichè non viene et gia siamo sotto le feste ho pigliato questo spediente di racordarli con questa mia il bisogno nostro, perchè se non habbiamo almeno un corpo che sia sano, non si fara cosa buona. O do che di Barga farono con dotti corti a Firenze alcuni giorni sono per giustitiarsi, quella vedra se si potesse haverne uno. L'anno passato stemmo molto male, che ci diedero uno vecchio che haveva havuta la q:ⁿᵃ [febbre quartana] molti mesi, et si corruppe in un tratto. Appresso non possiamo far' cosa buona senza simia per le cose di Galeno, hora l'hanno passato ci fu assegnata una che ha ex Lucca Martini. ma non ci furono date le lettere prima che fu fornita l'Anatomia. Pero V. S. sara contenta di commetter' che ci sia data a buon hora quest'anno, et non ci potendo haver' questa ne faccia procacciar un'altra. Acciochè possiamo far' compiutamente et con diligenza il nostro ufficio, per far' honor' (come merita) al nostro Ill:ᵐᵒ padrone. Non altro. Nostro S.ʳᵉ Dio la feliciti. In Pisa, il 27 Novemb. 1550. Di V. S. Ser.ʳᵉ affetti.ᵐᵒ Gabrielle Falloppio.

Annex 9

Archivio di Stato di Venezia, Lettere dei Riformatori dello Studio, 1555-1559, filza 63, n. c. (margin slightly cut): letter by Gabriele Falloppio to the *Riformatori dello Studio padovano* (Padua, December 12th, 1556):

Clar.mi et Ill.mi Signori. Gli tempi serenissimi aggiuntavi la neve et il [...]schio colle vacanze di Natale che vengono invitano all'anatomia et dopia[no] l'ardore immenso de scolari gli quali essendo stato due anni senza, non veggono l'hora che si venga a mostrargli la fabrica humana: Qua [sono] molti scolari Thedeschi et Poloni, gli quali non vedendo preparamento alcuno, et dubitando quasi che non si faccia per diffetto di soggietto, s'incominciano d'apparechiar[si] per andare a Bologna o a Ferrara, dove indubitatamente l'havranno queste feste. Io gli vado tratenendo con buone promesse, et che senza fallo in questo vacanze havranno l'Anatomia. Ma non so poi come attendergli se non sono aiutato da[lle] Illustrissime Magnificenze Vostre pero prego quelle riverentemente, che voglino scrivere una sua al Clarissimo Podestà et raccommandargli l'an[atomia] chiedendogli un soggietto quanto più presto sarà possibile e con [...] a gli massari dell'Anatomia, che esse segretamente se ne possano cacciare uno quando gli venga l'occasione di persona igno[bile] et non conosciuta per che io prometto alle Illustrissime Magnificenze Vostre di fare con gl'orsi et la simia una bellissima Anatomia in questi 30 giorni che non si leggerà, et compirla prima che vengano le lettioni dell'anno nuovo. Et havrei caro, che quelle fossero presente alla fattic. et diligenza che usero in mostrare questi occulti misteri d'Iddio par[...] nell'uomo, acciochè conoscessero se merito, che quelle mettano [...] parte o non et non mi facciano leggere (come ho già fatto un [...]) senza argomento. Alla buona gratia delle quali basciando humil[mente] la mano mi offero et raccomando, pregandole di nuovo che [...]ciano scrivere. Nostro S.r Iddio le conservi. In Padova il 12 Decembre 1556. Delle V. Ill.me et Cl. Sig. Humil ser[vitore].

Index